CAPITAL RETURNS

Wall Street's Wheel of Fortune

(illustration by David Foldvari)

CAPITAL RETURNS

INVESTING THROUGH THE CAPITAL CYCLE: A MONEY MANAGER'S REPORTS 2002–15

Edited by

EDWARD CHANCELLOR

 macmillan education palgrave

First published 2016 by
PALGRAVE

Palgrave in the UK is an imprint of Macmillan Publishers Limited, registered in England, company number 785998, of 4 Crinan Street, London N1 9XW

Palgrave Macmillan in the US is a division of St Martin's Press LLC, 175 Fifth Avenue, New York, NY 10010.

Palgrave is the global imprint of the above companies and is represented throughout the world.

Palgrave® and Macmillan® are registered trademarks in the United States, the United Kingdom, Europe and other countries

ISBN: 978-1-137-57164-9

This book is printed on paper suitable for recycling and made from fully managed and sustained forest sources. Logging, pulping and manufacturing processes are expected to conform to the environmental regulations of the country of origin.

A catalogue record for this book is available from the British Library.

Library of Congress Catalogingin-Publication Data

Capital returns : investing through the capital cycle : a money manager's reports 2002–15 / Edward Chancellor.
    pages cm
    ISBN 978-1-137-57164-9
    1. Business cycles. 2. Marathon Asset Management. 3. Speculation. I. Chancellor, Edward, 1962– editor. II. Marathon Asset Management.
HB3711.C353 2015
332.6—dc23   2015025955

CONTENTS

List of Charts, Illustrations and Tables   viii

Foreword   x

Preface   xii

Introduction by Edward Chancellor   1

Part I   Investment Philosophy

1   Capital Cycle Revolution   **25**
   1.1   Evolution of cooperation (February 2004)   25
   1.2   Cod philosophy (August 2004)   28
   1.3   This time's no different (May 2006)   31
   1.4   Supercycle woes (May 2011)   33
   1.5   No small beer (February 2010)   37
   1.6   Oil peak (February 2012)   40
   1.7   Major concerns (March 2014)   43
   1.8   A capital cycle revolution (March 2014)   45
   1.9   Growth paradox (September 2014)   48

2   Value in Growth   **52**
   2.1   Warning labels (September 2002)   53
   2.2   Long game (March 2003)   55
   2.3   Double agents (June 2004)   58
   2.4   Digital moats (August 2007)   60
   2.5   Quality time (August 2011)   62
   2.6   Escaping the semis' cycle (February 2013)   65
   2.7   Value in growth (August 2013)   68
   2.8   Quality control (May 2014)   70
   2.9   Under the radar (February 2015)   73

3   Management Matters   **76**
   3.1   Food for thought (September 2003)   76
   3.2   Cyclical missteps (August 2010)   80

3.3   A capital allocator (September 2010)   82
3.4   Northern stars (March 2011)   85
3.5   Say on pay (February 2012)   88
3.6   Happy families (March 2012)   91
3.7   The wit and wisdom of Johann Rupert (June 2013)   95
3.8   A meeting of minds (June 2014)   99
3.9   Culture vulture (February 2015)   102

Part II   Boom, Bust, Boom

4   **Accidents in Waiting**   107
4.1   Accidents in waiting: meetings with Anglo Irish
      Bank (2002–06)   109
4.2   The builders' bank (May 2004)   117
4.3   Insecuritization (November 2002)   120
4.4   Carry on private equity (December 2004)   122
4.5   Blowing bubbles (May 2006)   126
4.6   Pass the parcel (February 2007)   130
4.7   Property fiesta (February 2007)   132
4.8   Conduit Street (August 2007)   135
4.9   On the rocks (September 2007)   138
4.10 Seven deadly sins (November 2009)   141

5   **The Living Dead**   145
5.1   Right to buy (November 2008)   146
5.2   Spanish deconstruction (November 2010)   148
5.3   PIIGS can fly (November 2011)   151
5.4   Broken banks (September 2012)   154
5.5   Twilight zone (November 2012)   156
5.6   Capital punishment (March 2013)   158
5.7   Living dead (November 2013)   160
5.8   Relax, Mr. Piketty (August 2014)   163

6   **China Syndrome**   167
6.1   Oriental tricks (February 2003)   168
6.2   Dressed to impress (November 2003)   171
6.3   Game of loans (March 2005)   173
6.4   What lies beneath (February 2014)   176
6.5   Value traps (September 2014)   179
6.6   Devil take the hindmost (May 2015)   181

7   Inside the Mind of Wall Street   184
    7.1   A complaint (December 2003)   185
    7.2   Private party (December 2005)   189
    7.3   Christmas cheer (December 2008)   192
    7.4   Former Greedspin boss flees China (December 2010)   195
    7.5   Occupy Bundestag (December 2011)   197
    7.6   Season's greetings (December 2012)   200
    7.7   Lunch with the GIR (December 2013)   203

Index   207

LIST OF CHARTS, ILLUSTRATIONS AND TABLES

CHARTS

I.1	The capital cycle	4
I.2	Asset growth and investment returns	8
I.3	Investor overreaction and the capital cycle	14
1.1	Nominal changes in commodity prices (2001–10)	34
1.2	Mining capital spending in the MSCI World Index	34
1.3	Global M&A activity in metals & mining industry	35
1.4	Capital markets financing of metals & mining industry	35
1.5	Global market share of top four brewers	38
1.6	Brent crude oil price	40
1.7	The fade rate	46
1.8	Vestas Wind Systems: capex-to-depreciation ratio and relative share price performance	47
1.9	Global M&A, IPO and S&P 500 buybacks	50
2.1	The semiconductor cycle	65
3.1	European capital allocation	80
3.2	Average holding period for equities by geographic region	90
3.3	Credit Suisse Family Index	92
4.1	Anglo Irish Bank: extracts from Marathon meeting notes	108
4.2	Anglo Irish Bank EPS growth and customer advances	118
5.1	Irish banks lending share	152
5.2	US GDP recoveries after recessions	161
6.1	China's investment share of GDP	175
6.2	Bank of America and ICBC: loan growth and credit costs	180

ILLUSTRATIONS

	Wall Street's Wheel of Fortune (illustration by David Foldvari)	ii
4.1	Northern Rock headquarters	139
7.1	A Churn's-eye view of the World	185

TABLES

2.1 Amazon's net profit margin   61
6.1 Performance of Chinese government-sponsored equity
      issues (1993–2003)   168

FOREWORD

Marathon Asset Management LLP[1] will shortly celebrate its 30th birthday. Over three decades, our investment philosophy has evolved, but two simple ideas about how capitalism works have always been paramount.

The first notion is that high returns tend to attract capital, just as low returns repel it. The resulting ebb and flow of capital affects the competitive environment of industries in often predictable ways – what we like to call the capital cycle. Our job has been to analyze the dynamics of this cycle: to see when it is working and when it is broken, and how we can profit from it on behalf of our clients. The second guiding idea is that management skill in allocating capital is vital over the long-term. Picking managers who allocate capital in sensible ways is crucial to successful stock selection. The best managers understand the capital cycle as it operates in their industries and don't lose their heads in the good times.

We found that the kind of opportunities created by capital cycle analysis often have long gestation periods, as the timing of the pay-off was highly uncertain. As a result, we discovered that our approach has worked best when we invested in a relatively large number of stocks, holding onto them for long periods of time. This rather goes against the grain of our industry where the preference has been to hold concentrated portfolios, confirming a fund manager's conviction in his or her ideas, albeit for shorter and shorter periods of time.

While we have sometimes struggled to explain our stance to consultants and other professionals in the financial services arena, it has always proved easier when it came to our clients. The latter – pension funds, state funds, foundations and endowments, predominantly in the United States – are often staffed by individuals with experience of working in non-financial businesses. A common refrain from them when explaining our process is "that's just common sense." Fortunately for us, these ideas about how the capital cycle operates and how management allocates capital are not widely followed by our own competitors in the investment industry. This throws

---

[1] Trading under the name of Marathon-London in the United States.

up investment opportunities for us around the world. While we have made innumerable errors over the years, our overall record in terms of relative performance has been favourable.

Furthermore, the investment approach has fared well under conditions of extreme stress and market madness. The Asian Crisis of the late 1990s and the technology, media and telecoms (TMT) bubble of the turn of the millennium were documented in our last collection of essays, *Capital Account*.[2] Since 2004, the principal stress test was the long run up to, and calamitous aftermath of, the Global Financial Crisis (GFC). The challenges this posed for fund managers is the main story of this book. We were responsible for numerous howlers – catching "falling knives" from the detritus of both the TMT bubble and the GFC, as well as numerous errors of judgment when it came to picking management teams. Our hall of shame includes the likes of Bear Stearns, Bradford & Bingley, Blockbuster, MBIA, HMV etc., etc. Nevertheless, overall performance has been gratifying, giving us confidence in the robustness of the investment philosophy.

This good fortune is matched by our success in persuading Edward Chancellor to reprise his role as editor of this volume of essays taken from the period 2002–15, as well as to write an insightful introduction. We thank him, along with Marathon's employees, past and present, for their role in building this firm and creating this book.

Neil Ostrer, Founding Member
William Arah, Founding Member
June 2015

---

[2] Edward Chancellor (ed.), *Capital Account: A Money Manager's Reports on a Turbulent Decade 1993–2003* (2004).

PREFACE

Capital Returns appears just over a decade after the publication of Marathon's previous publication, *Capital Account*, which I also had a hand in editing. This new work is arranged along the same lines as its predecessor. The pieces here have been selected from the firm's *Global Investment Review*, which appears eight times a year and typically contains six essays of around 1,500 words in length. The review, or *GIR* as it is known in-house, is written to inform Marathon clients of the firm's investment approach and to provide real-time insights into developments in the investment world.

The essays collected in the current volume have been chosen because they exemplify Marathon's capital cycle investment philosophy, which Marathon believes to be of some interest to the wider investing public (and perhaps even the odd economist if any can bring himself or herself to read a book devoid of equations and mathematical models). The process of selection inevitably leads to what is known in the investment world as "survivorship bias": those essays which haven't survived the test of time, or have turned out to be plain wrong, have been jettisoned, while the better investment calls have largely avoided the cull. The result is to make Marathon appear more clairvoyant than is actually the case – one could quickly put together a far larger volume of duff pieces! My intention has not been to flatter the authors' prescience, but rather to find interesting examples of capital cycle analysis, as applied by Marathon's analysts over the past decade.

As before, I have been given a free hand in editing and have employed the same technique as formerly. Namely, I have edited the text to make it read more fluently than when it first appeared. Editing a text long after it has been written necessarily involves some hindsight bias. This diminishes to some extent the integrity of *Capital Returns* as original source material. My aim, however, has been to draw out the capital cycle analysis as clearly as possible without changing the meaning of the original piece.

The authors of the essays in this collection are (in alphabetical order): Charles Carter, David Cull, Mike Godfrey, Jeremy Hosking, Nick Longhurst, Jules Mort, Michael Nickson, Neil Ostrer, James Seddon, Nick Sleep, Mike

Taylor, Simon Todd and Qais Zakaria. I have received even more help putting together *Capital Returns* than with the earlier volume. Simon Todd valiantly started out the selection process, which in many ways is the most arduous aspect of the job (there were over 600 essays from which to pick). Quentin Carruthers undertook the initial sub-editing. William MacLeod has assisted with many of the footnotes. Nicola Riley has helped on the administrative side, printing off numerous drafts and sending me countless files. Bridget Hui kindly checked the proofs. As with *Capital Account*, the present volume is largely the product of my friend and former colleague Charles Carter. It has been a pleasure working with him again.

Edward Chancellor
June 2015

INTRODUCTION

This book contains a collection of reports written by investment professionals at Marathon Asset Management. What makes these reports stand out, in my opinion, is an analytical focus on the ebb and flow of capital. Typically, capital is attracted into high-return businesses and leaves when returns fall below the cost of capital. This process is not static, but cyclical – there is constant flux. The inflow of capital leads to new investment, which over time increases capacity in the sector and eventually pushes down returns. Conversely, when returns are low, capital exits and capacity is reduced; over time, then, profitability recovers. From the perspective of the wider economy, this cycle resembles Schumpeter's process of "creative destruction" – as the function of the bust, which follows the boom, is to clear away the misallocation of capital that has occurred during the upswing.

The key to the "capital cycle" approach – the term Marathon uses to describe its investment analysis – is to understand how changes in the amount of capital employed within an industry are likely to impact upon future returns. Or put another way, capital cycle analysis looks at how the competitive position of a company is affected by changes in the industry's supply side. In his book, *Competitive Advantage*, Professor Michael Porter of the Harvard Business School writes that the "essence of formulating competitive strategy is relating a company to its environment."[1] Porter famously described the "five forces" which impact on a firm's competitive advantage: the bargaining power of suppliers and of buyers, the threat of substitution, the degree of rivalry among existing firms and the threat of new entrants. Capital cycle analysis is really about how competitive advantage changes over time, viewed from an investor's perspective.

---

[1] Michael Porter, *Competitive Strategy* (1980), p. 3. See also *Capital Account*, pp. 6–7.

A STYLIZED CAPITAL CYCLE

Here's how the capital cycle works. Imagine a widget manufacturer – let's call it Macro Industries. The firm is doing well; so well, that its returns exceed Macro's cost of capital. The firm's CEO, William Blewist-Hard, has recently featured on the front cover of *Fortune* magazine. His stock options are in the money, and his wife no longer complains about being married to a boring industrialist. Of the nine investment bank analysts who cover Macro's stock, seven have buy recommendations and two have holds. The shares are trading at a price-earnings multiple of 14 times, below the market average. Macro's stock is held by several well-known value investors.

Macro's strategy department anticipates strong demand growth for its products, especially in emerging markets where widget consumption per capita is less than one-tenth the level found in the advanced economies. After discussions with the board, Macro's CEO announces his plans to increase manufacturing capacity by 50 per cent over the next three years in order to meet growing demand. A leading investment bank, Greedspin, arranges the secondary share offering to fund the capital expenditure. Stanley Churn of Greedspin, a close friend of Macro's Blewist-Hard, is the lead banker on the deal. The expansion is warmly received in the *FT*'s Lex column. Macro's shares rise on the announcement. Growth investors have lately been buying the stock, excited by the prospect of rising earnings.

Five years later, Bloomberg reports that Macro Industries' chief executive has resigned after longstanding disagreements over corporate strategy with a group of activist shareholders. The activists, led by hedge fund Factastic Investment, want Macro to shutter under-performing operations. Macro's profits have collapsed, and its share price is down 46 per cent over the last twelve months. Analysts say that Macro's problems stem from over-expansion – in particular, its $2.5bn new plant in Durham, North Carolina, was delayed and over budget. The widget market is currently in the doldrums, suffering from excess supply. Macro's long-established competitors have also increased capacity in recent years, while a number of new low-cost producers have also entered the industry, including Dynamic Widget, whose own shares have disappointed since its IPO last year.

The market for widgets is suffering from the recent slowdown in emerging markets. China, the world's largest consumer of widgets, has vastly expanded domestic widget production over the last decade and has lately become a net exporter. Macro is reportedly considering a merger with its largest rival. Although its stock is trading below book, analysts say there's little near-term visibility. Of the remaining three brokerages that still cover Macro, two have sell recommendations with one hold.

The ups and downs of this fictional widget manufacturer describes a typical capital cycle. High current profitability often leads to overconfidence among managers, who confuse benign industry conditions with their own skill – a mistake encouraged by the media, which is constantly looking for corporate heroes and villains. Both investors and managers are engaged in making demand projections. Such forecasts have a wide margin of error and are prone to systematic biases. In good times, the demand forecasts tend to be too optimistic and in bad times overly pessimistic.

High profitability loosens capital discipline in an industry. When returns are high, companies are inclined to boost capital spending. Competitors are likely to follow – perhaps they are equally hubristic, or maybe they just don't want to lose market share. Besides, CEO pay is often set in relation to a company's earnings or market capitalization, thus incentivizing managers to grow their firm's assets. When a company announces with great fanfare a large increase in capacity, its share price often rises. Growth investors like growth! Momentum investors like momentum!

Investment bankers lubricate the wheels of the capital cycle, helping to grow capacity during the boom and consolidate industries in the bust. Their analysts are happiest covering fast-growing sexy sectors (higher stock turnover equals more commissions.) Bankers earn fees by arranging secondary issues and IPOs, which raise money to fund capital spending. Neither the M&A banker nor the brokerage analysts have much interest in long-term outcomes. As the investment bankers' incentives are skewed to short-term payoffs (bonuses), it's inevitable that their time horizon should also be myopic. It's not just a question of incentives. Both analysts and investors are given to extrapolating current trends. In a cyclical world, they think linearly.

The Macro example also shows the lag between a rise in capital spending and its impact on supply, which is characteristic of the capital cycle. The delay between investment and new production means that supply changes are lumpy (i.e., the supply curve is not smooth, as portrayed in the economics textbooks) and prone to overshooting. In fact, the market instability created by lags between changes in supply and production has long been recognized by economists (it is known as the "cobweb effect").

The capital cycle turns down as excess capacity becomes apparent and past demand forecasts are shown to have been overly optimistic. As profits collapse, management teams are changed, capital expenditure is slashed, and the industry starts to consolidate. The reduction in investment and contraction in industry supply paves the way for a recovery of profits. For an

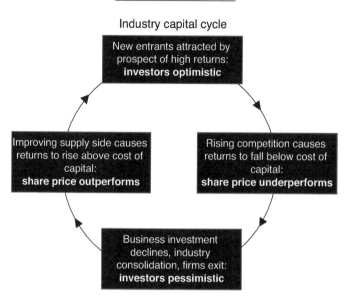

Chart I.1   The capital cycle

Source: Marathon.

investor who understands the capital cycle this is the moment when a beaten down stock becomes potentially interesting. However, brokerage analysts and many investors operating with short time horizons generally fail to spot the turn in the cycle but obsess instead about near-term uncertainty.

SOME RECENT CAPITAL CYCLES

The capital cycle described above might seem rather simplistic and contrived. Yet it is surprisingly common. Some industries, such as the semiconductor and airline industries, are particularly prone to violent capital cycles, resulting in frequent bouts of excess capacity and generally disappointing investment returns.[2] We have witnessed this boom-bust process in many other sectors in recent years. Marathon's earlier book, *Capital Account*, described the mistaken demand forecasts and overinvestment which accompanied the TMT bubble of the late 1990s.

During the tech boom, many telecoms companies operated on the mistaken assumption that Internet traffic was doubling every 100 days. This forecast was used to justify enormous capital spending by the likes of WorldCom, Global Crossing and a host of long-forgotten "alternative carriers" (as the

---

[2] For more on the semiconductor cycle, see below 2.6 "Escaping the semis' cycle."

minor telecoms players were then known). After the bubble burst, the misallocation of capital was revealed and, for several years afterwards, telecoms networks were plagued with massive excess capacity (known as "dark fibre," as much of the networks' expensively laid fibre optic cable remained unlit.)

Following the dotcom bust, a number of capital cycles appeared across a variety of industries. The global shipping industry provides a classic example.[3] Between 2001 and 2007, daily rates for "Panamax" class ships rose tenfold as China's rapidly increasing share of global trade boosted shipping demand. New orders in the shipbuilding industry are strongly correlated with daily spot rates. The supply response was inevitable if not immediate – it takes up to three years for a new ship order to be delivered. Between 2004 and 2009, however, the global dry bulk fleet doubled from 75 to 150m deadweight tonnes.[4] The effect of this new supply combined with the global slowdown resulted in a 90 per cent fall in Panamax daily rates, which wiped out all the gains from earlier in the decade. An investor who bought into shipping in the summer of 2007, before the onset of the global financial crisis, would have lost two-thirds of his money. Shares in global shipping companies, such as Denmark's Maersk Group, were down a similar amount. New ships, which had been ordered during the boom years, continued to be delivered long after the downturn. At the time of writing, the shipping industry is still suffering from poor capacity utilization and low rates.

Rising house prices after 2002 prompted another capital cycle in the US homebuilding industry. By the time the US housing bubble peaked in 2006, the excess stock of new homes was roughly equal to five times the annual production required to satisfy demand from new household formation. Spain and Ireland, whose real estate markets had even more pronounced upswings, ended up with excess housing stocks equivalent to roughly 15 times the average annual supply of the pre-boom period. Whilst under way, housing booms are invariably justified by references to rosy demographic projections. In the case of Spain, it turned out that recent immigration had largely been a function of the property boom. After the bubble burst and the Spanish economy entered a depression, foreigners left the country by the hundreds of thousands.

---

[3] See "Waves in Ship Prices and Investment," by Robin Greenwood and Samuel Hanson, NBER Working Paper, 2013.

[4] "Shipping Sector Report: Supply Finally Conquered but will Spot Rates be Liberated?," DNB Markets, 8 April 2013.

Several well-known "value" investors who ignored capital cycle dynamics were blindsided by the housing bust. In the years before US home prices peaked in 2006, homebuilders had grown their assets rapidly. After the bubble burst, these assets were written down. As a result, investors who bought US homebuilders' stocks towards the end of the building boom when they were trading around book value – towards their historical lows – ended up with very heavy losses.[5] From a capital cycle perspective, it's interesting to note that although UK and Australia experienced similar house price "bubbles," strict building regulations prevented a supply response. Largely as a consequence, both the British and Australian real estate markets recovered rapidly after the financial crisis.[6]

THE COMMODITY SUPERCYCLE

The commodity "supercycle," as the brokers called it, took off in the period of low interest rates following the dotcom bust of 2002 (see below, 1.3 "This time's no different" and 1.4 "Supercycle woes"). Rising prices for commodities were propelled by China, whose investment-heavy economy was experiencing consistent double digit annual GDP growth. After the financial crisis, China's investment share of GDP rose even further to some 50 per cent of GDP, a higher level than seen before in any other economy. By 2010, China accounted for more than 40 per cent of global demand for a number of commodities, including iron ore, coal, zinc and aluminium. China's share of incremental demand for these commodities was even higher.[7] The prices of these commodities and several others were far above their historic trends, arguably at bubble levels.[8]

---

[5] For instance, the large US homebuilder KB Home experienced a 28 per cent compound annual growth in assets between 2001 and 2006. By summer of 2006, its shares were trading at 1.2 times book. From that point, KB's book value declined by 85 per cent, and its shares, already well below their peak, fell a further 75 per cent.

[6] The fact that UK housing supply didn't respond to the British housing bubble is reflected in the superior performance of UK homebuilding stocks relative to their US counterparts over the last decade.

[7] Sanford C. Bernstein estimates that China contributed 92 per cent of total growth in iron ore consumption between 2000 and 2013. See "US Metals and Mining: Super-cycle... Where is the Super-Cycle?," July 2014.

[8] At the Boston-based investment firm GMO, my former employer, we defined an asset price bubble as a two-standard deviation from trend. By 2010, iron ore was 4.9 s.d. above trend, copper 3.9 s.d., coal 4.1 s.d., zinc 1.9 s.d. and aluminium 1.4 s.d. See Jeremy Grantham, "The Time to Wake Up: Days of Abundant Resources and Falling Prices Are Over Forever," GMO, April 2011.

As the price of commodities rose, the profitability of global mining companies took off. Their return on capital employed rose from around 7.5 per cent at the turn of the century to peak at nearly 35 per cent in 2005, rebounding after the financial crisis to around 20 per cent.[9] Even after the Lehman bust, most analysts extrapolated recent commodity demand growth into the distant future on the grounds that China's economy was destined to converge with, and eventually overtake, the mighty US economy. This combination of high commodity prices, strong profitability and robust expected future demand spurred the miners to increase production.

Annual global mine production (in USD terms) rose by 20 per cent annually between 2000 and 2011, more than half of this growth coming from iron ore and coal.[10] In volume terms, iron ore production doubled over the same period. Mining capital expenditure climbed more than fivefold, from around $30bn a year at the turn of the century to peak at over $160bn.[11] Changes in iron ore supply materialize after a long lag – it takes up to nine years to develop a greenfield site. New supply is particularly lumpy owing to the huge size of some of the new mines – Vale's Serra Sul project in Brazil, which had a capex budget of nearly $20bn, is expected to add nearly 5 per cent to global iron ore production.

During the years of rocketing commodity prices, supply also came on stream from non-traditional producers, including Iran and parts of Africa. Although the global mining industry is concentrated among a handful of major players, competition has been fierce – Australia's Fortescue Metals Group, a relative newcomer, expanded aggressively to become the 4th largest iron producer by 2011. Many smaller mining companies came to the market, including a number of rather dubious foreign outfits floated on the London Stock Exchange.[12] High prices also increased the supply of scrap metal.[13]

The commodity supercycle appears to have turned in 2011, roughly coincident with a slowdown in China's growth rate. By April 2015, the price of seaborne iron ore was down roughly 70 per cent from the peak (in USD terms). New mining capacity, commissioned when prices were high, is destined to come on stream for the next several years, contributing further to

---

[9] "A Long Lasting Mining Capex Correction," UBS, June 5, 2014.

[10] See Bernstein, op. cit.

[11] The ratio of the miner's capex to depreciation, which rose from 1.1x in 2001 to peak at 3x in 2012, UBS, ibid.

[12] On a 12-month basis, global junior and mid-tier equity raisings in the mining sector went from just $1bn in 2005 to $30bn by mid-2011, falling back to around $2bn by early 2014 (Bernstein, ibid.).

[13] Scrap metal consumption rose from 401m to 573m metric tonnes, between 2000 and 2011.

overcapacity.[14] The profitability of the global miners has declined in tandem with commodity prices, and their shares have underperformed.[15] Thus, the great commodity supercycle bears the hallmarks of a classic capital cycle: high prices boosting profitability, followed by rising investment and the arrival of new entrants, encouraged by overly optimistic demand forecasts; and the cycle turning once supply has increased and demand has disappointed.

THE CAPITAL CYCLE ANOMALY

So much for some recent anecdotal evidence in support of the capital cycle approach. What do the finance professors have to say? When I wrote the introduction to Marathon's *Capital Account* just over a decade ago, little academic work had been published on this subject. More recently, however, a number of papers have appeared, observing an inverse relationship between capital expenditure and investment returns. Firms with the lowest asset growth have outperformed those with the highest asset growth, as the chart from Société Générale strategist Andrew Lapthorne shows (see Chart I.2).

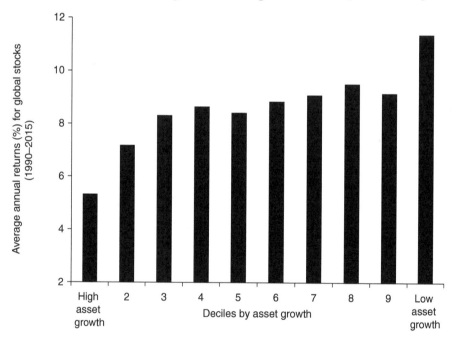

Chart I.2   Asset growth and investment returns

Source: SocGen.

---

[14] A recent research note from Sanford C. Bernstein (*supra*) suggested that potential new capacity in the pipeline amounted to 50 per cent of current global iron ore production.

[15] Fortescue's share price fell 44 per cent in the five years to June 2015.

Modern finance theory is based on the notion that while markets are efficient, certain "factors" – namely, size, value and momentum – have historically beaten the benchmark index. Nobel laureate Eugene Fama and his colleague Ken French have suggested adding two more factors to their model: profits and investment.[16] With regards to the capital cycle, Fama and French observe that companies which have invested *less* have delivered higher returns. This finding has been termed the "asset-growth anomaly." A paper in the *Journal of Finance* reports that corporate events associated with asset expansion – such as mergers & acquisitions, equity issuance and new loans – tend to be followed by low returns.[17] Conversely, events associated with asset contraction – including spin-offs, share repurchases, debt prepayments and dividend initiations – are followed by positive excess returns. The negative impact on shareholder returns from expanding corporate assets was found to persist for up to five years.

The *Journal of Finance* authors conclude that firm asset growth is a *stronger* determinant of returns than traditional value (low price-to-book), size (market capitalization), and momentum (both long and short horizon). Other finance economists have found that companies often accelerate investment after their stocks have done relatively well and that these same companies later underperform. This suggests that asset growth may explain the phenomenon of momentum reversal.[18]

In short, recent research is edging towards the conclusion that the excess returns historically observed from value stocks and the low returns from growth stocks are not independent of asset growth. This leads to a key insight of the capital cycle investment approach: *when analyzing the prospects of both value and growth stocks, it is necessary to take into account asset growth, at both the company and the sectoral level.* One researcher goes so far as to claim that the value effect disappears after controlling for capital investment.[19]

---

[16] Eugene Fama and Kenneth French, "A Five-Factor Asset Pricing Model," Working Paper, September 2014.

[17] Michael Cooper, Huseyin Gulen, and Michael Schill, "Asset Growth and the Cross-Section of Stock Returns," *Journal of Finance*, 2008. See also, Sheridan Titman, John Wei and Feixue Xie, "Capital Investment and Stock Returns,"*Journal of Financial and Quantitative Analysis*, 2004; Yuhang Xie, "Interpreting the Value Effect through Q-Theory: An Empirical Investigation," Working Paper, 2007; and S.P. Kothari, Jonathan Lewellen, and Jerold Warner, "The Behavior of Aggregate Corporate Investment," Working Paper, September 2014.

[18] Christopher Anderson and Luis Garcia-Fijóo, "Empirical Evidence on Capital Investment, Growth Options, and Security Returns," *Journal of Finance*, 2006.

[19] Xie, ibid.

MEAN REVERSION

The "asset-growth anomaly" can be viewed from the perspective of mean reversion.[20] Mean reversion is not driven by the ebb and flow of animal spirits alone. Rather, it works through differential rates of investment. Companies which earn above their cost of capital tend to invest more, thereby driving down their future returns, while companies which fail to earn their cost of capital behave in the opposite way. This point is recognized by Benjamin Graham and David Dodd in *Security Analysis* (1934), the bible of value investing:

> A business which sells at a premium does so because it earns a large return upon its capital; this large return attracts competition; and generally speaking, it is not likely to continue indefinitely. Conversely in the case of a business selling at a large discount because of abnormally low earnings. The absence of new competition, the withdrawal of old competition from the field, and other natural economic forces, should tend eventually to improve the situation and restore a normal rate of profit on the investment.

Investment drives mean reversion for both individual companies and whole markets. A researcher at the University of Arizona has demonstrated that corporate investment in most developed economies (comprising US and EAFE) is a significant negative predictor of aggregate profitability, stock market returns, and even GDP growth.[21] During the US stock market bubble of the late 1990s, for instance, the investment share of GDP rose above average levels. After the bubble burst and the misallocation of capital of the boom years was revealed, both aggregate investment and profitability declined and the US economy went into recession.

All this suggests that asset allocators should consider market valuation in tandem with the capital cycle. Normally, the two run together. The US stock market in recent years, however, has proved something of a conundrum. Since 2010, US stocks have looked expensive when viewed from a valuation perspective (e.g., the cyclically-adjusted price-earning ratio) largely due to the fact that profits have been above average. Yet US corporate investment has been lacklustre since the global financial crisis.

---

[20] For a discussion of mean reversion and the capital cycle, see *Capital Account*, p. 28.

[21] Salman Arif, "Aggregate Investment and Its Consequences," Working Paper, March 2012. The exceptions to this finding are Hong Kong, Switzerland and Sweden.

With the key driver of mean reversion missing, profits have remained elevated for longer than expected, and the US stock market has delivered robust returns.[22] China provides an example at the opposite end of the spectrum: stock prices have often appeared cheap from a valuation perspective, but investment and asset growth have been elevated resulting in poor corporate profitability.

EXPLANATIONS FOR THE CAPITAL CYCLE ANOMALY

The market inefficiency observed by capital cycle analysis can be explained in terms of the conventional findings of behavioural finance – namely, some combination of overconfidence, base-rate neglect, cognitive dissonance, narrow-framing and extrapolation appear to account for the fact that companies with high levels of investment tend to underperform. These behavioural factors are reinforced by agency-related problems. Skewed incentives encourage both investors and corporate managers to adopt short-term perspectives which are inimical to capital cycle analysis. Rational investors are unable to impose their views on the market as the capital cycle poses a number of "limits to arbitrage."

OVERCONFIDENCE

Why do investors and corporate managers pay so little attention to the inverse relationship between capital spending and future investment returns? The short answer is that they appear to be infatuated with asset growth. Corporate expansion fires the imagination of both managers and shareholders. This mistaken fetishism for growth is reflected in the historic poor performance of stocks with higher growth expectations (higher valuations). Behavioural finance suggests that investors (and corporate managers) are prone to overconfidence when it comes to making forecasts. As Yogi Berra says, "It's tough to make predictions, especially about the future." As we shall see, this is especially the case when it comes to predicting future levels of demand.

COMPETITION NEGLECT

Overinvestment is not a solitary activity; it comes about because several players in an industry have been increasing capacity at the same time. When

---

[22] This is not to say that unorthodox monetary policies from the Federal Reserve have played no part in recent years in inflating US stock prices.

market participants respond to perceived increases in demand by increasing capacity in an industry, they fail to consider the impact of increasing supply on future returns. "Competition neglect," according to Harvard Business School professors Robin Greenwood and Samuel Hanson, is "particularly strong when firms receive delayed feedback about the consequences of their own decisions."[23] The authors of a paper in the *American Economic Review* sought to explain why so many new entrants into business frequently fail. They found that managers so overestimate their own skills they neglect competitive threats.[24]

This failure to pay attention to the outward shift in the supply curve can be linked to another common behavioural trait, known as "base-rate neglect." Namely, the tendency of people not to take into account all available information when making a decision. With regards to the workings of the capital cycle, investors focus on current (and projected) future profitability but ignore changes in the industry's asset base from which returns are generated. At times, this tendency morphs into what psychologists call "cognitive dissonance" – a wilful refusal to consider disconfirming evidence once a course of action has been decided upon.

INSIDE VIEW

Such narrow-framing arises by decision-makers taking the "inside view," a term coined by the psychologist Daniel Kahneman.[25] The inside view is generated when individuals in a group focus on "specific circumstances and search for evidence in their own experiences."[26] As investment strategist Michael Mauboussin (formerly of Legg Mason) writes:

---

[23] Robin Greenwood and Samuel Hanson, "Waves in Ship Prices and Investment," NBER Working Paper, July 2013. On the phenomenon of excess investment, Greenwood and Hanson comment that "models in which market participants over-extrapolate exogenously given cash flows are well understood in economics... But in most industries, the cash flows are not exogenous but are an endogenous equilibrium outcome that is impacted by the industry supply response to demand shocks. It follows that firms may over-extrapolate current profits either because they (i) overestimate the persistence of the exogenous demand shocks facing the industry or (ii) fail to fully appreciate the long-run endogenous supply response to those demand shocks."

[24] Colin Camerer and Dan Lovallo, "Overconfidence and Excess Entry: An Experimental Approach," *American Economic Review*, 1999.

[25] See Michael Mauboussin, "Death, Taxes and Reversion to the Mean," Legg Mason Capital Management, December 2007.

[26] Daniel Kahneman, *Thinking Fast and Slow*, 2011, p. 247.

An inside view considers a problem by focusing on the specific task and the information at hand, and predicts based on that unique set of inputs. This is the approach analysts most often use in their modeling, and indeed is common for all forms of planning. In contrast, an outside view considers the problem as an instance in a broader reference class. Rather than seeing the problem as unique, the outside view asks if there are similar situations that can provide useful calibration for modeling. Kahneman notes this is a very unnatural way to think precisely because it forces analysts to set aside all of the cherished information they have unearthed about a company. This is why people use the outside view so rarely.[27]

Analysts with highly specialized knowledge of an industry are prone to adopting the inside view. They assume that their own case is unique. When it comes to investment analysis, looking for relevant historical parallels (e.g., comparing the US real estate boom of the 2000s to the Japanese real estate market in the 1980s) is an example of taking the outside view. "In the inside view," write the *AER* authors in their paper on new entrants' failures, "there is no special role for anticipation of the number of competitors or their abilities. In the outside view, the fact that most entries fail cannot be ignored."

EXTRAPOLATION

The inside view is linked with our tendency to extrapolate. Behavioural finance – a branch of economics established by Kahneman and his late colleague Amos Tversky – describes how we "anchor" on the information placed in front of us and are overly influenced by our immediate experiences ("recency bias.") Another common heuristic is the tendency to draw strong inferences from small samples. These weaknesses reinforce the propensity of investors to make linear forecasts, despite the fact that most economic activity is cyclical – there are trade cycles, credit cycles, liquidity cycles, real estate cycles, profit cycles, commodity cycles, venture capital cycles and, of course, industry capital cycles. Our inclination to extrapolate must be hard-wired.

---

[27] Mauboussin, ibid. The failures of analysts who take an "inside view" is discussed below, see 3.1 "Food for thought."

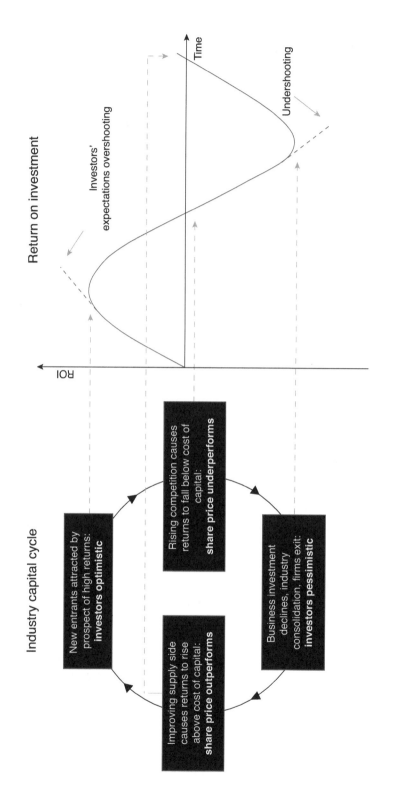

Chart I.3   Investor overreaction and the capital cycle
Source: Marathon.

Value investors who buy cheap stocks with depressed earnings are protected against the extrapolation tendency. As the author of a recent investment text book writes:

> The main behavioral explanation for value stocks' long-run outperformance is excessive extrapolation by investors of multiyear growth rates. In reality, growth mean reverts faster than the market expects, making growth stocks more likely to disappoint.[28]

The capital cycle analyst would agree with these comments, adding crucially that mean reversion is driven by changes on the supply side which value investors who consider only quantitative measures of valuation are inclined to overlook.

SKEWED INCENTIVES

Skewed incentives exacerbate these well-known behavioural weaknesses. CEO compensation is often linked to short-term performance measures, such as annual changes in earnings-per-share or shareholder returns. Stock prices often react positively to announcements of major capital spending.[29] Companies which invest more often attract premium valuations. The stocks of high asset growth companies often exhibit positive momentum.[30] Executive pay is also frequently linked to a company's size, as measured by revenue or market capitalization. The incentives are thus skewed for managers to favour growth and to downplay any adverse long-term consequences. There is some evidence that managers with a large ownership stake are more likely to shrink capital employed – through buybacks – if they see few profitable alternatives.

Investors whose compensation is linked to short-term performance are also inclined to myopia. Investment bankers who drive the capital cycle – raising money to finance investment with debt and equity issuance and launching IPOs – are compensated according to their fee generation rather than the outcome their capital-raising activities may have for clients and shareholders. Investment bank analysts serve as cheerleaders; their pay is linked to brokerage commissions, generated by stock turnover. They too have little interest in long-term outcomes.

---

[28] See Antti Ilmanen, *Expected Returns,* 2011, Chapter 12.
[29] See Titman et al., op. cit.
[30] Ibid.

PRISONER'S DILEMMA

Game theory can also explain overinvestment within an industry. Managers in a business with high current profitability may face a problem akin to the prisoner's dilemma. Take a situation where future demand growth can profitably accommodate expansion by a single player, but no more. If several players simultaneously expand their operations, their aggregate profits will decline at some future date. Under such circumstances, it's collectively rational for the incumbents to prevent any expansion – since gains only accrue to one of their number. If the industry is competitive or has low barriers to entry, there is an incentive for one player to break ranks and enjoy the fruits of expansion. The remainder may feel obliged to follow suit, as they can't abide a competitor leaving them standing and may wish to protect market share. Thus, excessive asset growth can result from a lack of cooperative behaviour within an industry (see Section 1.1 "Evolution of cooperation").

LIMITS TO ARBITRAGE

If high asset growth companies consistently underperform, why don't smart investors simply short these stocks? Or, if they are constrained from going short, at least not go long? The answer is that the fast-growing companies often have volatile share prices and going short volatility can be very expensive – as short-sellers of Internet and technology stocks discovered to their cost in the late 1990s. Furthermore, companies with strong asset growth often have large market capitalizations – as was the case with many of the telecoms companies in the 1990s and more recently with the global mining stocks. Investors who avoid buying high asset growth stocks may be forced to take large bets against the benchmark. Short-term underperformance may result in the only risk which keeps professional investors awake at night, namely "career risk."[31] It should also be noted that capital cycles vary in length, and nobody knows in advance when they will turn. This uncertainty adds yet another limit to arbitrage. Marathon's private ownership and longstanding client relationships

---

[31] See Eric Lam and John Wei, "Limits-to-Arbitrage, Investment Frictions, and the Asset Growth Anomaly," *Journal of Financial Economics*, forthcoming. Harvard's Andrei Shleifer and Robert Vishny demonstrated that markets become inefficient when rational investors face high costs, which come, for example, from shorting volatile stocks. They coined the phrase "limits to arbitrage" to describe this phenomenon (see eponymous paper in the *Journal of Finance*, 1997). Lam and Wei argue that the inverse relationship between high asset growth and subsequent returns is most pronounced for stocks that are difficult to arbitrage, because they have larger market caps, greater trading costs, or are more volatile.

enable the firm to adopt a long-term approach, more tolerant of benchmark deviation, which is necessary to apply capital cycle analysis.

FUNDAMENTALS OF CAPITAL CYCLE ANALYSIS

Marathon's approach is to look for investment opportunities among both value and growth stocks, as conventionally defined.[32] They come about because the market frequently mistakes the pace at which profitability reverts to the mean. For a "value" stock, the bet is that profits will rebound more quickly than is expected and for a "growth stock," that profits will remain elevated for longer than market expectations.

FOCUS ON SUPPLY RATHER THAN DEMAND

Given that the future is uncertain, why should Marathon's approach fare any better? The answer is that most investors spend the bulk of their time trying to forecast future demand for the companies they follow. The aviation analyst will try to answer the question: How many long-haul flights will be taken globally in 2020? A global autos strategist will attempt to forecast China's demand for passenger cars 15 years hence. No one knows the answers to these questions. Long-range demand projections are likely to result in large forecasting errors.

Capital cycle analysis, however, focuses on supply rather than demand. Supply prospects are far less uncertain than demand, and thus easier to forecast. In fact, increases in an industry's aggregate supply are often well flagged and come with varying lags – depending on the industry in question – after changes in the industry's aggregate capital spending. In certain industries, such as aircraft manufacturing and shipbuilding, the supply pipelines are well-known. Because most investors (and corporate managers) spend more of their time thinking about demand conditions in an industry than changing supply, stock prices often fail to anticipate negative supply shocks.[33]

---

[32] See below, 2.1 "Warning labels" and 2.7 "Value in growth."

[33] Several accounting based measures provide insights into the capital cycle. As observed above, stocks with the fastest asset growth tend to underperform. When a company's capital expenditure relative to depreciation rises above its average level it may be a sign that the capital cycle is deteriorating (see 1.4 "Supercycle woes" and Chapter 1, "A capital cycle revolution"). A rising gap between reported earnings and free cash flow is another warning sign (see 1.7 "Major concerns"). The Herfindahl Index provides a statistical measure of industry concentration which may reveal changes in competitive conditions. Anecdotal signs prove just as useful in gauging the capital cycle. It's generally a bad sign when a company starts building a grandiose new head office (see 4.9 "On the rocks").

ANALYZE COMPETITIVE CONDITIONS WITHIN AN INDUSTRY

From the investment perspective, the key point is that returns are driven by changes on the supply side. A firm's profitability comes under threat when the competitive conditions are deteriorating. The negative phase of the capital cycle is characterized by industry fragmentation and increasing supply. The aim of capital cycle analysis is to spot these developments in advance of the market. New entrants noisily trumpet their arrival in an industry. A rash of IPOs concentrated in a hot sector is a red flag; secondary share issuances another, as are increases in debt. Conversely, a focus on competitive conditions should alert investors to opportunities where supply conditions are benign and companies are able to maintain profitability for longer than the market expects. An understanding of competitive conditions and supply side dynamics also helps investors avoid value traps (such as US housing stocks in 2005–06).

CAVEAT INVESTMENT BANKER

The capital cycle analyst is particularly wary of the actions of investment banks, and the work of their in-house propagandists, the brokerage analyst.[34] Besides generating fees for themselves, the main economic function of the investment bank is to supply finance to capital-hungry businesses – for which they earn generous fees. Bankers are paid to drive capital cycles, not to worry about the negative long-term consequences that capital expansion may have for clients.

Brokers also pay little attention to the capital cycle which operates beyond their short-term time horizon. Instead, they spend their time trying to forecast the next quarter's earnings, which is good for generating turnover and commissions, and occasionally going "over the wall" to help their banker colleagues market a new share issuance. In fact, brokers have never been adept at anticipating movements in the capital cycle:

> "Rarely does one find a brokerage house study that point outs," wrote Benjamin Graham, "with a convincing array of facts, that a popular industry is heading for a fall or that an unpopular one is due to prosper. Wall Street's view of the future is notoriously fallible... [especially when it] is directed towards forecasting the course of profits in various industries."

---

[34] For a humorous take on this, see Chapter 7.

Yet the broker's continual failure to analyse the capital cycle doesn't mean that all effort is futile! The good capital cycle analyst is a contrarian by nature and always sceptical of the siren call of Wall Street.

SELECTING THE RIGHT CORPORATE MANAGERS

Marathon is fond of repeating two comments of Warren Buffett. The first being to the effect that most chief executives have risen to the top of their companies because they "have excelled in an area such as marketing, production, engineering – or sometimes, institutional politics." Yet they may not have the capital allocation skills required of managers. Such skills are essential, according to the Sage of Omaha, since, "after ten years on the job, a CEO whose company retains earnings equal to 10 per cent of net worth will have been responsible for the deployment of more than 60 per cent of all capital at work in the business." Capital cycle analysis involves keeping a sharp eye on managers to assess their ability to allocate capital. Marathon spends a lot of time meeting and questioning managers to this effect (see 3.8 "A meeting of minds").

GENERALISTS MAKE BETTER CAPITAL CYCLE ANALYSTS

Industry specialists are prone to taking the "inside view." Having got lost in a thicket of detail, industry specialists end up not seeing the wood for the trees. They may, for instance, spend too much time comparing the performance and prospects of companies within their sector and fail to recognize, as a result, the risks that the industry as a whole is running. Marathon prefers to employ generalists who are less likely to suffer from "reference group neglect" and better able to employ an understanding of capital cycle dynamics across industries.

ADOPT A LONG-TERM APPROACH

Capital cycle analysis, like value investing, requires patience. It takes a long time for an industry's capital cycle to play out. The Nasdaq started bubbling in 1995. Yet it wasn't until the spring of 2000 that the dotcom bubble finally burst. New supply comes with varying lags in different industries. As we have seen, it can take nearly a decade for a new mine to start producing. Marathon warned of the dangers of rising mining investment back in May 2006 (see 1.3 "This time's no different" – yet after rebounding in the wake of the financial crisis, the commodity supercycle didn't turn down for another five years. Marathon's long-term investment discipline, with its very low portfolio turnover, is well suited to applying the capital cycle approach.

CAPITAL CYCLE BREAKDOWNS

Capital cycle analysis requires patience, a certain doggedness (willingness to be wrong for a long period) and a contrarian mindset. Once the cycle has turned and overcapacity in an industry has been exposed, the progression of events appears inevitable. That's hindsight bias. At the time, the outcome never seems so certain. Besides, on occasion the normal operation of the capital cycle breaks down. Over the last two decades, the Internet has destroyed many long-established business models – in advertising (Yellow Pages), media (newspapers), retailing (bookshops), and entertainment (music industry and video rental). Investors who underestimated the disruptive impact of new technology have lost money.[35] The capital cycle also ceases to function properly when policymakers protect industries (see 5.4 "Broken banks" and 5.5 "Twilight zone") and under conditions of state capitalism, as found in modern China (see Chapter 6, "China Syndrome").

THE TENETS OF CAPITAL CYCLE ANALYSIS

The essence of capital cycle analysis can thus be reduced to the following key tenets:

- Most investors devote more time to thinking about demand than supply. Yet demand is more difficult to forecast than supply.
- Changes in supply drive industry profitability. Stock prices often fail to anticipate shifts in the supply side.
- The value/growth dichotomy is false. Companies in industries with a supportive supply side can justify high valuations.
- Management's capital allocation skills are paramount, and meetings with management often provide valuable insights.
- Investment bankers drive the capital cycle, largely to the detriment of investors.
- When policymakers interfere with the capital cycle, the market-clearing process may be arrested. New technologies can also disrupt the normal operation of the capital cycle.

---

[35] For Marathon's experience, see footnote to 5.6 "Capital punishment."

- Generalists are better able to adopt the "outside view" necessary for capital cycle analysis.
- Long-term investors are better suited to applying the capital cycle approach.

A BRIEF OUTLINE OF THE BOOK

I have arranged the essays from Marathon's *Global Investment Review* in the following order: *Chapter 1 – Capital Cycle Revolution*: This chapter looks at the operation of the capital cycle in a number of industries, from fishing to wind turbines. As noted above, the capital cycle enters a dangerous phase when high profitability leads to rising capital spending, as has occurred in both the mining and oil sectors in recent years. In these cases, increases in miners' capex to depreciation ratio and the decline in energy companies' cash conversion rate served as red flags for investors. The capital cycle enters a benign phase when low profitability results in industry consolidation, as the global beer industry experienced at the turn of the century. Alternately, the capital cycle takes a positive turn when industry players cease competing virulently against each other and learn to cooperate.

Chapter 2 – Value In Growth: The essays contained in this chapter eschew the conventional growth/value dichotomy. Marathon rejects the label "value investor," which is generally associated with buying stocks that are cheap based on accounting measures. Instead, the aim is to look for stocks which are selling below Marathon's estimate of intrinsic value and have strong competitive positions: such companies may benefit from network effects, occupy secure niches, be firmly embedded an industry's supply chain, or enjoy pricing power because their products are sold through third parties more concerned with quality than price. Marathon argues that high valuations are often justified for companies protected by deep moats. Fast-growing companies with little or no profits and high valuations, such as Amazon, can still make good investments provided their industry's supply side remains supportive.

Chapter 3 – Management Matters: Over the medium term, the performance of companies depends on how well managers allocate their assets. It's important therefore that investors meet with management in order to assess their asset allocation skills. Marathon argues that much can be learned from meeting CEOs – the ones who fly around in private jets, spend their time constructing lavish new headquarters, or are greedy and vain, generally deliver poor returns for shareholders. The greatest managers, like Björn Wahlroos at

Finland's Sampo, understand their industry's capital cycle and invest in a contrarian fashion.

Chapter 4 – Accidents in Waiting: The financial crisis took most of the world by surprise. Yet banks can also be analysed from a capital cycle perspective. When bank assets (loans) are growing strongly, this is generally a negative indicator. In the years prior to the Lehman bust, Marathon's investment professionals held meetings with a number of banks and became increasingly concerned by what they saw – particularly at the Anglo-Irish Bank, whose failure imperilled the sovereign credit of Ireland. One European bank, Sweden's Handelsbanken, provides a model of how to overcome many of the flaws inherent in modern banking, including asset-liability mismatching and chronic short-termism.

Chapter 5 – The Living Dead: Policymakers have responded to the financial crisis by lowering interest rates and supporting stricken industries, such as European automakers. Their actions have interfered with the economic process of creative destruction. Low return businesses are able to survive in the era of ultra-low rates, creating the possibility that Europe is entering an era of "zombie" capitalism – akin to Japan's lost decades. Low rates have also encouraged investors to chase yield, which poses the threat of capital losses at some future date.

Chapter 6 – China Syndrome: Many investors believe that investment returns follow economic growth. Yet the returns from the Chinese stock market since it reopened in the early 1990s have been dreadful – notwithstanding the occasional bubble. Poor returns from Chinese equities are largely the result of Beijing's investment-intensive growth model, which relies on cheap capital, debt forgiveness and never-ending asset growth. The fact that many Chinese IPOs have been carved out of larger state-owned enterprises and dressed up with artificial profits has further damaged investors' interests.

Chapter 7 – Inside the Mind of Wall Street: As outlined above, Marathon is inherently suspicious of the modern investment banker, who prizes fees (and bonuses) above all else. The book concludes with a satirical take on Wall Street provided by the antics of a fictional banker, Stanley Churn, head of the investment bank Greedspin. Any resemblance to real bankers and real banks, living or dead, is purely coincidental!

PART I

INVESTMENT PHILOSOPHY

1

CAPITAL CYCLE REVOLUTION

The following essays describe the operation of the capital cycle in a variety of industries, from cod fishing to global brewers and wind turbine manufacturers. A common theme linking these pieces is the importance of understanding how competition – or the supply side – evolves over time, and the role it plays in determining both industry and individual company returns on capital. In addition, some of the essays highlight the malign influence of regulation and the potentially disruptive impact of technology on particular industry capital cycles. An understanding of the capital cycle helps to identify and avoid speculative bubbles. All too often, high returns attract capital, breeding excessive competition and overinvestment. In recent years, for instance, there has been an epic burst of capital spending in the field of resource extraction. Four of the articles presented below highlight the dangers posed to shareholders over the last decade by ever rising levels of investment in the mining and the oil and gas sectors.

1.1 EVOLUTION OF COOPERATION (FEBRUARY 2004)

Instability within an industry can create the conditions for improved future returns

In the 1980s, Robert Axelrod, an American political scientist and author of *The Evolution of Cooperation*, invited game theory experts to participate in repeated rounds of the best-known problem in their field – the prisoner's dilemma game.[1] Axelrod found that a policy of "tit for tat," or reciprocity,

---

[1] The "prisoner's dilemma" involves two prisoners, kept apart, who are separately offered inducements to betray each other. If one betrays the other while the other stays silent, then the squealer goes free and the one who stayed silent is harshly punished. If both prisoners betray each other, they each receive harsh punishment. If both stay silent, they each receive a lesser penalty. The rational solution to a single game is for both prisoners to betray each other. When the game is played several times, a successful strategy of "tit for tat" evolves in which each betrayal is met by retaliation.

was the most successful strategy to adopt in the long-run. He pointed to an intriguing example of "tit for tat" in the trenches of World War I. When stationed for long periods opposite each other, unspoken truces emerged spontaneously between British and German troops. If either side reneged on the compact, revenge would be exacted by the injured party, after which the truce would return.

From an investor standpoint, a similar kind of cooperation in basic industries is crucial to shareholder value creation. The trick is to identify conditions where cooperative behaviour can exist or may evolve, while avoiding those industries where this is unlikely to happen. For contrarian investors, a history of poor returns in an industry can represent a potential opportunity, since cooperative behaviour is more likely to break out if companies are responding to the imperative of balance sheet repair. Just as Hyman Minsky, the US economist and author of *Stabilizing an Unstable Economy*, observed that financial stability is destabilizing since it leads to all kinds of excessive behaviour, so instability can, from a capital cycle standpoint, create conditions of stability.

The ideal capital cycle opportunity for us has often been one in which a small number of large players evolve from a situation of excess competition and exert what is euphemistically called "pricing discipline." Having a small number of players is important, since retaliation (say a price cut) is likely to be a more powerful weapon in the hands of a dominant price setter, although barriers to entry are also required to deter opportunistic entrants from taking advantage of any price umbrella.

Certain industries having evolved oligopolistic industry structures, have a potentially favourable capital cycle, and yet persist in generating poor returns. Partly, this is because "tit for tat" is only likely to work where the strategy can be properly discerned. In the auto industry, for example, there is too much noise in the everyday competitive battle. Carmakers have to decide not just on price, but also on specification, customer financing terms, new model launches, service and warranty terms etc., leading to the paradoxical conclusion that product differentiation can be an impediment to achieving supernormal returns. Contrast this with the steel or paper producer, whose product is relatively undifferentiated.

Politics can also hinder the operation of the capital cycle. In the European auto industry, for instance, Volkswagen has for many years pursued a market share strategy. At VW, the agenda of the State of Lower Saxony (the largest single shareholder, with 18.2 per cent) has more of a stakeholder than shareholder bent, with an eye to local employment conditions. In airlines, the habit of protecting "national champions" has not died out in Europe as yet.

Transaction frequency is another feature that can confuse, such as in the airline industry, where decisions on pricing have been devolved to front-line managers, creating a competitive battleground akin to death by a thousand cuts. Again, contrast this with an industry such as the automotive glass industry in Europe, where the three remaining participants enjoy long-term supply agreements and infrequent decisions on new capacity that are signalled clearly in advance.

Axelrod attributes the success of the "tit for tat" strategy in his repeated prisoner's dilemma game to what he calls the "shadow of the future," which has a bearing on decision-making in the current game. Participants are less likely to defect in the current game if they think that a competitor will retaliate in the subsequent game. The generals of WWI, infuriated by the policy of "live and let live" adopted by their troops realized that the way to change behaviour was to remove the "shadow of the future." This they did by reducing the time served by troops in a particular trench, making it harder for the soldiers to establish cooperative rules of (non-)engagement with the opponent. Industries where managers can be seen to be extending the "shadow of the future," by signalling how they will respond to competitor behaviour, are thus wholly welcome.

Biological evolution works by natural selection, and so it is with the evolution of cooperation. Employment or anti-trust concerns blunt the efficacy of this process, most notably via Chapter 11 bankruptcy protection. Again, we have noted in the past how the imposition of exit barriers can lead to "survival of the unfittest." Likewise on a broader macroeconomic level, the low interest rate policy of the Federal Reserve – replacing an investment/tech bubble with a housing/credit bubble – has (so far) stymied many of the natural evolutionary forces. But that's another story....

A basic industry with few players, rational management, barriers to entry, a lack of exit barriers and non-complex rules of engagement is the perfect setting for companies to engage in cooperative behaviour. It is relatively easy to identify those industries where these conditions exist currently (just look at existing returns on capital), and it is for this reason that the really juicy investment returns are to be found in industries which are evolving to this state. The joy from a capital cycle perspective is that most investors are, for a variety of behavioural reasons, taken by surprise. Across many competitive battlefronts, we are always looking out for the next outbreak of peace.

1.2   COD PHILOSOPHY (AUGUST 2004)

The cod fishing industry provided a marvellous example of the capital cycle in action until governments intervened

Thoughtful investment managers probably packed *Capital: The Story of Long-Term Investment Excellence* by Charles Ellis for their beach reading this year. Instead, our pick of the holiday reading this year is *Cod* by Mark Kurlansky. In this wonderful book, Kurlansky describes the rise and fall of the cod fishing and processing industry from the perspective of a social historian and gastronome, and the book takes the form of a culinary travelogue peppered with recipes. The recipes look appealing, but our advice is to read the book from the perspective of the capital cycle; then the industry's rise and fall becomes even more interesting.

While there has always been plenty of cod in the sea, so to speak, the identity of the trade's beneficiaries has changed constantly. What follows here is a précis of the book from an investor's perspective, with apologies to Mr Kurlansky for reinterpreting his fine work.

Cod is prized because it is high in protein and low in oils and fats. Fresh, the meat flakes and falls from the bone, so it is easy to prepare. When it is dried, the water evaporates and the residue is more than 80 per cent protein. Almost the entire fish can be put to use: in Iceland, the organs are used as fertilizer and even the bones are softened with milk and fed to children. The fish is large and easily caught – so easily caught it is of little interest to sport fishermen. Markets for the fish stretch from North America, throughout Europe and to the Caribbean. In fishing, cod's where the money is (or, at least was).

In the early sixteenth century, cod was so prized that Portuguese fishermen sailed to Newfoundland to catch cod for the Basque market in Spain. This was no easy trip, and Kurlansky notes that "European ambition was simply too far ahead of technology, and until better ships and better navigation were developed, shipwrecks and disappearances were a regular part of this new adventure." It is probably a safe bet that the price of cod reflected these trials, enough at least to fund industry development, as by the mid-sixteenth century over 60 per cent of the fish eaten in Europe were cod, a percentage that remained relatively unchanged for almost two centuries.

To prepare the fish for the long journey to market, cod was gutted, sun dried and salted. Space was limited on small, sail-powered trawlers, and so processing took place in port. Harbours with natural exposed rock slabs for drying cod, located near the cod fields, as can be found on the Newfoundland, New England and Icelandic coasts, became the natural pinch-point between the abundance of fish in the sea and the households of Europe. The result was a cod processing boom, and "men of no particular skill, and with very little capital, made fortunes." However, the pinch-point in the system, where the excess profits were made, did not stay with the fishing ports for long, as their harbours were too small to berth transatlantic cargo vessels. Instead, the bottleneck naturally migrated to the nearest sizeable port with a central market, which in New England was Boston.

Until the American Revolution, Britain's trade monopoly with Massachusetts required the colony to sell Boston salted cod to selected British ports. But England had its own cod industry and a taste for fresh, not salted fish. The market for New England cod remained in Continental Europe and especially with the Basques in Spain and in Portugal. So the British authorities turned a blind eye to the illegal trade, and New England entrepreneurs sold salt cod directly to the Europeans in exchange for currency and materials, with lower quality scraps sold directly to the sugar plantations in the Caribbean in exchange for molasses.

A three-way trade evolved: ships took New England salted cod to Europe, African slaves to the Caribbean sugar plantations, and Caribbean molasses to the newly established New England rum distilleries. By the eighteenth century, the three-way trade, powered by cod, had lifted New England from a distant colony of starving settlers to an international commercial power with a fully-fledged "cod aristocracy."

This phase lasted until technology caught up, or rather at least three technologies working in combination. The first was developed in the 1920s by Clarence Birdseye (who else?) who, after a series of home experiments which included irritating his wife by keeping live pickerel in the bathtub, successfully developed food-freezing. Second, came the introduction of steam-powered trawlers, which were larger and more efficient than their sail-powered forerunners and could in theory strip the ocean of its contents. Third, was sonar, which for the first time could accurately locate shoals of cod and by the 1930s had become standard issue on British vessels. Once food-freezing technology was incorporated into the new steam-powered trawlers, there was no need to dock in the old harbours to cure fish or pay commission to the Boston market. Instead, Spanish vessels fished off the Newfoundland coast and docked fresh fish in La Rochelle, France. The old harbours and the Boston market went into decline.

However, the new equipment was expensive; certainly, "men of no capital" were barred from entering the industry, and those that remained borrowed heavily to stay competitive. Each individual's financial incentive was to catch more fish to repay debts, and over-fishing became commonplace. As the price of fish declined, fishermen became caught in a "prisoner's dilemma" and opted to land more fish. "Cod wars" broke out over rights to fish, and the industry went into crisis.

The first government to intervene in the cod wars was Iceland, which asserted sovereignty over its coastal waters to a distance of one mile, then four miles, then 50 miles and, in 1973, 200 miles. The effect was to nationalize the waters for the purpose of supporting the local industry and force foreign vessels elsewhere. The governments of Canada, the US and the EU had little choice but to follow suit, and soon the North Atlantic had been carved up into four exclusive zones, with fish quotas set to restore depleted stocks.

When viewed from the perspective of the capital cycle, the intervention has been a disaster. Ordinarily capital would leave the industry, productive capacity would shrink, and prices rise toward an economic rate of return. Instead, government support financed, of course, by taxes has kept industry capacity high and the price of fish low. Worse still, the quota system is administratively complex, hard to enforce, and is often flouted. The Canadian government, which is reported to have invested three dollars in the industry for every dollar the fisheries earn, has set the high water mark for bureaucratic inefficiency.

Over approximately 150 years, the cod fishing and processing industry has evolved from one where excess profits were earned at the ports, then the market, then the food processors, to one where it is the consumers of fish that are the industry's chief beneficiaries. The primary driver of the process has been the decline in the cost of technology, which has removed the excess profits earned at the pinch-points in the industrial process.

It is for this reason that Marathon research focuses on not just the magnitude of a company's profitability (the size of the pinch-point – what is the capacity of Boston's port?) but also its sustainability (why dock at Boston at all?). The longer one owns shares, the more important sustainability becomes, and so we focus on companies that control their own pinch-point. Is Nike's $1bn media budget high enough? Is Ethan Allen's advertising spending sufficient? Is Invensys' research and development proprietary? And for firms with less control of their destiny, we focus on the industry supply side for signs of rising levels of competition. Is the Thai cement industry expanding again? Is Shimano increasingly vulnerable to niche competitors?

The same capital cycle process that hollowed out the profits from the cod industry can been seen throughout the economy: it has taken around 70 years from the introduction of the Bessemer Process to reach commoditization in the integrated steel mill industry, mainly through competition from asset-light mini mills. Department stores have been commoditized in 30 years by big box retailing. In semiconductors, excess profits are wrung out in less than two years. The question for investors today is how long will the same process take in media distribution, telecommunication, or online auctions? Which of these businesses will end up being the twenty-first century equivalent of the Newfoundland harbours or Boston fish market?

1.3   THIS TIME'S NO DIFFERENT (MAY 2006)

High commodity prices are eliciting a supply side response

These are tough times to be a signalman on the French railways, if recent newspaper reports are to be believed. They are having to cope with unprecedented levels of theft of signalling copper cable, from wires overhead or buried in the ground, as the recent rise in the price of copper attracts the attention of the light-fingered. Seven tonnes of copper are reported to have been stolen from one stretch of track alone. Meanwhile, in the UK, the Royal Mint has warned people not to think about melting down their pennies, which some believe are now worth more for their copper content than as currency. These strange circumstances are a result of the general rise in commodity prices over the past few years. The price of copper has risen six-fold since the end of 2001, and the prices of a number of other metals – including iron ore, zinc, aluminium and, of course, gold – have also taken off.

Part of the reason for the boom is demand from emerging countries, notably China and India, whose economies are growing rapidly with high levels of construction and relatively inefficient production. A commodities "supercycle" is said to be under way.[2] Supply has been constrained by underinvestment in the mid- to late-1990s, when commodity prices were lower. Commodity bulls say that this cycle will be different from previous cycles since better investment discipline is supposedly keeping supply levels in check. Moreover, there is a shortage of mining equipment (a common complaint from mining companies these days). A recent brokerage report claimed that rising extraction costs – costs are said to have risen by around 30 per cent over the past two years – would ensure ever rising commodity prices, as the miners would continue to be able to charge ever higher prices. Such is the circular logic of bull markets.

The rise in commodity prices has naturally attracted interest on Wall Street. Commodities, asset allocation experts claim, should be considered a vital part of every investment portfolio. Hedge funds are now commodities

---

[2] The expression "commodity supercycle" surfaced in a Morgan Stanley report published in March 2004, just as the commodity bull market was taking off.

experts. Banks are planning to double the size of their commodities trading staff, and there are breathless reports of seven-figure, sign-on bonuses
for commodities traders (who were probably unemployable a few years ago).
Several investment banks have developed specialist commodity indices,
which no doubt they use to sell derivative products to clients. At Marathon,
we are bombarded with invitations to attend exotic conferences on specialist areas of commodities (which stand alongside invites to conferences on
wind power, solar power and carbon emissions). The increasing popularity
of commodity-related funds suggests that that well known trend-follower,
the retail investor, is getting in on the act.

A simple analysis of the economics suggests that the rapid rise in price
in a number of commodities is unsustainable. Take copper, for example. The
current cost of production is roughly $0.80–0.90 per pound, with the mar-
ginal cost of production somewhat above that, say $1.20 per pound. Yet the
current price is $3.60 per pound, three times the cost of production (five
years ago, copper traded for as little as 60 cents). It is hard not to see speculation at work, as hedge funds and other non-industrial buyers push up prices,
hoping to get out before the price turns.

Commodity bulls attribute high prices to supply shortages, and argue
that higher prices are needed as an incentive to invest in production. All the
same, one can be sure that additional supply will be forthcoming at some
point.[3] Indeed, mining companies have certainly responded to the pricing
situation in the way that one would expect: initially they were sceptical of
the price rises, but later they started investing heavily to bring on new supply. Mining exploration costs doubled between 2003 and 2005. Much of this
additional spending is a consequence of having to absorb higher production
costs, but not all of it. Indeed, some mining companies believe that there is
enough supply coming on stream in copper for there to be a sizeable market
surplus in a couple of years' time. Supply bottlenecks do not last forever.

Demand is the other part of the equation. Chinese demand is indeed
growing very strongly, but it is very tricky to know just how far into the future
this can be extrapolated. What we can say is that countries generally become
more efficient in their use of raw materials as their economies develop, and
so we should not be surprised to see the same thing happening gradually in
China. Indeed, the Chinese government have spoken of their desire to move
more towards a service-based economy in the future. Attempts to slow down
the Chinese juggernaut could have the same impact on demand but rather

---

[3] The World Steel Association estimates that global iron ore production doubled between
2002 and 2013.

more quickly. It also seems reasonable to expect that a prolonged period of elevated commodity prices will have a negative impact on demand, just as high oil prices in the 1970s forced improved oil efficiency on industry. This already appears to be happening in Germany, where demand for copper pipes is said to have halved from 90,000 tonnes to 45,000 tonnes over the past year, as the construction industry switches to cheaper PVC plastics.

As the capital cycle plays out in commodities, it is perhaps worth highlighting the outcome of another recent minor bubble: namely, that of the container shipping industry. Here, too, a couple of years back we were promised a "supercycle," as earlier underinvestment led to a shortage of new ships, and strong Chinese growth was producing annual double-digit increases in shipping demand. Indeed, we even spotted the odd specialist container shipping conference invite. Spurred on by these "once-in-a-generation" conditions, shipping companies indulged in an M&A boom in mid-2005. Shipyards working flat out were fully booked out for years to come. Predictably, this frenzy marked the peak of the cycle, and shipping rates (and shipping company share prices) have now fallen sharply, while supply continues to increase.[4] A sign of things to come in the commodities world?

1.4 SUPERCYCLE WOES (MAY 2011)

The commodity industry is showing the classic signs of a capital cycle peak
A cursory analysis of the capital cycle for the commodity industry – in particular the huge expansion of commodity capital expenditure in recent years, and the precarious nature of Chinese demand for raw materials – suggests that the much hyped commodity "supercycle" is entering a downturn.

This capital cycle started a few years back after the pick-up in commodity prices led to a material improvement in the returns on equity for mining companies. Initially, the miners' response to improved conditions in their industry appears to have been quite controlled – capital expenditure relative to cash flow somewhat declined in the early 2000s as commodity prices began to rise. Nor was there a bubble in the stock market. Mining shares performed well because their fundamentals had never been better.

The bad news is that commodity industry is showing signs of a classic capital cycle peak – higher returns on invested capital are attracting more

---

[4] According to Clarksons Research, dry bulk new building orders rose from 33m deadweight tonnes in 2004 to a peak of 164m tonnes in 2007, falling back to 31m in 2009. The Baltic Dry Index, a composite measure of the cost of moving major raw materials by sea, peaked at nearly $12,000 in May 2008. Six months later it had fallen 94 per cent to $663, and by the end of 2014 it was only slightly higher at $782.

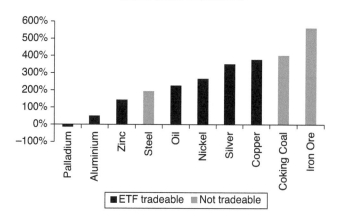

Chart 1.1   Nominal changes in commodity prices (2001–10)
Source: Macquarie.

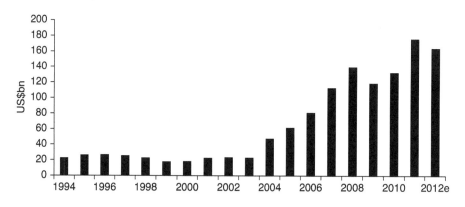

Chart 1.2   Mining capital spending in the MSCI World Index
Source: Factset, Bloomberg, Marathon.

capital and higher share prices, leading to more mergers and acquisitions and IPOs. Total mining capex from 124 companies in the MSCI All Country World Index is predicted to rise to a whopping $180bn in 2011 from less than $30bn ten years ago – a six-fold increase (see Chart 1.2).

The impact of all this investment has come with a lag. After a delay of several years, the surge in mining capex, however, has propelled production volumes to new highs. Merrill Lynch estimates that between 2000 and 2014, global nickel production will have climbed from around 1,000 metric tonnes to around 2,000 (a rise of 100 per cent), copper from some 15,000 metric tonnes to over 20,000 (33 per cent increase), aluminium from roughly 25,000 metric tonnes to over 50,000 (100 per cent increase), and most impressively, global iron production is set to rise from 1bn metric tonnes at the turn of the century to around 2.25bn by 2014, an increase of 125 per cent in just over a decade.

This change in mining fortunes has not been lost on investment bankers who, true to form, have brought ever more seductive commodity-themed IPOs to market. Between 2005 and 2010, the number of metals & mining flotations rose by climbed by 50 per cent. The bankers have also abetted their mining clients in an M&A frenzy, as deals in the sector have become larger and larger. Large numbers of IPOs and high M&A activity in any sector tend to occur in the later stages of the capital cycle.

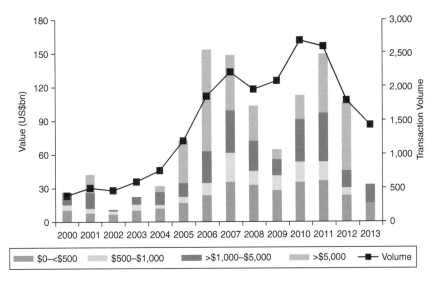

Chart 1.3   Global M&A activity in metals & mining industry

Source: PricewaterhouseCoopers.

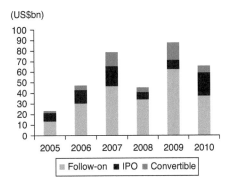

Chart 1.4   Capital markets financing of metals & mining industry

Source: Dealogic, Credit Suisse.

Thus, ever rising amounts of capital are coming into the sector at a time when commodity prices are well above marginal costs of production, even for the high cost producers. When this supercycle eventually turns, there is potentially a long way for commodity prices to fall before they reach replacement cost. This could pose a problem for benchmark-hugging investors, since the metals and mining sector – up more than three times from its 1999 low – is currently close to its all-time high as a share of the FTSE World Index.[5]

Many commentators enthuse about a "new paradigm" for commodities associated with China's rise. Almost all of the demand growth for commodities is due to China's insatiable appetite for raw materials. The Middle Kingdom now consumes around half the global production of iron ore, nickel, copper and zinc. The commodity bulls, however, seem to be overlooking some troubling signs. The most obvious of these is the inexorable rise of Chinese fixed asset investment to around 50 per cent of GDP – even in Japan, with its penchant for building roads to nowhere, investment peaked at only 30 per cent of GDP. It is not surprising that much of this capital is being wasted. The Chinese industrial sector's return on net operating assets is low and continues to trend downwards. Low profitability doesn't stop Chinese SOEs from investing, however. In the power industry, for instance, capital expenditure is running at over 100 per cent of operating cash flow (cement and steel capex relative to EBITDA is running at only marginally lower levels). To make matters worse, all the above mentioned sectors are also over-indebted. Optimists are hoping that Beijing will encourage industrial consolidation and reduce capacity. But even if this does occur, a lower pace of investment growth in these industries won't be good news for overall commodity demand.

Investors are ignoring signs of an over-heated Chinese economy and are enamoured of a commodity sector that has attracted, and continues to attract, large amounts of capital and where supply is inexorably increasing. To our minds, all this is clear evidence that the current chapter in the commodity story appears much closer to its conclusion, than the beginning.

---

[5] Between 1 January 2012 and 31 December 2014, the MSCI Metals & Mining Index underperformed the MSCI World Index by 79 percentage points.

1.5   NO SMALL BEER (FEBRUARY 2010)

Consolidation has improved the pricing power of the global brewing
industry

"Most people hate the taste of beer to begin with. It is, however, a
prejudice that many have been able to overcome."

Sir Winston Churchill

For a number of years, the only exposure of Marathon's European portfolios
to beer (and we are of course talking investment exposure here, as opposed to
any stock picking inspiration brought about by its consumption!) was a holding
in Heineken. Being a shareholder in the Dutch brewer between 2002, when we
made our initial purchase, and 2008 was not a particularly happy experience,
with the shares underperforming the wider European market by some 30 per
cent over the period, although some of this was recovered in 2009.

In part, Heineken's underperformance was due to a series of poor and overpriced acquisitions, with the company investing some $9.5bn over the decade to
2009, over which period its return on capital dropped from 20 per cent to below
10 per cent. This run culminated in the unfortunate acquisition of Scottish &
Newcastle's UK brewing assets in 2008, just as the UK entered recession and the
currency turned against them. While some of the other brewers did not fare so
badly, the overall return on capital for the brewing sector declined steadily from
13 per cent in 2000 to 9 per cent in 2008. Given all this, it may come as a surprise to some that we are overcoming our prejudice and have been increasing
our exposure to the brewing sector, now owning positions in three of the four
listed brewers – Heineken, Carlsberg and AB Inbev – in European portfolios,
and in the other – SABMiller – in UK-only portfolios.

The acquisition activity which has driven down returns sharply over the
past few years has been part of a wider industry consolidation. This began
in earnest in 2002, when the South African brewer SAB bought Miller of
the US, with other significant M&A activity including the merger between
the Brazilian AmBev and the Belgian Interbrew in 2004; the joint venture
between SABMiller and Molson Coors in the US in 2007; Heineken and
Carlsberg buying S&N in 2008; and then the huge ($60bn!) InBev acquisi-
tion of US market leader Anheuser-Busch in the same year. Most recently,
Heineken has bid $7.6bn for the Mexican brewer FEMSA, which is no.2 in its
home market and no.4 in Brazil.

Apart from providing endless fees to investment bankers and confusing
investors as various company names got shunted together to form new ones,

this long phase of deal-making activity brought about the situation illustrated in Chart 1.5 below, in which the global beer market concentrated into
the hands of four major (and European listed) players, having around 50 per
cent share of global beer volumes between them.

This process has been more pronounced in some markets than others,
with certain markets becoming extraordinarily concentrated. For example
in the US, the world's largest beer market by value, 80 per cent is now shared
between just two players, AB InBev and the Miller Coors joint venture, while
in the 5th largest market (the UK), the top three – Heineken, Molson Coors
and AB InBev – have 67 per cent of the market. There is a similar picture in
the 6th largest market where AB InBev alone has a 70 per cent market share,
while in the no.7 market of Russia, Carlsberg, AB InBev and Heineken have
70 per cent of the market between them.

Aside from the sheer scale of the consolidation, the other encouraging
point is that each of the four major players has a different area of profitability
focus, with, as one might expect, the greatest proportion of profits coming
from areas in which they have the greatest market shares.

So what implications did this have for profitability? Global beer volumes
grew at a fairly steady 4 per cent between 2005 and 2010. All this growth
came from emerging markets, notably China (9 per cent growth p.a.) and
Brazil (5 per cent), which were becoming increasingly affluent and had lower
starting levels of per capita beer consumption. By contrast, Western markets
experienced pretty flat volume growth, or in some cases declining volumes.
So it was interesting to note that US and Western European markets have
registered some fairly decent price increases over the same period. While
there is undoubtedly an element of "cost push" in these figures – the largest raw material cost is barley and the price of this rose by some 60 per cent

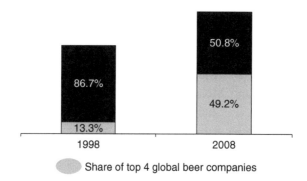

Chart 1.5   Global market share of top four brewers (volume)

Source: Bernstein, Eurostat.

between 2005 and 2007 – it is also an indication of how the larger brewers were able to use their greater scale to push back against the retailers, without much fear of interference from a disruptive third party.

This encouraging process is continuing with, for example, the largest players in the UK market all having announced price rises of 4 per cent already in 2010. In emerging markets, pricing growth has been easier to achieve, in part due to the greater fragmentation of the retail channel and generally higher levels of inflation which have made it possible to hide price increases. Here, as well as volume growth, the story is one of increased "premiumization" – persuading consumers to trade up as they become wealthier. In Europe, premium lager accounts for nearly 25 per cent of the market (and 15 per cent in the US), but this figure is well below 5 per cent in most emerging market countries. A consolidated market is not a prerequisite for premiumization, but having high volumes in a market makes it more economic for a brewer to offer a wider range of products at different price points.

On the supply side, there is an encouraging capital cycle angle as the consolidation process has seen a reduction in brewery capacity, particularly in Europe where the fragmented regional nature of the market meant that there had been persistent overcapacity to be exploited by retailers. Several markets have experienced quite meaningful capacity reduction. In the UK, for example, 10 per cent of brewing capacity was taken out of the market following Heineken's acquisition of Scottish & Newcastle. Markets such as Ireland, Finland and France experienced similar levels of capacity reduction, while a lesser amount of capacity was taken out of the Danish market. Brewers have also worked hard to generate savings in areas such as procurement, looking at the potential for greater cross-border supply to improve utilization rates, as well as simplifying product ranges.

Following the M&A splurge, which pushed debt levels to an average net debt/EBITDA across the sector of around 3 times, compared to a long-run average of 1.5 times, there has been a greater focus on balance sheet discipline, with less need to defend market share by attempting to grow volumes aggressively. So whereas historically, companies were spending around 2 times depreciation on capex, on average this has come down to below 1.5 times, or from nearly 10 per cent of sales to below 8 per cent. There has also been more of an emphasis on working capital, with several of the companies adopting explicit reduction targets.

Taking all these things together – the emphasis on pricing, the focus on cost reduction and balance sheet efficiency – an improvement in both margins and return on capital was to be expected. As for valuation, the average free cash flow yields of 6–7 per cent imply growth rates of around GDP or a little less, which suggests that the stock market is underestimating the potential long-run benefit to be derived from market consolidation and improved discipline. In the light of an improving capital cycle among brewers, we find ourselves able, to paraphrase Sir Winston, to overcome our prejudice and begin increasing our exposure to beer.[6]

1.6   OIL PEAK (FEBRUARY 2012)

In the energy markets, as elsewhere, "there is no cure for high prices like high prices"

Following a relatively good stock market performance over the past 12 months for the energy sector (which is dominated by major oil companies), and with the oil price approaching its all-time high (Chart 1.6), it makes sense to review our significant underweighting of the energy sector.

Various theories have been put forward to justify high oil prices and an increased asset allocation to commodities, chief among which is the idea of "peak oil." Bullish forecasts suggest that increasing energy demand from emerging markets, together with declining oil reserves and rising production costs, will propel the price of crude oil to $200 a barrel or more. While a high oil price, however, is perceived to be beneficial for oil company profits

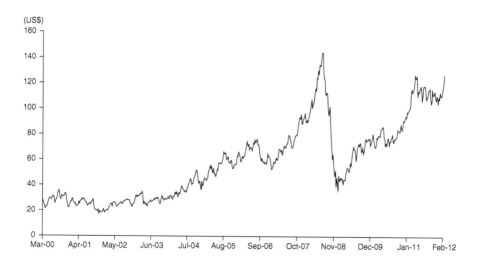

Chart 1.6   Brent crude oil price

Source: Bloomberg.

---

[6] From the time of writing to the end of 2014, all of the abovementioned beer companies outperformed the MSCI Europe Index with the exception of Carlsberg, which has experienced problems with its Russian operations.

in the short run, there are trends developing which will severely undermine both the oil price and energy shares during the coming years.

It is said that "there is no cure for high prices like high prices." Thus, while the price of crude appears to be suspended at an elevated level, the very persistence of the oil price above $100 per barrel is encouraging developments which pose an increasing risk to energy investors. There has been a surge in natural gas supply in North America, where new technology and better drilling techniques have helped to boost the production and lower the cost of natural gas from conventional resources, as well as from shale gas. US shale gas reserves are estimated to be huge. Extraction techniques continue to improve and we are still at the very early stages of the fracking revolution, so potential reserves from shale gas are probably still underestimated, as was the case in the early days of the oil industry. These extra and cheaper sources of energy have brought down natural gas prices in the US and opened up a huge price differential between crude oil and gas. In the US, at least, these developments have resulted in a dramatic shift towards natural gas, away from oil and coal, as a primary source of energy.

Those who argue that the surge in gas supply will only impact North America are ignoring the fact that not only is the US still the largest consumer of crude oil (and is currently a net importer) but also that significant investment is being undertaken to be able to export this cheap gas. We are seeing gas import plants in the United States being reengineered to enable exports and new gas export facilities planned. In addition, to capitalize on the lowest US natural gas prices in a decade, industries are starting to shift production to the US and are even moving physical assets. In the case of Methanex, the world's largest methanol maker, there are plans to dismantle an idled Chilean factory and ship it to Louisiana to be reassembled.

The high oil price is fuelling other significant changes in the energy markets. The transport industry is becoming much more fuel efficient (airlines are ordering new fuel efficient aircraft/engines, and new fuel efficient ships are being ordered despite low cargo rates and a glut of older vessels). And there's the increasing use of non-oil fuel for transport. Just look around. In Thailand, natural gas is already outselling petrol because of new technology used by taxis, tractors, buses and now some cars; in the US and in the UK (where there are tax incentives for "green" vehicles), there's increasing evidence of not just hybrid vehicles but now fully electric cars (from economy models such as the Smart to the sporty Tesla), and facilities are being built to recharge these vehicles on the move; businesses are developing natural gas powered trucks (manufactured by Navistar and Clean Energy Fuels Corp) and hydrogen cell cars (by Acal). In short, there is no shortage of investment directed towards reducing the use of expensive crude oil.

Meanwhile, oil producing countries within OPEC have become some-what complacent about the high oil price. Some are using the extra revenue generated by the high oil price to pour billions of dollars into social spending. Saudi Arabia now requires an oil price of $90 per barrel to cover its planned expenditure (other OPEC countries "need" even higher prices). But these high spending commitments require decent volumes as well as high prices. This makes any volume discipline to control prices more difficult, and so undermines the ability of OPEC to influence oil prices in the future.

Recent meetings with several of the largest global oil companies have also revealed some worrying signs. Senior oil executives appear to be anchoring their expectations about the future oil price on current market levels. Total, for instance, has raised its projection for long-term oil prices, which it uses to justify exploration and acquisition spending, from around $20 per barrel a decade ago to a range of $80 to $100. The French oil major claims it is willing to spend $20bn a year based on this elevated oil forecast. Increased spending promises to boost Total's annual oil production, something which the company believes will lead to a rerating (upwards) of its shares.[7]

Total is not alone. The whole industry is justifying rising levels of investment based on the inflated expectations of future oil prices. BP has raised the oil price it uses to test new projects from $16 per barrel in 2002 to above $60. Even the well managed Imperial Oil, with substantial low cost oil and gas assets in Canada (over 100 years of reserves at current production), is now using a forecast of $50–60 per barrel compared to $35–40 ten years ago. Petrobras is aiming to spend $225bn in the next five years and to more than double its already substantial production in the next decade. The Brazilian oil giant assumes the crude oil price will be $80–95 per barrel for the next five years. Its record breaking $70bn rights issue last year shows there's no shortage of funding for new oil projects while the oil price remains elevated.[8]

---

[7] From the date of this article to the end of 2014, Total SA's share price declined by 9 per cent in US dollars, underperforming the MSCI Europe Index by nearly 26 per cent.

[8] In September 2010, Petrobras conducted the largest share sale in history, raising $73bn on the Brazilian stock exchange – a capital cycle red flag if ever there was one. Not all this money, however, found its way into increasing oil production. In March 2014, federal police arrested Paulo Roberto Costa, former chief of refining at Petrobras, in a money laundering investigation. Mr Costa, seeking leniency, confessed to far more than that, according to *The Economist*. Construction companies that won contracts from his division diverted 3 per cent of their value into slush funds for political parties, Mr. Costa claimed. Police identified nearly $6bn of suspicious payments making petrolão (the "big oily") Brazil's biggest corruption scandal.

On current earnings, oil company valuations do not looked stretched: cash flow is lowly rated and dividend yields are above average. But there is now a risk that oil companies' new assumptions about a high oil price are fixing their costs at a high level. The more of their healthy cash flows these companies spend on high cost projects, the lower their current earnings and cash flows are likely to be valued. The operational leverage of oil company profits is rising, so their earnings are particularly vulnerable to a severe correction in the oil price. And the longer the high oil price persists, the greater the risk of a correction. With this in mind, a modest and stock- specific weighting in the energy sector within our global portfolios seems prudent. It should at some stage add significant value to performance, at least on a relative basis.[9]

1.7   MAJOR CONCERNS (MARCH 2014)

Energy companies are suffering from the delayed consequences of their capital spending boom

Is now the time to increase exposure to the oil majors? Stocks of the largest five global oil companies, which in aggregate account for over 40 per cent of the MSCI World Oil and Gas Index, are trading at significant discounts to the MSCI World price-earnings ratio and provide, on average, close to double the dividend yield. These valuations may look attractive, but a closer examination of the recent financial performance of the five oil majors reveals a fairly worrying picture.

Over the period 2003 to 2012, as the Brent oil price increased by 16 per cent a year, the net income of the oil majors grew by only 8 per cent a year. Total growth in their earnings per share (EPS), including the effect of share buybacks, was 10 per cent – lagging the S&P, which compounded earnings at 12 per cent over this same period. A surge in the Brent crude price between 2003 and 2007 (increasing at 33 per cent a year) resulted in the aggregate return on equity for the oil majors rising to 27 per cent. As capital cycle theory would suggest, this led to a dramatic rise in capital expenditure, which increased from 1.2 times depreciation and amortization between 2003 and 2007 to 1.7 times between 2007 and 2012. Despite this rise in capex, net income has actually fallen slightly in aggregate, which explains the marked drop in returns on

---

[9] By the end of 2014, the Brent Crude oil price had fallen to $57, a decline of over 50 per cent from the date of this article (February 2012). Over the same period, the FTSE All-World Oil & Gas Index fell by 16 per cent, underperforming the broad FTSE All-World Index by over 48 per cent.

equity for the large energy companies – from 27 per cent in 2007 to 17 per cent in 2012, at a time when the oil price increased by nearly 20 per cent.

Why has the higher oil price and rising capex not produced faster earnings growth? The main issue is that the majors have had a real fight just to stand still. The yield of an oil and gas field steadily falls over its lifetime, in the order of 5 per cent annually, so a material amount of capital expenditure is required just to offset the decline rate. Lately, the quality of oil exploration projects coming on stream has not matched that of the legacy assets. Newer fields are both harder to access technically, as well as being in riskier jurisdictions. An ever greater amount of capital has been required to deliver the same level of production, resulting in the inevitable decline in return on invested capital. This explains why net production growth has been so depressed over recent years – in aggregate, the oil majors' production has declined by approximately 2 per cent a year over the last five years.

Of course, given the long-term nature of oil projects – the average time lag to reach full productive capacity is around six years – the impact of recent capex spending may yet be seen over the next five years, with an attendant rise in earnings. However, an analysis of company guidance and analyst expectations for the next four years (2014–17) does not support this contention. The ratio of capex-to-depreciation is expected to remain high, at 1.6 times, with a forecast cash conversion rate of only 50 per cent, even lower than over the last five years.[10] Furthermore, production growth is expected to remain muted, growing at around just 2 per cent a year. While this, in theory, is above the growth rate of the last five years, reality has often fallen short of expectations.

So it is difficult to argue that the majors are "cheap" today. On cash earnings, valuations are much higher than the low earnings multiple suggests – indeed, if forecasts are correct, the majors are trading on a price to free cash flow multiple of 22 times, a premium to the wider market. Yet the earnings growth outlook for the sector is below that of the market, even assuming a reasonably resilient oil price. And there is the very real possibility that the oil price falls in the medium term – witness the progress in the way energy is both produced and used.

In addition, there are particular reasons why investors should demand a discount on a cash flow multiple, before committing capital to the oil sector. First, the sheer quantum of capex required on an annual basis means the investor is forced to place a large degree of faith in the management team to allocate capital correctly. This has been a problem historically, given the bias

---

[10] The cash conversion rate measures the extent to which reported profits *convert* into free cash flow.

of management to focus on growth over returns, particularly in periods of strong oil price appreciation. Second, oil fields are captive assets. The risk of government intervention and profit claw-backs is higher than average, and the risk is increasing as the mix of the industry's asset base shifts towards less politically stable regions.

Are there any grounds for optimism? By virtue of the capital cycle, an extended period of growing capital intensity and low returns should eventually lead to a supply side contraction, laying the foundations for an inflection in returns on capital and more healthy stock returns. In this sense, a weak oil price could even be a blessing in disguise for investors – much as its rapid rise since 2003 has been somewhat of a curse, accompanied as it has been by an increased focus on production at the expense of capital discipline.

1.8   A CAPITAL CYCLE REVOLUTION (MARCH 2014)

A Scandinavian wind turbine maker experiences the ups and downs of the capital cycle

Marathon looks to invest in two phases of an industry's capital cycle. From what is misleadingly labelled the "growth" universe, we search for businesses whose high returns are believed to be more sustainable than most investors expect. Here, the good company manages to resist becoming a mediocre one. From the low return, or "value" universe, our aim is to find companies whose improvement potential is generally underestimated. In both cases, the rate at which a company reverts to mediocrity (or "fade rate") is often miscalculated by stock market participants. Marathon's own experience suggests that the resultant mispricing is often systematic for behavioural reasons.

Chart 1.7 illustrates the "fade rate" of corporate returns, an idea developed by Holt Value Associates (now part of Credit Suisse). Holt's concept of the stock market-implied fade rate chimed well with our focus on competitive conditions within industries and the flow of capital into (and out of) high (and low) return industries. Using this framework, two purchase candidates are identifiable. Purchase Candidate A is a company capable of sustaining high returns beyond the market's expectation (the upper dotted line) – that is, the company remains above average for longer than average. Candidate B is a company which can improve faster than the market generally expects (the lower dotted line).

Marathon's experience suggests that the stock market is often poor at pricing superior fade characteristics. For Purchase Candidate A, mispricing stems from a number of sources. One is the underestimation of the durability of barriers to entry. Another is the underappreciation of the scale and

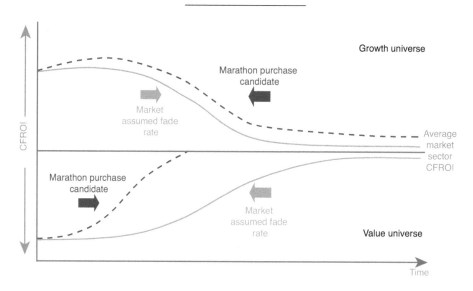

Chart 1.7   The fade rate
Source: Marathon, Credit Suisse HOLT.

scope of the addressable market. Management's capital allocation skills are also often overlooked. A recent meeting with the CEO of Bunzl, the leading specialist business-to-business distributor, was instructive in this regard. While sell-side analysts covering the stock have made reasonably accurate forecasts of returns from the core business, they have consistently failed to give management credit for adding value via bolt-on acquisitions, despite 20 years or so of supporting evidence. Investors also appear to be biased against "boring" high return companies, such as Bunzl, which do not offer the prospect of immediate high share price appreciation.

The conditions leading to Purchase Candidate B often stem from the market misjudging the beneficial effects of reduced competition as weaker firms disappear, either through consolidation or bankruptcy. Alternately, an unruly oligopoly may tire of excess competition and enjoy an outbreak of peaceful coexistence. The turn in the capital cycle often occurs during periods of maximum pessimism, as the weakest competitor throws in the towel at a point of extreme stress. When the pain of losses coincides with a depressed share price, investors can find wonderful opportunities, particularly if they are willing to take a multiyear view and put up with short-term volatility.

Management skill at dealing with problems may also be overlooked. This is especially true when a new leader is recruited externally, maximizing the possibility of change. The turnaround achieved at Fiat by Sergio Marchionne in recent years is one outstanding example.[11] Highly competent managers are often attracted by the challenge of turning around a troubled company, not least because of the financial rewards. This factor was evident in a recent meeting with Rupert Soames, who is shortly to take on the role of CEO at Serco, the embattled UK outsourcing company.

A recent example from Marathon's European portfolio illustrates the perils and opportunities faced by investors in low return companies. In the case of Vestas Wind Systems, Marathon's initial investment took place in 2003, when the company was suffering from a temporarily weak US market due to change in tax incentives. Partly in response, Vestas acquired a local rival. Subsequently, demand for wind turbines recovered and Vestas' share price multiplied by around 40 times from its trough to the 2008 peak.

The good news didn't last. With the advent of the financial crisis, wind farm projects around the world were quickly shelved at just the point when the new wind turbine capacity came on stream. Although we had reduced clients' holdings by a quarter at near-peak levels (see Chart 1.8 below), the residual holding then suffered an ignominious "Return to Go" with a 96 per cent decline in value.

Vestas had become a victim of the alternative energy capital cycle. Its capex-to-depreciation had risen from just over 1 times in 2005 to nearly 5

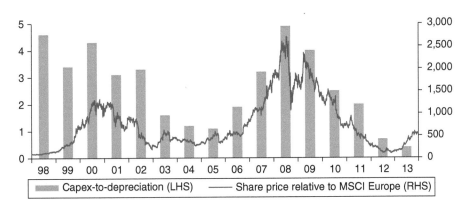

Chart 1.8 Vestas Wind Systems: capex-to-depreciation ratio and relative share price performance

Source: Capital IQ, FactSet.

---

[11] Sergio Marchionne was appointed Chief Executive of Fiat SpA in mid-2004. Since that date, Marchionne has revitalized Fiat's car operations and spun off the company's agricultural equipment division (Case New Holland). An investment in Fiat at the time of Marchionne's appointment was worth 183 per cent more by the end of 2014 (based on the combination of FCA and CNH's share prices, excluding dividends).

times in 2008, contributing to excess capacity in the wind turbine sector. With the benefit of hindsight, it would have made sense to dispose of our entire holding after the crisis struck, as the share price subsequently endured four more years of under-performance. This would have saved us having to answer awkward questions from consultants and clients about why our position had been maintained!

Nevertheless, continued contact with the company provided the opportunity to buy more shares at a later date, an option which might have been lost had we washed our hands of the embarrassing position. Following a meeting with the impressive new Swedish chairman in early 2013, Marathon bought more shares, increasing the holding by 90 per cent and becoming the company's largest shareholder. New management has since been able to implement significant restructuring at a time when investor fears about weak industry demand have proved too pessimistic. Capex has been slashed to 0.4 times depreciation in 2013, boosting cash flow and helping to repair the weak balance sheet. The subsequent 360 per cent share price rise has partly spared our blushes from failing to sell more at the peak.

The example of Vestas shows how a company can morph from being a "value" buying opportunity to being an expensive "growth" stock and then cheap value again in the course of a few years. Investors can take advantage of Mr. Market's shifting moods. Our Vestas experience also demonstrates the benefits of well-timed contrarian purchases, notwithstanding the valid questions the case raises about selling discipline.

1.9 GROWTH PARADOX (SEPTEMBER 2014)

The capital cycle partly explains why corporate profitability lags GDP growth

Investors who assume corporate earnings will increase in line with the economy should look at the historical data. Since 1960, US earnings have compounded by 2 per cent a year in real terms, while the US economy has grown by 3.1 per cent. With an average dividend pay-out of 45 per cent, companies effectively ploughed back the majority of earnings into the business only to trail growth in the wider economy. Even more puzzling, corporate profits as a share of GDP actually increased significantly during the period, rising from 6 per cent in 1960 to over 10 per cent by 2013. What has gone wrong?[12]

---

[12] This example comes from the US market. The problem is even more pronounced globally. The real growth in dividends on a global basis has only been 0.6 per cent in the period 1900–2013 (Credit Suisse Global Investment Returns Sourcebook, 2014).

The first issue is that new share issuance exceeded stock buybacks over time, diluting the equity holder. For example, in a 2003 paper, Bernstein and Arnott estimated net share issuance to have been in the order of 2 per cent a year in the US market.[13] One explanation for this phenomenon is the procyclical behaviour of management, specifically the tendency to buy back stock when confidence is high and valuations heady, only then to be forced to issue equity when circumstances are less favourable and share prices lower. The recent experience of the banking sector is a particularly savage example of management's buy high and sell low tendency.

Mergers and acquisitions show the same pro-cyclicality, with activity typically reaching a crescendo in the later stages of bull markets. Deals struck at high valuations lead to shareholder value destruction. Finally, management issuance of share options to employees has also been a drag on shareholder returns. Today a "burn rate" of 1 per cent is not uncommon – and it was even higher prior to the mandatory expensing of options through the profit and loss account.[14]

Another explanation for surprisingly low earnings growth is that a disproportionate portion of new profits are generated by unlisted companies.[15] This is partly because private firms, less encumbered by agency problems and the pressure of meeting near-term earnings expectations, tend to invest more than public companies. Additionally, new business models and technology are often developed by unlisted companies and only reach the public market once they are relatively mature and past the high growth phase. For investors in public equity, this poses two problems. First, new businesses and technologies have a disruptive impact on the returns of publicly listed companies. Secondly, as with buybacks and M&A activity, the level of IPO activity is strongly procyclical (see Chart 1.9). This means valuations at the time of listing are typically elevated, effectively causing dilution of earnings per share at the aggregate level. To make matters worse, the subsequent inflow of capital following a stock market debut often directly contributes to an eventual deterioration in returns, especially when multiple companies are listing from the same industry (a classic example being the rash of telecoms IPOs in the late 1990s which were raising capital to invest in fibre optic networks).[16]

---

[13] William Bernstein and Robert Arnott, "Earnings Growth: The Two Percent Dilution," *Financial Analysts Journal*, 2003.

[14] Prior to 2006, FASB accounting rules did not require the expensing of stock options.

[15] See John Asker *et al.*, "Comparing the investment behavior of public and private firms," National Bureau of Economic Research, 2011.

[16] See Jay Ritter, "Initial Public Offerings: Updated Statistics" (2013) for a comprehensive statistical study showing that IPOs on average under-perform the wider market in the first three years.

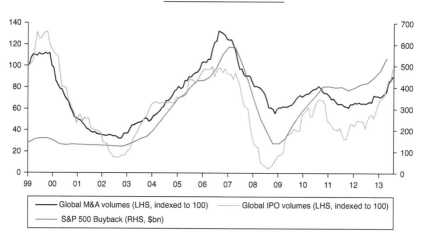

Chart 1.9   Global M&A, IPO and S&P 500 buybacks
Source: Citi, Dealogic.

The concept of the capital cycle provides a broader explanation as to why corporate profitability lags GDP. The primary driver of healthy corporate profitability is a favourable supply side – not high rates of demand growth. Hence, it is possible for there to be rapid growth in an industry which brings little or no benefit to investors. In fact, strong growth in demand is often the direct cause of value destruction as it encourages a flood of capital into the industry, eroding returns.

It is not hard to think of examples. Technological advancement in digital semiconductors has revolutionized technology and economic productivity. Yet the experience of investors in the semiconductor industry has been a depressing one. A fragmented supply side allied with high capital intensity and low product differentiation has led to long-term destruction of economic value. It is only very recently, with an improvement in the supply side via consolidation, that the outlook has improved. The airlines have revolutionized travel over the last 60 years, with attendant economic benefits, but again a poor supply side has led to a very bumpy ride for investors.[17] Even the

---

[17] The capital cycle for the airline industry has been so poor – largely owing to the fact that supply has generally not diminished during times of industry losses and bankruptcy – that the aggregate profits of US airlines between 1960 and 2000 would have been sufficient to pay for the delivery of just two 747 jumbo jets. Over the last decade, however, the capital cycle has turned positive as the industry consolidated (following mergers between US Airways and American, Delta and Northwest Airlines, United and Continental, and Southwest and Airtran Airways.) After this bout of mergers, US airline stocks performed strongly. There are signs, however, that the industry is once again losing capital discipline. Southwest and

most bullish tech analyst would not have predicted how widespread mobile phones have become, and yet such foresight would not have helped long-suffering shareholders in Nokia, Motorola or Blackberry-maker RIM.

Thus procyclical management behaviour alongside the destructive power of the capital cycle largely explain why real earnings growth of the US stock market has not kept pace with broader economic growth. Evidence suggests that these problems intensify the higher the rate of GDP growth, with no correlation between long-term GDP growth and equity market return. The Chinese stock market is perhaps the most obvious example of this – despite stellar GDP growth since 1993, the real return from Chinese equities has been negative, declining by 3 per cent per year.

Investors should not expect earnings to grow in line with economy. Rather, they should look out for those rare examples of management who are prudent in their use of capital. The starting point for company analysis is not the outlook for end demand but rather the supply side. Our goal is to find investments in depressed industries at positive inflection points in the capital cycle and in sectors with benign and stable supply side fundamentals.

---

several other US airlines are currently committed to growing "available seat miles" by 10 per cent annually, or around four times faster than underlying economic growth.

2

VALUE IN GROWTH

Capital cycle analysis, as it originally evolved at Marathon, looked to invest in companies from sectors where capital was being withdrawn and to avoid companies in industries where assets were increasing rapidly. The insight being that both profits and valuations should generally rise after capital has exited an industry and decline after capital has poured in. In other words, capital cycle analysis was all about the drivers of mean reversion. Yet the same mode of analysis can be used to identify companies which, for one reason or another, are able to repel competition.

Companies with such strong competitive advantages, possessing what Warren Buffett calls a wide "moat," are able to maintain profits, often for longer than the market expects. Mean reversion is suspended. From a capital cycle perspective, it can be observed that a lack of competition prevents the supply side from shifting in response to high profitability. Acquiring stocks in companies which defy mean reversion has been a particularly fruitful investment strategy for Marathon over the last decade.

Somewhat confusingly, this style of investment is known generally as "growth" investing in fund management industry parlance, as distinct from "value" investing. Having acquired the "value" investor label from industry consultants before and during the dotcom bubble, Marathon was wary of being accused of style drift as it invested increasingly in stocks with higher valuations and better growth prospects. As the essays below point out, the "value/growth dichotomy" is false – at least, to a true *value* investor, whose aim is not to buy stocks which are "cheap" on accounting measures (P/E, price-to-book, etc.) and to avoid those which are expensive on the same basis, but rather to look for investments trading at low prices relative to the investor's estimate of their intrinsic value.

2.1 WARNING LABELS (SEPTEMBER 2002)

**Labelling fund managers as "value" or "growth" investors risks
distorting the investment process**

Marathon has often been pigeon-holed as a value manager, a description
that we resist because it oversimplifies and misrepresents our investment
approach. The traditional definition of a value manager is one who invests
solely in companies with low valuations as measured by price-to-book, PE,
price-to-sales or price-to-cash flow. The value approach is associated with
Benjamin Graham, who sought unloved stocks with low stock price multiples which could deliver more than was generally expected – what was
termed "cigar-butt" investing in the sense that the object had been discarded
as worthless but nevertheless could provide one last puff. A growth manager
is one who invests at the other end of the spectrum in companies with high
stock price multiples.

Companies in the Marathon portfolio have tended to have below average
multiples, but this is not because we have been engaged in seeking "cigar-
butts." In fact, the stocks in our European portfolios have relatively strong
earnings growth. Part of the reason for this apparent contradiction is that
we have found that smaller companies with above average growth prospects
are often cheap.

While smaller companies have, in the recent past, tended to have low
valuations, large-cap stocks have attracted unjustifiably high valuations.
The growth of very large fund managers is largely to blame. In Europe,
the MSCI Europe Index consists of 540 stocks of which only 88 have a
market capitalization above $10bn. Liquidity reasons (that is, the amount
of time it takes to trade in and out of a stock) preclude fund managers
with vast assets under management from investing in stocks with market
valuations below this threshold. The trouble is that the largest cap stocks
are concentrated in certain sectors and underrepresented in others. Since
three-quarters of industrial stocks have a market cap of less than $10bn,
industrials are essentially "screened out" by the large-cap managers. By
contrast, 85 per cent of the healthcare stocks have market caps above
$10bn. As a result, pharma stocks attract disproportionate attention from
institutional investors.

The issue with style labelling is somewhat deeper, however. Similar to
the recent obsessions with tracking error, indexation and understanding
the "new economy," it risks grossly distorting the investment process and
requires/encourages managers to use inappropriate tools and measurement
systems to construct portfolios. Many great investors will interpret value

according to their perceptions of value. The renowned "value" investor Bill Miller of Legg Mason has championed Amazon.com and AOL, while Warren Buffett, that great disciple of Ben Graham, has preferred growth franchises such as Coke and Disney. The latter, however, believes (or at least did believe) that these high-quality businesses were cheap (i.e., good value relative to the present value of their expected future returns) and still regarded himself as buying value.

The fact is that one person's growth stock is another's value stock. Recently, the investment data company Lipper has reported that Citigroup, AIG and IBM are among the top 15 mutual fund holdings in both the large company "value" and "growth" categories. This brings us to our next point, which perhaps best explains why Marathon should never be labelled as a pure value investor. Our capital cycle process examines the effects of the creative and destructive forces of capitalism over time. A growth stock usually becomes a value stock after excess capital, lured in by large current profitability, brings about a decline in returns. When this becomes extreme, as was the case during the technology bubble, the resultant bust can turn growth stocks into value stocks almost overnight.

The telecoms sector provides a good demonstration of this. Energis, the UK alternative telecoms carrier, was bid up to a value of 10 times invested capital during the "New Economy" boom of the late 1990s due to the perceived growth potential for broadband and data networks. After an excessive amount of money had been invested in the sector, Energis's shares were sold down to a tiny fraction of capital invested. They continue to languish. The lesson here recently is not only the slim dividing line between value and growth but also the danger of "value traps," since Energis (like Worldcom) never turned out to be cheap however much the stock fell.[1]

Marathon's portfolio strategy in Europe and elsewhere is now shifting from the deep value biases, maintained over the last five years, to more of a relative valuation orientation, as stocks that were previously overvalued on their perceived growth potential have slumped. At the same time, yesterday's deep value sectors – such as basic materials, paper, chemicals and certain capital goods – now do not appear such good buys from an intrinsic value viewpoint. Our thinking is best illustrated by two recent portfolio trades. Assa Abloy is a world-leading lock company, owner of well known brands such as Yale, VingCard and Vachette. It has grown sales at 25 per cent per annum for the last ten years and compounded earnings by 38 per cent a year

---

[1] Energis was placed in administration in July 2002. It was subsequently turned around and sold to Cable & Wireless in 2005.

over the same period, helped in part by acquisitions. Its shares have fallen by 56 per cent as growth stocks have derated. Having been bid up to 4 times sales, Assa Abloy's stock now trades at less than 1.5 times sales, a discount to our estimate of intrinsic value. We are buyers. On the other hand, we are disposing of Stora Enso, a Finnish paper company that we have long owned, but whose corporate strategy we have issues with. No longer a deep value stock, Stora Enso remains cheaper than Assa Abloy on every single valuation metric other than the one which matters but which can't be screened on a quantitative basis – namely, intrinsic value.[2]

Investment style labelling is another convenient box-ticking, quantitative oriented procedure beloved of consultants. Investors who adhere to one particular style are likely to end up in trouble, sooner or later. Our belief is that stocks should be viewed not as "growth" or "value" opportunities, but rather from the perspective of whether the market is efficiently valuing their future earning prospects.

2.2   LONG GAME (MARCH 2003)

Long-term investing works because there is less competition for really valuable bits of information

There are many ways to describe investment approaches, indeed a consulting industry has emerged whose primary function is to do just that. However, there is one attribute that separates investors better than most, in our opinion, and that is portfolio turnover. Marathon's portfolios have an average holding period of around five years, a figure which in all likelihood will rise in the coming years as the quality of the companies in the portfolio (as measured by normalized returns on capital and growth potential) has risen, post bubble.[3] We can therefore perhaps be expected to argue vigorously in favour of low turnover investment strategies.

While the case for long-term investment has tended to centre around simple mathematical advantages such as reduced (frictional) costs and fewer decisions leading (hopefully) to fewer mistakes, the real advantage to this approach, in our opinion, comes from asking more valuable questions.

The short-term investor asks questions in the hope of gleaning clues to near-term outcomes: relating typically to operating margins, earnings per

---

[2] From the date of writing (September 2002) to the end of 2014, Assa Abloy's share price rose by 452 per cent in US dollars, comfortably outperforming Stora Enso, which was up by 0.7 per cent over the same period.

[3] Marathon's holding period in its main EAFE product has subsequently risen to 7.5 years.

share and revenue trends over the next quarter, for example. Such information is relevant for the briefest period and only has value if it is correct, incremental, and overwhelms other pieces of information. Even when accurate, the value of the information is likely to be modest, say, a few percentage points in performance. In order to build a viable, economically important track record, the short-term investor may need to perform this trick many thousands of times in a career and/or employ large amounts of financial leverage to exploit marginal opportunities.

And let's face it, the competition for such investment snippets is ferocious. This competition is fed by the investment banks. Wall Street relies heavily on promoting client myopia to earn its crust. Why else would Salomon Smith Barney produce a research report which begins "We are focusing on the three month sales momentum model this month"; or Deutsche Bank publish a "Weekly Autos" review? Can there really be much of value to say about industry developments over such limited time frames? Of course not. Even so, we would hate to discourage such research as, from time to time, what the short-term guys are selling can turn out to be wonderful long-term investments.

The operative word here is "quick." The longer one owns the shares, however, the more important the firm's underlying economics will be to performance results. Long-term investors therefore seek answers with shelf life. What is relevant today may need to be relevant in ten years' time if the investor is to continue owning the shares. Information with a long shelf life is far more valuable than advance knowledge of next quarter's earnings. We seek insights consistent with our holding period. These principally relate to capital allocation, which can be gleaned from examining the company's advertising, marketing, research and development spending, capital expenditures, debt levels, share repurchase/issuance, mergers and acquisitions and so forth.

Take marketing, for instance, which can be vital to long-term value creation, yet is often ignored. An understanding of the economics of line extensions and an advertising strategy would have proved useful to investors in consumer products companies. Colgate Palmolive introduced its first line extension – a blue minty gel – in the early 1980s, and supported this new product with a hefty advertising spend. This was Colgate's first new toothpaste in a generation, and line extensions, which had been used successfully in other household goods, were novel to the toothpaste market. By advertising heavily, the firm hoped to change the buying habits of a generation of shoppers who would subconsciously think of Colgate as they approached the toothpaste section of a supermarket, and when they got there, would find a product which was new, superior and, because of advertising spend, trusted.

We did not attend any Colgate meetings in the early 1980s, but if they were anything like their equivalents today the questions might have been along the lines of: what does the rise in advertising spend mean for margins next quarter (an almost worthless piece of information)? Or, how will the increase in depreciation from the new product line for minty gel affect earnings (yawn)? Brokerage reports following the meeting may have been like one which crossed our desks this morning, entitled "Thinking Outside the Box, but near term outlook remains dreary," recommendation: underperform. Few investors would have understood, and even fewer would have cared, about the transformation that was taking place.

Even today, Colgate presentations do not mention the company's advertising spend, which remains in excess of market share in all countries except Mexico, where market share is around 90 per cent. And this is despite 20 years of the firm demonstrating that line extensions and advertising support are powerful competitive weapons. "Most people don't think it is important," confessed the firm's investor relations spokeswoman. Even though we don't own the shares, Marathon is the only fund manager to have sought and gained a meeting with Colgate's director of advertising and marketing.[4]

In the two decades since its first line extension, Colgate's share price has risen 25 fold, handsomely beating the market. This shows how important it is for long-term investors to understand a firm's marketing strategy. Yet, given the annual 100 per cent turnover in Colgate shares, very few of the firm's shareholders have benefited fully from its success. And since Colgate's investment returns didn't outperform the S&P 500 in any meaningful way for a full ten years after the introduction of its first line extension, investors with short time horizons wouldn't have cared about such matters.

Why did so few Colgate investors stay the course? There are a range of psychological forces stacked up against the long-term investor. In particular, there is strong social pressure from peers, colleagues and clients to boost near-term performance. Even if one has developed the analytical skills to spot the winner, the psychological disposition necessary to own shares for prolonged periods is not easily come by. J.K. Galbraith observed that: "nothing is so admirable in politics as a short-term memory." Why should politics have a monopoly on sloppy thinking? Which makes us think that long-term investing works not because it is more difficult, but because there is less competition out there for the really valuable bits of information.

---

[4] At the time, Marathon believed that the share price was too expensive for Colgate to be buying back so much stock. Since March 2003, Colgate has modestly outperformed the S&P 500 Index.

2.3   DOUBLE AGENTS (JUNE 2004)

Conflicts of interest in the business world sometimes play to an investor's advantage

In a recent lecture given at the University of California, Charles T. Munger described a test he had performed at a number of US business schools.[5] This test involved the Berkshire Hathaway vice-chairman asking the MBA students the following question: "You have studied supply and demand curves. You have learned that when you raise the price, ordinarily the volume you can sell goes down, and when you reduce the price, the volume you can sell goes up. Is that right? That's what you've learned?" The business school students all nod in agreement. Munger then goes on: "Now tell me several instances when, if you want the physical volume to go up, the correct answer is to increase the price?" Some students come up with the luxury good paradox, whereby higher prices indicate superior quality which, in turn, leads to greater sales.

Very few students identify Munger's answer, namely that when the customer is not involved directly in the purchasing decision, then higher prices can be used to bribe the purchaser's agent and can result in both higher profit margins and sales volumes. From an economist's perspective, the customer experiences an agency problem. Agency creates the potential for supernormal profits for both agents and producers. Investors who understand the process can profit, too. It's worth examining how the agency issue – hitherto something discussed mainly in relation to the dysfunctionality of the investment management industry – relates to a number of companies we own or may purchase at some stage in the future (price permitting, that is).

Normal relations between provider, intermediary and consumer are distorted when the consumer lacks understanding and relies on a supposedly independent intermediary. In many cases the relationship between the intermediary and the product provider has developed to the point where these parties form a tacit alliance to exploit consumer ignorance. We came across this phenomenon with Geberit, the Swiss sanitary systems manufacturer. The company sells its product to plumbers via wholesalers who then install them in the end-customer's home or commercial building. Geberit has a push-pull marketing strategy whereby plumbers are educated to "pull" the product through the wholesale channel, and company sales representatives "push" the product to wholesalers. When we asked senior management about pricing pressure, we were told that plumbers welcomed price

---

[5] See www.tilsonfunds.com/MungerUCSBspeech.pdf

increases, since they were paid on a percentage commission basis for the system installation.

This model encourages innovation – in Geberit's case, it might be a new pre-wall installation system (don't ask) – as the plumber-agent finds it easier to persuade customers to pay up for novelty. This had led to frantic product development at Geberit, where around a third of the company's sales derive from products introduced over the last three years. The somewhat unholy alliance between Geberit and plumbers has produced a deep profit pool, from which Geberit takes a healthy share (it enjoys margins of over 15 per cent at the group operating profit level). The company's high market share – around 50 per cent in its seven core European markets – and the fragmentation of the plumbing industry help to maintain profitability.

Of course, the company would argue that these arrangements ultimately benefit customers, as profits finance new product development. That's as may be. What's clear is that Geberit has an extremely effective business model, with 8 per cent annual growth at the top line level over two decades.

An unholy alliance between producers and distributors exploiting customer ignorance is also prevalent in the healthcare sector. Without going into the dubious marketing ethics of the pharmaceutical industry, we have found agency models similar to Geberit's among European dental implant and hearing aid manufacturers. Nobel Biocare and Straumann are Swiss leaders in the field of dental implant technology. Constant innovation and customer (in this case, the dentist) education has driven strong growth and high margins. Nobel Biocare has grown revenues at 17 per cent p.a. since 1995, and its latest operating profit margin was 24 per cent. Dentists who adopt its implant technique, which replaces the traditional crown and bridge solution, earn higher revenues. Customers end up with better teeth, and shareholders are smiling!

In the upscale hearing aid market, a field dominated by European firms – Siemens, William Demant, GN Store Nord, and Phonak – there is a similar emphasis on continuous innovation. The fitters of hearing aids, like dentists, are keen to sell high-end products which earn them more money. We understand from William Demant (a portfolio holding with margins above 20 per cent after spending around 7 per cent of sales on R&D) that one of the defining characteristics of the high-end products is that they require a customized fitting, since everyone's "ocular canal" is unique. Their hearing aids cost around $1,000; on top of this, the fitter charges another $2,000 for customized service. As with Geberit's plumbing business, innovation in hearing aid technology has been a boon for raising product prices. Once again, the customer (the fitter-agent) is not price-sensitive. The producers of hearing aids and dental implants are helped by the fact that the markets into which they sell their products are so fragmented.

Another example of the agency model is when the paying customer doesn't actually choose the service. Labtest is the Hong Kong subsidiary of Intertek, a company listed on the London Stock Exchange. The company's role is to serve as a gatekeeper between Chinese consumer goods manufacturers and American retailers. We understand that the US firms select Labtest to check the prototypes of new Chinese products to ensure that they meet the appropriate specifications. Intertek charges the Chinese firms, rather than the US retailers, for this service, a fee that constitutes a relatively low proportion of the product price (less than 1 per cent of the manufacturer's cost). This distancing of payer from the service selector lies at the heart of Labtest's remarkable profitability – with margins around 33 per cent – alongside more obvious network and scale effects.

Munger is right. Customers will often pay more when agents are involved. In each of the cases we've discussed, the business models – whether in plumbing, dentistry, hearing aids, or product testing – involved value being transferred from the person who pays to the agent, with the producer taking a large slice of the pie. Each of these models has evolved over time and appears reasonably robust, even as consumers become better informed in the Internet age. Just as agency problems in the fund management industry have shown remarkable persistence, we expect the superior profitability of companies that exploit agency to endure.[6]

2.4   DIGITAL MOATS (AUGUST 2007)

Internet companies investing in their competitive positions can afford to ignore short-term profitability

Eight years ago, when it looked as though the future belonged to Internet companies, it was possible to double your money in a matter of months by investing in any company with dotcom attached to its name. At the time, we were unable to justify the valuations of any of these companies, nor identify any which we could safely say would still be going strong in years to come. Consequently, Marathon's global portfolios avoided any exposure to Internet companies. Yet some of the best recent performers in our global portfolios are companies which execute all of their business online. Two of them are even former highfliers

---

[6] Between August 2007 and the end of 2014, Intertek's share price rose by 83 per cent in US dollars, Geberit was up by 152 per cent, and William Demant fell by 13 per cent. The MSCI Europe Index, over the same period, was down by 21 per cent.

from the dotcom bubble, Amazon.com and Priceline.com. Given that these firms have little in the way of current profitability, why do we own them?

For a start, these companies are building sustainable competitive advantages. Their strategy is to use the low cost and scalability of Internet technology to provide savings for their customers. They recognize the importance of securing a dominant position in their respective markets by operating their businesses with low margins, in the short-term, so as to maximize their earnings potential in the long-term.

Amazon.com is the best known and most established of the businesses, having expanded well beyond its origins as an online discount book retailer. A lot of scepticism surrounds the stock, partly because of its high profile at the time of the Internet bubble, and more recently because of the volatile progression of the company's margins. The variation in the margin stems from Amazon's desire to continue to expand its offer, and the fact that a number of the new services – including Amazon Web Services, which provides computing services for clients, and "Fulfilment by Amazon," which enables other retailers to use Amazon's expertise in processing inventory and orders – have required large up-front investments and will take some time to develop into profitable businesses. This investment, most of which is written off as an expense in the accounts, has made margins rather volatile over recent years (as can be seen below).

While Wall Street fretted about the collapse in margins, without thinking of the longer-term benefits of the investment, the stock declined from $60 to $40. Now there are signs that Amazon's margins are recovering, while sales are growing at 35 per cent year-on-year. The stock has almost doubled since the start of 2007. Amazon gives frustratingly little long-term guidance about the potential profitability of its new initiatives, but hints at an ambition for margins in the high single digits once these businesses have reached maturity. The company's track record gives us confidence that they

Table 2.1   Amazon's net profit margin

Year	Net margin (%)
2003	0.7
2004	8.5
2005	4.2
2006	1.8

Source: Bloomberg.

can achieve this, and at the current valuation of 2.3 times current sales, the shares are far from overvalued.[7]

Priceline.com shares took one of the biggest tumbles when the Internet bubble burst, falling from a peak of $974 to a low of $7. The company had been operating an undifferentiated "name-your-own-price" model, until the acquisition of Booking.com in 2005 shifted the corporate strategy towards developing its European agency hotels business. Some 32,000 hotels have signed up so far; with over 100,000 hotels to target, along with increasing Internet use by Europeans, Booking.com is well placed to capture a much larger share of hotel bookings in Europe. Operating the platform requires minimal cost, and the company is already generating good cash flow which is being used to repurchase stock. It may be that the management of Priceline.com stumbled on this European opportunity by chance, but they have been smart enough to recognize the potential to create a business which could be generating enough cash in three to five years' time to make the valuation of the company look far too conservative.

The basic corporate model of low margins in order to maximize long-term absolute profit is a well-trodden path, with Wal-Mart the most notable exponent. It is not surprising that some companies will have the good sense to apply this old model to the new medium of the Internet. This strategy dramatically reduces business risks (via reduced competition) while simultaneously raising long-term rewards (via likely growth). Internet technology will help these firms secure competitive advantage, and investors should benefit in the long run.

2.5 QUALITY TIME (AUGUST 2011)

Our portfolios have shifted towards higher quality companies with sustainable barriers to entry

A few discordant commentators question whether the elevated current levels of corporate profits in the US and Europe are sustainable. As bottom-up investors, however, we are more interested in the capital cycle as it affects individual companies than in aggregate corporate profitability. We are on the lookout for factors which might lead to improved returns on equity, in

---

[7] The positions in Amazon.com and Priceline were eventually sold in February and September 2013, having risen respectively by 231 per cent and 1,055 per cent since the date of this piece. Amazon's stock has continued to perform strongly, up 18 per cent from the date of sale to the end of 2014, yet the company still shows nothing in the way of profit (its net margin in 2014 was −0.3 per cent.)

particular: (1) the emergence of oligopolies in industries hitherto characterized by low returns and excessive competition; (2) the evolution of business
models with high and rising barriers to entry; and (3) management behaviour which encourages these trends.

Even if European corporate profits decline in aggregate, our portfolio companies should be able to resist the trend. That's because over time,
Marathon's European portfolio has shifted gradually towards higher quality
companies with superior barriers to entry.

We have discussed at length our investments in so-called agency business
models, including medical devices and building equipment (locks, electrical
and plumbing fittings, etc). Essentially, these companies rely on an intermediary to sell their products (a doctor, plumber, locksmith etc.) whose advice
is relied upon by uninformed consumers who do not perceive the common
interest of the producer and agent to sell high-margin products. These business models account for approximately 10 per cent of Marathon's European
portfolio and have an average estimated RoE for 2011 of 27 per cent, some 11
percentage points above the average for European non-financials. Exposure
to branded consumer goods has also increased in recent years – including
additions of beer stocks, Unilever and Swedish Match – and now represents
around 9 per cent of the portfolio, with an average RoE of 48 per cent.

Another class of business whose weight in our portfolios has expanded
in recent years has been subscription-based service companies with annu-
ity-like revenue streams. Excluding telecom companies, which also have a
high degree of subscription-based revenue, these companies now account
for around 12 per cent of the European portfolio and have a forecast RoE of
42 per cent. The common theme here is a longer-term commitment made by
the customer, together with an element of inertia when it comes to renewals.
These factors, in combination with the scale economies which often arise in
the provision of subscription services, make for significant barriers to entry
and high and sustainable returns.

This is particularly true where the cost of the service is only a small
proportion of the customer's total spending, as is the case for a number of
our portfolio companies, including Rightmove, Capita and a handful of
information providers. Rightmove, the UK property listings website, enjoys
a winner-takes-all network benefit from being the most popular website
for property searchers. The company charges estate agents a subscription
price per office which is well below the cost of less effective print advertising. When we met the company in March 2011, 65 per cent of subscriptions
for the year had already been received, and a further 20 per cent were to be
received in May. Price increases this year are in the order of 16 per cent.

In the area of dialysis treatment, Fresenius Medical Care (FMC) has a 34 per cent market share in the US and makes substantial profits from private insurers for whom the cost of dialysis care is only 2 per cent of total outgoings. Negotiations with private insurers are on a state-by-state basis, limiting customer buying power, and increasingly insurers are moving to multiyear contracts with built-in price escalators. Capita, the UK business processing outsourcing company, has built up a base of multiyear contracts with local and central government and, increasingly, in the life insurance and pensions administration market. It has been able to improve its margins over time by delivering substantial cost savings for customers and in some cases building competence centres whose costs are spread across a number of clients.

In the area of information providers, portfolio companies such as Experian, Reed Elsevier, Wolters Kluwer and Informa have businesses with unique information whose value for customers depends on having a complete data set. Hence, it is hard to consider cancelling subscriptions even during economic downturns. Even Experian, whose data collection business is linked to the growth of credit markets generally, delivered modest growth during the financial crisis.

Together, the above three categories of stocks account for approximately 31 per cent of Marathon's European portfolio. To these, one can add holdings in pharmaceutical and telecom companies, which have high returns (although there are more doubts about their sustainability), and one arrives at a total of close to 40 per cent of the total portfolio (nearer 50 per cent ex-financials). The average RoE of this group of stocks is 39 per cent, 2.4 times the average for non-financial stocks generally.

Although there is variability among this group in terms of sensitivity to the economic cycle and some business models will undoubtedly prove more durable than others, these high RoE business models are likely to outperform more discretionary areas, particularly those exposed to weak domestic European consumption. Other more cyclically sensitive portfolio holdings are increasingly oriented towards global growth, especially in relation to emerging markets, whose prospects appear more promising than those in the mature Western economies. This shift to quality should render Marathon's European portfolios less dependent on a precise answer to the question of whether aggregate corporate profits, whether for cyclical or structural reasons, are about to be squeezed.[8]

---

[8] Of the 11 companies referred to in this article (Assa Abloy, Legrand, Geberit, Unilever, Swedish Match, Rightmove, Capita, Fresenius Medical Care, Experian, Reed Elsevier and

2.6 ESCAPING THE SEMIS' CYCLE (FEBRUARY 2013)

Niche semiconductor businesses have escaped the ravages of the industry's capital cycle

Driven by Moore's law, the semiconductor sector has achieved sustained and dramatic performance increases over the last 30 years, greatly benefiting productivity and the overall economy. Unfortunately, investors have not done so well. Since inception in 1994, the Philadelphia Semiconductor Index has underperformed the Nasdaq by around 200 percentage points, and exhibited greater volatility.

The reason for this poor performance is no secret. No part of the technology world has been more prone to cyclical booms and busts than the semiconductor industry. In good times, prices pick up, companies increase capacity, and new entrants appear, generally from different parts of Asia (Japan in the 1970s, Korea in 1980s, Taiwan in the mid-1990s, and China more recently). Excess capital entering at cyclical peaks has led to relatively poor aggregate industry returns.

While the history of the semiconductor business provides a classic example of the capital cycle, there are companies operating in niches of the industry which have delivered excellent long-term returns for shareholders. Two of them are recent additions in our US portfolio: Analog Devices, based in Norwood, Massachusetts, and Linear Technology, headquartered in Milpitas, California.

Chart 2.1 The semiconductor cycle
Source: Marathon.

Wolters Kluwer), 10 outperformed the MSCI Europe Index between August 2011 (date of publication) and the end of 2014 – the exception being Swedish Match.

Semiconductors are essential electronic building blocks for electronic systems and equipment. Analog semiconductors represent around 15 per cent of the total semiconductor market, with the rest being digital. The function of an analog semiconductor is to bridge the gap between the real world and the electronic one – monitoring, amplifying and transforming phenomena such as temperature, sound and pressure. End-markets include mobile phone handsets (e.g., the digitization of voice), automobiles (e.g., the crash sensor in an airbag) and the industrial economy (e.g., a temperature sensor in process automation equipment). This is in contrast to digital semiconductors which operate, predominantly, in the purely digital world of binary code.

The analog sub-sector has been a notable exception to the low and volatile investment returns of the semiconductor industry. Analog Devices, for example, has consistently generated high margins over many years, with robust profits even in stressed environments. On average, between 2000 and 2012, the company's gross margin was 60 per cent and operating margin was 25 per cent. The level of capital intensity required to achieve these impressive returns was relatively low. Capex to sales at Analog Devices has averaged 6 per cent since 2000, and has fallen to 4 per cent over the last five years. This low level of capital intensity has allowed free cash flow conversion at a consistently high level, on average at over 100 per cent of net income.

Linear Technology has displayed even stronger economics. Since the turn of the century, it has enjoyed an average gross margin of 76 per cent and average operating margin of around 50 per cent. The ratio of capex to sales has hovered around 5 per cent, with cash conversion again greater than 100 per cent. In addition to having robust margins, both companies have historically experienced strong sales growth, driven by the increasing penetration of technology into everyday life. Since 1990, Analog Devices's revenue has compounded at 8 per cent annually, and Linear's sales have grown by 14 per cent a year.

How have these companies generated such high returns and to what extent are these returns sustainable? The answer lies in an understanding of the supply side of this industry – the specifics of the production process, market structure, competitive dynamics and pricing power, which together constitute the essence of capital cycle analysis. Consider first the mechanics of the analog semiconductor business. As the real world is far more complex and heterogeneous than the digital one, the product design required to capture it has to be more complex and heterogeneous. This means that product differentiation of analog semiconductors is higher and company-specific intellectual property (whether physical or human capital) more important.

The human capital component is especially hard to replicate because engineering talent deepens with experience. The design process is much more trial and error than in other technology disciplines, and less reliant on computer modelling and simulation. To become an expert in analog semiconductor design takes many years – the tenure of the average engineer at Analog Devices is 20 years. This forms an important barrier to entry. In addition, each analog company's process technologies are quite distinct (digital utilizes a more generic process).

Thus, it is difficult for an engineer to be poached by another analog company without his productivity being significantly impaired. The supply of new engineers tends to be constrained for the analog sector – new science graduates are much more likely to pursue the digital semiconductor route. This is largely because the learning curve is less steep in digital, and experience on the job less valued. As a result, research capacity in the world of analog semis has been, and will likely to continue to be, constrained.

These factors – a differentiated product and company-specific "sticky" intellectual capital – reduce market contestability. These strategic advantages are compounded by the fact that analog has a more diverse end market than digital, with a much wider range of products, numbering in the thousands, and smaller average volume size. Such market characteristics make it difficult for a new entrant to compete effectively. Thus pricing power tends to be robust and market positions relatively stable over long periods. While the overall market is relatively fragmented – the five firm concentration ratio is around 50 per cent – it is more consolidated in the various market sub-segments. Analog Devices, for instance, has over a 40 per cent share in data converters.

Pricing power is further aided by the fact that an analog semiconductor chip typically plays a very important role in a product (for example, the airbag crash sensor) but represents a very small proportion of the cost of materials. The average selling price for Linear Technology's products is under $2. As a result, competition tends to be less on price and more on product quality. In addition, once a chip has been designed into an application – a process on which the original equipment manufacturer and the analog company often collaborate, it is costly for the manufacturer to replace it, as the whole production process has to be revised. Hence switching costs are high, both improving pricing power over the product lifecycle (often ten years or more) and the degree to which revenues are recurring.

Finally, and of critical importance, the analog production process is less standardized than most tech components, and thus far less vulnerable to obsolescence from the endless march of Moore's law, significantly reducing capital intensity. More than a third of sales at Analog Devices come from products which are more than ten years old. This shelters the sector from the destructive force of the capital cycle which has wreaked such havoc in the digital semiconductor industry. Hence there are good reasons to believe that the high returns historically achieved by these companies can be sustained into the future.

We are also confident that management will allocate future surplus cash flow for the benefit of equity investors. Historically, most of the growth of these businesses has been organic, with excess cash returned to shareholders. This is a significant achievement for companies in the technology sector, an area where the temptation to do strategic deals has been strong, often to the detriment of shareholders. We expect the long-serving management teams of both companies to continue to allocate capital prudently. Both Analog Devices and Linear Technology currently offer free cash flow yields of 5 per cent. With long-term growth in free cash flow likely to be similar to historical levels, our total annual return expectation is in the low double digits.[9]

2.7 VALUE IN GROWTH (AUGUST 2013)

A Chinese Internet firm's market dominance justifies its high valuation
It should never be forgotten that, in its most basic form, investing is always and everywhere about price and value. Price is what you pay, says the Sage of Omaha, and value is what you get. By this definition, every serious investor must be a value investor. This is not to say that investors should restrict themselves to buying companies with low valuation multiples. The business of investment is ultimately about buying stocks at a discount to intrinsic value.

So how do you calculate value? Well, in theory the value received is derived from future cash flows discounted back to today at the appropriate discount rate. The trouble is that we are rather poor at making predictions, especially about the future. But that doesn't put us off. We suffer from what Nassim Taleb calls the "epistemic arrogance" – in plain English, we think we are better at making predictions than we really are.[10] The result is that we

---

[9] Between inception in 1994 and the end of 2014, the Philadelphia Stock Exchange Semiconductor Index rose by 474 per cent, underperforming the Nasdaq Composite by nearly 19 per cent. Over the same period, Linear Technologies was up 729 per cent and Analog Devices up 1,059 per cent.

[10] Nassim Taleb, *Black Swan: the Impact of the Highly Improbable*. The glossary of this book defines epistemic arrogance as a measurement of "the difference between what someone actually knows and how much he thinks he knows. An excess will imply arrogance,

have a misplaced sense of confidence in our forecasts. Investors like modelling because it appears scientific (the more spreadsheet tabs, the greater the effect).

Investment models, however, encourage anchoring. Most models are calibrated to produce a current value for a company within a reasonable range of the current price. Another wrinkle is the discount rates. If you don't accept that historical volatility (beta) is a good measure of risk (which we do not), then it's not clear how to calculate the appropriate discount rate. At Marathon, we believe that detailed forecasting adds little value.

One common response to the difficulty of forecasting is to turn to simple value proxies, such as the price-to-book ratio, price-to-earnings (PE) ratio, and free cash flow yield. Many "value" investors advocate buying a basket of stocks which are cheap by these measures. There's nothing inherently dumb about this approach. Each of the measures is a very useful indicator of potential value, but there's a danger of oversimplification. Traditional valuation measures say nothing about the specific context of an investment – for instance, a company's business model, its industry structure, and management's ability to allocate capital – which determines future cash flows.

Quantitative valuation measures also tend to encourage a narrow categorization of investment styles. Take for example the S&P US Style Indices. Value stocks are defined by their ratios of price-to-book, price-to-earnings, and price-to-sales. The growth index, on the other hand, is defined by the three-year change in earnings per share, three-year sales per share growth rate, and 12-month price momentum. While some of these factors are powerful, they are too crude to be the sole framework for assessing value. An analysis of our portfolios often creates confusion as to which box Marathon fits best. Conventional labels – "growth" or "value" – tend not to suit our capital cycle approach to investment.

Take Baidu, for example, the dominant Internet search engine in China, which happens to be a recent addition to the Marathon portfolios. At the time of purchase, the stock was priced at 7.2 times book and 18 times earning, neither of which look particularly appetizing from a value perspective.

Consider, however, that Baidu has a 70 per cent market share in an industry where profits accrue disproportionally to the market leader, making it difficult for competitors to thrive. Baidu also operates a business model which requires little capital investment and converts profit to cash at a rate in excess of 100 per cent. The asset-light nature of the balance sheet is helpful in

a deficit humility. An epistemocrat is someone of epistemic humility, who holds his own knowledge in greatest suspicion."

managing overinvestment and working capital creep, the two great dangers of a rapid growth model. Baidu's current level of monetization per search is less than a tenth of that achieved by its developed market peers, leaving significant opportunity for improvement. Furthermore, the founder, CEO and Chairman Robin Li has a 20.7 per cent stake, which aligns his interests with those of outside investors. Although there are a number of risks to the investment case (not least that that of supply side disruption), we believe that the "expensive" Baidu stock provides a compelling value opportunity for long-term investors.

2.8   QUALITY CONTROL (MAY 2014)

Capital cycle analysis helps to identify investments with high and sustainable returns

The capital cycle approach to investing is often associated with stocks from the "value" universe, where low and falling returns lead to capital flight, laying the foundations for an eventual recovery in profitability and valuations. It is perhaps less well understood how the capital cycle can also be applied to companies which have high and sustainable returns. This class of business has produced some of Marathon's best performers over the last ten years – Coloplast, Intertek, Geberit, Gartner, Kao and Priceline, to name a few. How do such investments fit in the capital cycle framework?

Pricing power has arguably been the most enduring determinant of high returns for these investments. It has come from two main sources. The first is a concentrated market structure, closely associated with effective management of capacity through the demand cycle which encourages a rational approach to pricing. The second is "intrinsic" pricing power within the product or service itself. Intrinsic pricing power is created when price is not the most important factor in a customer's purchase decision. Most often, this property is generated by the existence of an intangible asset. There are several classes of intangible assets, examples of which can be found among Marathon's holdings.

An obvious one is consumer brands. In the toothpaste category, private label penetration is only 2 per cent, supporting Colgate's excellent economics.[11] An intangible asset can also derive from a long-term customer relationship, as in case of the agency business models (Legrand, Assa Abloy or Geberit), where the customer relies on intermediaries (electricians, architects

---

[11] See above, 2.2 "The long game."

and plumbers respectively). The agent's interest is safety, quality, reliability, availability, and perhaps his own ability to earn a commission. Under such circumstances, price is a pass-through to the end customer, for whom product costs represent a small part of the total bill.[12]

Sometimes a product is so embedded in a customer's workflow that the risk of changing outweighs any potential cost savings – for instance, in subscription-based services like computer systems (Oracle) or payroll processing (ADP, Paychex). Networks where the customer benefits from a company's scale, as in the security business (Secom), industrial gases (Praxair, Air Liquide), car auctions (USS) or testing centres (Intertek) are another example. Finally, technological leadership (Intel, Linear Technology) can be another important intangible asset – although this is perhaps one of the less durable sources of pricing power, unless combined with others. The very best economics appear when some of the above characteristics combine in a situation in which the cost of the product or service is low relative to its importance: for example, the analog semiconductor chip which activates the car airbag, yet costs little more than a dollar.

The presence of intangible assets acts as a powerful barrier to entry. They are by nature durable, difficult to replicate and tending to economies of scale. Importantly, these barriers often strengthen over time, as high returns on capital throw off abundant free cash flow which is in turn reinvested in the business. For example, over the last five years, P&G has spent over $40bn in advertising, while Intel has invested roughly the same amount on R&D. This repels new entrants, short-circuiting the destructive side of the capital cycle – whereby excess profits normally attract competitors, which over time erodes profitability. Thus, the presence of intangible assets creates a virtuous cycle, allowing intrinsic value to compound over sustained periods at above average rates, an extremely powerful combination for the long-term shareholder when allied with prudent use of free cash flow. (The importance of management in this process is paramount – high organic returns can be diluted quickly by poorly conceived investment decisions or badly timed buybacks.)

Critically, this higher rate of compounding comes at a lower level of risk as the economics of a high return business tend to be more resilient to adverse shocks. This is partly mathematical – a 1 per cent fall in margin has a greater impact on a 5 per cent margin business compared to one that earns 20 per cent. Equally though, the factors which create sustainably high returns – intangible assets, strong market position and rational management – also

---

[12] See above, 2.3 "Double agents."

make a business more robust in the face of adverse changes in the business environment, whether of a macroeconomic or industry-specific nature.

For investors with short-term horizons, the virtue of compounding at a higher rate can appear insignificant. Over short time periods, share prices are generally driven by other factors such as macroeconomic or stock-specific news flow. Investing in a high-quality company can seem dull and unrewarding in the near-term. The lower risk which comes from investing in quality companies is only properly observed over the long-term. The fact that investors are often focused more on the short-term is partly a function of psychology – the human brain is simply not attuned to multiyear planning, being far better at responding to short-term threats and stimuli. This is seen in several behavioural heuristics – notably hyperbolic discounting[13] and recency bias. Short-termism can be intensified in an institutional setting. Performance-related pay for money managers at most investment firms is weighted to annual performance, which discourages long-term thinking.

Finally, there is another more technical reason why the virtues of a high return business are not always fully appreciated by investors. This is the tendency of investors to focus on the income statement. This fosters a fixation on price-earnings (P/E) valuation metrics and not price to free cash flow (P/FCF). Thus, all earnings growth is seen as equal, even though it is materially more value creative when return on capital and cash flow generation is higher. Faced with a choice between investing in two companies with the same earnings growth, we are prepared to pay materially more (in P/E terms) for the business with high returns on equity and superior cash flow generation.

In short, there are any number of good reasons to invest in businesses with durable high returns. Now appears an especially good time to do so. The rationale is simple – across nearly all sectors, margins are close to peak levels. It is sensible, therefore, to consider whether current profitability is sustainable given the historical tendency of margins to mean revert. In addition, tail risks lurking in the background – namely elevated debt levels in the private and public sectors, and the uncertain consequences of the unprecedented degree of monetary stimulus – are likely to impact the profits of lower quality firms at some stage in the future. Current valuation levels do

---

[13] There is evidence that investors' discount rate increases when cash flows are further out – a phenomenon known as "hyperbolic discounting." See, for example, Andrew Haldane, "The Short Long", Bank of England (Speech May 2011).

not require investors to pay a premium for this superior durability, hence the preponderance of higher return names in our global accounts.[14]

2.9   UNDER THE RADAR (FEBRUARY 2015)

Companies which provide indispensable services to their customers often prove to be excellent investments

The typical growth stock starts out with high returns, rising turnover, and glorious prospects, only to stumble in later years. The trouble is that profitable and growing businesses tend to attract lots of competition, especially when they operate in exciting areas, such as technology. Investors who buy growth at high starting valuations generally end up disappointed. There is, however, a certain class of company which we have found is well worth paying a premium for. Our preferred growth stocks undertake apparently unglamorous activities that are essential to their customers – so essential, in fact, that customers pay little attention to what they're being charged.

When Marathon encounters such companies, the common refrain of managers is that their products (or services) constitute only a small part of the customers' total cost and yet are of vital importance to them. It may be that a particular component is "mission critical" for an industrial process or a company's workflow. For instance, customers may face a very high cost if they have to shut down a production line when a crucial component fails. Hence, reliability weighs more highly than price. The product may also be essential by virtue of its quality, safety or performance attributes.

Having a high perceived value for customers often combines with some other advantages, which limits competition, ensuring high and sustained returns. These may be economies of scale in manufacturing and distribution, regulatory barriers and high switching costs. Companies talk about "value based," or "technical" selling, which often involves having highly qualified sales staff "embedded" in the R&D departments of their customers. Sometimes this means that the component is mandated for use over the lifecycle of a product, as is commonplace in the automotive and aerospace industries.

We have observed such "under-the-radar" companies in a diverse range of industries. In the technology field, analog semiconductor companies such

---

[14] At the time of writing, Marathon's top ten positions in its global accounts had an aggregate operating margin and return on equity of 25 per cent, while trading on a similar trailing P/E multiple (18 times) to the MSCI World Index. The superior free cash flow conversion of these businesses (92 per cent vs. 65 per cent) means that they trade at a discount on a price to free cash flow basis.

as Linear Technologies (return on capital employed a stupendous 141 per cent) and Analog Devices (ROCE at 25 per cent) fulfil a vital function, linking real world phenomena (heat, sound, light) to the digital world. The cost of the chips is just small percentage of the total cost of the equipment [as discussed above.] Certain software companies display similar characteristics. Payroll processing companies such as Paychex (ROCE at 35 per cent) and ADP (ROCE at 25 per cent) provide an important service, which, in the case of ADP, costs the employer around $3 per pay check. Small companies don't want to be bothered with this detailed, time-consuming work which carries a high risk of error for the inexperienced administrator. Better to outsource to Paychex, which has been able to raise prices regularly by over 3 per cent a year without losing clients. In Europe, CAD-CAM software companies such as Aveva and Dassault Systèmes provide mission critical services to design engineers. Operating as an essential link in the supply chain provides their businesses with an effective barrier to entry.

In the consumer goods area, flavour and fragrance companies sell key ingredients that are important for the ultimate consumer purchase decision. And yet their products account for only a small fraction of the merchandise. In the case of enzymes, dominated by Novozymes of Denmark, numerous processes now use small quantities of enzymes which provide both efficiency savings and product differentiation. Enzymes used in detergents typically represent less than 5 per cent of the total cost. Novozymes, with its 50 per cent plus global market share, also enjoys huge economies of scale.

Similarly, speciality chemical companies can earn very high margins on specific products. Executives at Croda (ROCE at 23 per cent), a UK listed company, once described to us how they made a 90 per cent margin on a particular active ingredient for an anti-ageing cosmetic. Given the success of the product (Matrizyl), they now regret not negotiating a royalty fee since the price charged represented less than one per cent of the total sale price. Another UK niche chemical company, Victrex, which is the world leader in the production of polyetheretherketone (a polymer used in engineering applications), described to us how their specialist sales teams worked with OEMs like Apple in the design phase for new products. The company generates impressive operating margins of more than 35 per cent and earns a return on capital of around 25 per cent.

The market for laboratory supplies is highly profitable. The key here is that the customer (scientist/lab technician) cares more about product quality, availability and service and not so much about price, orders are regular (daily) and relatively small. So price is scarcely perceptible to the customer.

Examples include Waters (liquid chromatography), Pall Corporation (filtration), and Mettler-Toledo (measurement) which sell both equipment and then consumables. Scientists are extremely reluctant to change suppliers – Waters claims that they cannot even displace their own old technologies! Regulations create barriers to entry. Products often require FDA approval as part of the drug manufacturing process, raising potential switching costs. If they attempt to switch a single small supplier, pharma companies may need to get the FDA to recertify the entire production process.

Engineering companies can also generate very high returns from seemingly mundane products, like valves and actuators. Actuators made by Rotork (ROCE at 24 per cent) are used to control flows and feedback data in huge oil and gas refineries. These are so crucial to the function and safety of the plant that the owner of the facility, say Royal Dutch Shell, may specify that subcontractors use Rotork actuators. Over the past decade, Rotork's organic sales have compounded by 12 per cent annually. Spirax-Sarco, whose return on capital employed (ROCE) is around 17 per cent, sells engineered kits for steam-based applications in industrial processes. Its large army of engineers visit customer plants to demonstrate how their products can improve energy efficiency and environmental impact. The company enjoys margins of 20 per cent. Finally, IMI (ROCE at 20 per cent plus) has refocused its business on products which control liquids and gases in critical applications.

While the high profitability of the companies under discussion may be below the radar of their customers, it has not escaped the attention of investors. In the past, when we encountered such wonderful businesses we were prone to assume that high valuations meant they were fairly priced, or even overpriced, in the stock market. A few years later, however, when we reengage with the same firms, we often find that their share prices have shot up. When we first met with Spirax-Sarco in 2005, for instance, it was valued at 17.5 times earnings and the shares were trading around £8. We demurred. Five years later, at our next meeting, the stock was trading above £18. Again, we concluded that it was fully valued. Since then, the share price has almost doubled again. The lesson seems to be that a full price is often justified for high quality, "under-the-radar" businesses.[15]

---

[15] Spirax-Sarco shares were recently changing hands for around £35.

3

MANAGEMENT MATTERS

Like many other investors, Marathon never tires of quoting Warren Buffett. One particular comment of the Sage of Omaha has become something of a mantra at the firm: namely, Buffett's observation that "after ten years on the job, a CEO whose company retains earnings equal to 10 per cent of the net worth will have been responsible for the deployment of more than 60 per cent of all capital at work in the business." What this means is that investors should pay particular attention to the capital allocation skills of management.

As Marathon's investment holding periods became more extended, in contrast to the fund management industry as a whole, the notion that a manager's skill in capital allocation is decisive to the investment outcome has been reinforced. The study of management, via face-to-face meetings and general observation, has become one of the main elements of the daily job at Marathon. The case of Björn Wahlroos of Finland's Sampo, outlined in this chapter, shows how the ideal corporate manager is one who understands his industry's capital cycle and whose interests are aligned with those of outside investors.

3.1   FOOD FOR THOUGHT (SEPTEMBER 2003)

The failure of specialist analysts to anticipate a Dutch corporate collapse comes as no surprise
It is often said that one can learn more from failure than from success. Having experienced a fair number of failures in our European portfolios over time, we can confirm that this maxim applies to investment. Looking at the failures of others can also be instructive (and replete with *Schadenfreude*). The case of Ahold, the Dutch-based international food retailer, provides one of

Europe's most significant implosions of shareholder value in recent years.[1] Fortunately, our small team of generalist investment professionals spotted in advance the dangers created by capital misallocation, mismanagement and murky accounting at the world's third largest supermarket group. The question remains why teams of highly specialized (and highly paid) analysts failed to do so. We have retrospectively examined research on Ahold, published by some of the leading brokers. To our mind, this research reveals systematic flaws in the specialist analyst model, which largely derive from the relationship between research analysts and the companies they follow.

1. Too close to management

There is always a danger that an analyst is "captured" by management. This risk rises for specialist analysts who spend most of their time covering a small handful of companies, whereas a generalist might cover a few hundred. Capture poses the threat that an analyst lands up becoming the mouthpiece of management. In the case of Ahold, capture was a real and present danger. Take, for instance, the titles of one brokerage analyst's reports: "Live From Zaandam" (the company's headquarters), "Visit with Stop & Shop," and "A day with top performing CT Stop & Shop team and a night with the CFO." The analyst's choice of titles reveals, to our minds, an unhealthy proximity to Ahold's management.

Ahold was also notoriously opaque when it came to disclosure. By occasionally giving privileged information to particular analysts, the recipient may have felt (consciously or not) that he or she owed management a favour – what is known as "reciprocation tendency." And when things started to go wrong, the weird and wonderful effects of Stockholm syndrome – whereby the hostage becomes the mouthpiece for his captor – may have taken hold.[2]

2. Too much information

Having more information doesn't necessarily improve decision-making. We know from studies of horse racing that when handicappers receive more information about the horses and riders, they become proportionately more confident even though they are no more likely to pick the winner. When

---

[1] On 24 February 2003, shares in Royal Ahold fell 63 per cent on the NYSE after the Dutch supermarket group announced earnings had been overstated by close to $500m. The accounting problems related to the operations of its US foodservice business.

[2] In *The Economist* (27 February 2003), a brokerage analyst complained of Ahold management's "attempt to frighten us."

analysts have too much data, there's a danger they won't see the wood for the trees. Obsessing over Ahold's quarterly like-for-like sales per square foot and a multiplicity of other metrics did not provide a good insight into what was to come. Analyzing the company's cash flow over a five-year period, on the other hand, got one quickly to the key point that Ahold's management had failed to generate cash from its core business.

Then there's the danger of "cognitive dissonance," when information which conflicts with a previously formed conviction is blocked out. This appears to have afflicted one broker who, having reached the conclusion that Ahold had been unfairly derated (in valuation terms) after diversifying into the foodservice business, subsequently appeared blind to negative information about the company. It later transpired that the profitability of the foodservice operations had been fraudulently misstated. Our racecourse punters apparently become more confident of their opinion after having placed their bet. The danger is that the analyst reaches a conclusion based on a single line of thought and then sticks with this view, come what may.

3. Living in a cocoon

Specialist analysts operate in a cocoon, in which they are overexposed to company management and peer analysts and underexposed to what is going on in the rest of the world. Herding instincts may tend to reinforce similar opinions among peer analysts. Their thinking starts to reflect what Daniel Kahneman calls the "insider view." In the case of Ahold, the specialist retail analysts spent a great deal of time comparing the company's performance, on a range of measures, with US peers such as Albertson's and Kroger. As global investors, however, we find it more useful to compare the returns of a company in a particular industry with those in other industries and countries. A specialist analyst couldn't say whether Ahold was a good investment relative to, say, a Scandinavian paper company or a Thai cement plant.

4. Poor incentives

Management has a huge influence over the capital allocation of a business. Decisions taken by senior executives are likely to be influenced by their incentives. Yet specialist research rarely addresses the key issue of incentives. (In the brokerage reports on Ahold, there was no comment on the subject of incentives.) Perhaps, this oversight on the part of sell-side analysts relates to their own incentives and the bad feeling that such a discussion might provoke with their colleagues across the Chinese Wall in corporate finance. While there was a good deal of spin from Ahold about the introduction of incentives schemes based on Economic Value Added (EVA), we were told that the chief executive was primarily rewarded on the basis of earnings per share (EPS) growth – a metric which can be boosted with acquisitions and by the use of leverage. This did not give us a very warm feeling, given the malleability of Dutch GAAP accounting and Ahold's acquisition roll-up growth model. Things appeared even worse when we discovered that the CEO owned fewer than 1,700 shares (worth $70,000 at their peak) in the company.

5. An even worse performance metric

Unsurprisingly, in the light of these incentives, Ahold turned out to be exceptionally good at delivering earnings per share (EPS) growth. The company achieved the notable feat of 23 consecutive quarters of double-digit EPS growth. This record turned out to be too good to be true: Ahold's annual results for 2000, 2001, and the first three quarters of 2002 were all restated. Why do specialist analysts pay so much attention to earnings per share? One reason relates to short measurement periods. As we observed above, quarterly cash flow statements are relatively meaningless. Using the principles of accrual accounting, management has a certain leeway in what numbers they report. Unfortunately, there is a good deal of scope for cheating. Quarterly EPS figures also play a role in a stock market game. Once analysts set the market's EPS expectations for the next quarter and management beats the expected numbers, the share price can be expected to rise. We have previously discussed the futility of this game, vulnerable as it is to "Goodhart's Law" (namely, that once a data point is widely used as a measuring stick, it ceases to be reliable).[3]

The above is not to say that specialist analysts are without merit. We call on them to help us cut through the jargon that each industry produces and to help us stay abreast of key industry trends. At the same time, we have no intention of importing the specialist analyst model in-house because of the dangers we have outlined above. The difficulty we have is in persuading others that "expertise" (i.e., a lot of knowledge) doesn't necessarily lead to superior investment results. The reasons, we believe, are subtle and complex. The sorry tale of Ahold sheds some light on what can go wrong.[4]

---

[3] See *Capital Account*, pp.209–12.

[4] Marathon subsequently acquired shares in Ahold in mid-2014, after the company had shrunk its business and shifted the focus of executive remuneration from an EPS target to return on capital employed.

3.2 CYCLICAL MISSTEPS (AUGUST 2010)

A great mystery of the corporate world is the tendency of management to buy high and sell low

Now that the capital markets have settled somewhat, it's an interesting exercise to look at how managements behaved both before and after the Lehman crisis. It is generally the case that most managements, and indeed whole industries, engage in procyclical behaviour. It is greatly dispiriting to see companies repeatedly buying back their shares as the cycle peaks, only to raise fresh capital at the trough. Shareholders invariably lose out in the process. Alas, this time was no different.

It remains one of the great mysteries of corporate behaviour, why companies tend to buy high and sell low, even when this involves their own equity. This has been very much the case over the last few, tumultuous years. As the markets climbed towards their 2007 highs, companies spent a record amount on acquiring overvalued equity through cash-based M&A transactions and buybacks, as Chart 3.1 shows. Although equity issuance also reached a peak level, one suspects most of that was used to purchase overvalued equity in other companies. This was certainly the case with the €19bn Fortis rights issue, which funded the purchase of certain parts of ABN Amro, and the Veolia equity issuance of some €3bn at the top of the market, which was used to purchase assets that were clearly overvalued (if the subsequent 66 per cent decline in Veolia's share price fall is anything to go by).

The herd-like behaviour of companies and their managements never loses its power to astound. All too often, when one company decides that buybacks are the thing to do, then its competitors will play the game too. By

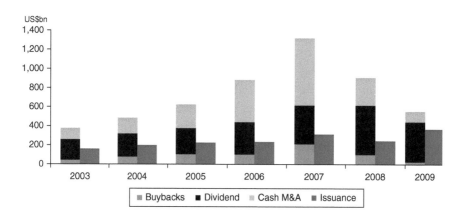

Chart 3.1   European capital allocation

Source: Nomura, Dealogic.

the same token, capital raising (secondary issues) often appears at the same time among multiple companies in the same industry. One reason they act together is that no company wants to see competitors gain a funding advantage. For instance, European building material groups – including Holcim, Lafarge and Saint-Gobain – raised a total of nearly €10bn around the market low in early 2009, having been marginal repurchasers of their equity in 2008. These same companies invested heavily at the top of the cycle, spending a phenomenal €46bn in the 2005–08 period, before making disposals of €9bn in 2009. Lafarge, the French cement group, exemplified this value destruction by buying Egyptian cement group Orascom in late 2007 for €10.2bn in cash and shares, only to be forced into a rights issue in 2009 at the market low. Lafarge's share price has fallen by around 64 per cent since that acquisition.

Procyclical behaviour has not been exclusive to the building materials industry. European homebuilders also bought back €1.95bn of stock in 2003-08, only to raise more than that amount in fresh equity in 2009 and 2010 – the sector is now capitalized at a third of its peak level in 2007. The European auto sector has performed true to type, being a modest net retirer of equity throughout the 2000–08 period to the tune of €7bn (of which nearly two-thirds was done at the top in 2008), before producing a deluge of paper in 2009–10 of some €12.1bn to refinance an industry laid low by the financial crisis.

A small number of companies took advantage of the crisis and were able to conclude deals at what may well turn out to be bargain basement prices. These took place mostly in the banking sector, where BNP pounced on Fortis (the Belgian and Luxembourg businesses); Barclays bought the Lehman's US business; Sampo acquired a significant stake in Nordea (which is already showing a €1bn profit); Santander snapped up Alliance & Leicester, Sovereign Bancorp and parts of BNP. In the auto sector, Fiat acquired Chrysler for nothing and some government guarantees. These acquisitions may prove to be the European equivalent of Warren Buffett using his cash pile to invest in GE, Harley Davidson, Swiss Re and Goldman Sachs near market lows.

While boards acting on behalf of shareholders have generally mistimed their equity purchases and sales, insiders have done rather better when trading for their own account. In the case of the aforementioned Veolia, the CEO sold most of his exposure (€4m worth) near the top. While insiders were net sellers of equities in the run-up to the financial crisis, an examination of director dealings over this tumultuous period shows that directors then became net buyers rather too early and remained so throughout the period of the market decline until the end of Q1 2009, from which point they became heavy net sellers, just as the market was beginning to recover. This may have been because they had been forced to defer sales during the market turmoil, and also because they were responding to widespread concerns about a double dip.

Looking back over recent years, our overwhelming impression is that the most companies mistimed the cycle and misjudged the crisis. As a result, poor capital allocation decisions were made over that period. The lure of cheap debt and apparently rosy growth prospects enticed many managements into thinking that not only were their own shares cheap, but that the equity of other companies also offered good value, particularly given the extremely low cost of capital at the time. This herd-like behaviour was exacerbated by the private equity bubble. The inevitable appearance of corporate excess at a high point in the cycle represents a significant drag on returns for investors in public equities.

3.3   A CAPITAL ALLOCATOR (SEPTEMBER 2010)

The best managers understand their industry's capital cycle and invest in a countercyclical manner

When an investor makes a long-term investment in a company, success or failure generally turns on the investing skills of senior management. Over the medium term, return on capital is generally determined by the CEO's decisions about capital expenditure, merger and acquisition activity, and the level of debt and equity used to finance the business. In addition, the question of whether to issue or buy back shares, and the stock price at the time of these decisions, can have a huge impact on shareholder returns. When portfolio managers buy shares, they are effectively outsourcing investment responsibilities to the incumbent management team. The CEO's "fund management" skills can be just as important as his skills in managing day-to-day operations. Unfortunately, as we have noted elsewhere, European business leaders tend to be herd-like and procyclical when it comes to capital allocation.

The problem is they often lack the right skills. As Warren Buffett has pointed out: The heads of many companies are not skilled in capital allocation. Their inadequacy is not surprising. Most bosses rise to the top because they have excelled in an area such as marketing, production, engineering – or sometimes, institutional politics.

Financial companies are probably the most challenging of all for CEOs to manage, as they require many more capital allocation decisions compared with, say, running a large food retailer or consumer products company. In recent years, there have been too many examples of bank CEOs wrecking their firms with ill-conceived capital allocation, of which the most notorious example is perhaps Fred "the Shred" Goodwin's decision to blow RBS's balance sheet on the acquisition of ABN Amro assets immediately prior to the onset of the global financial crisis.

Occasionally, though, a managerial exception to the general rule emerges. A case in point is Björn Wahlroos' tenure as CEO and now chairman of Sampo, a Finnish financial services group. This has been a long-term Marathon holding and is one of the largest financial positions in our European portfolios.

Björn Wahlroos arrived at Sampo in 2001, after selling his boutique investment bank (Mandatum) with excellent timing to Sampo for €400m. The consideration was paid in Sampo shares, with Wahlroos' 30 per cent holding in Mandatum converting into a 2 per cent stake in Sampo. The transaction was effectively a reverse takeover, with Wahlroos becoming CEO as part of the agreement. At the time, Sampo comprised three domestically-oriented businesses in banking, property & casualty (P&C) insurance, and life insurance. The group owned around 1 per cent of Nokia's outstanding shares, at the time worth €1.5bn or 22 per cent of Sampo's net asset value. One of Wahlroos' first acts as CEO was to sell down the Nokia stake from 35m to 6.7m shares by November 2001 at an average price of €35 per share. Today, the Nokia share price stands at €7.2 per share.

His next step involved the company's primarily Finnish P&C insurance business, which enjoyed a 34 per cent market share in the domestic market but was essentially mature. Wahlroos injected this asset into a pan-Nordic P&C business called "If" for which Sampo received a 38 per cent share (and half the voting rights), plus €170m of cash. The combined group controlled a 37 per cent market share in Norway, 23 per cent in Sweden and 5 per cent in Denmark. New discipline (read: oligopolistic pricing) was introduced, and the combined ratio[5] was quickly reduced from 105 per cent in 2002 to 90 per cent by 2005.

In 2003, before the full benefits of the new strategy were realized, Sampo took advantage of the financial distress of its partners and bought out 100 per cent of the equity in the P&C operations at an implied value for the whole business of €2.4bn. Today, the lowest valuation of "If" in brokers' sum-of-

---

[5] Used in both insurance and reinsurance, the combined ratio is calculated as the sum of incurred losses and expenses, divided by earned premium. A combined ratio of more than 100 per cent indicates an underwriting loss, while below 100 per cent indicates an underwriting profit.

the-parts valuations of Sampo is €4bn, and Mr Wahlroos has an open invitation to potential buyers of the business at a price tag of €8–9bn. The next major strategic move came in 2007, immediately before the global financial crisis struck, when Sampo announced the sale of its Finnish retail banking operation to Danske Bank. For this transaction, Sampo achieved a top of the market price of €4.1bn in cash. Gradually, this cash has been reinvested in a higher quality retail banking franchise, as Sampo has since built up a stake of over 20 per cent in Nordea, the largest Nordic banking group. They have now invested €5.3bn in Nordea at an average price of €6.39 per share, which compares with the current price of €7.70. Almost half of the position was acquired at a price of around 0.6 times book value, implying an impressive arbitrage compared with the 3.6 times book value achieved on the sale of the Finnish business.

The capital allocation masterstroke before the Lehman bust was Wahlroos' decision to reduce the weighting in equities down to 8 per cent of Sampo's investment portfolio, while maintaining a large position in liquid fixed income assets. As a result, the company was able to invest €8bn–€9bn in commercial credit in autumn 2008, purchased at bargain prices from distressed sellers. Sampo was particularly active in acquiring bonds in Finland's largest paper company, UPM-Kymmene, which at the time yielded over 8 per cent. The decision to invest in the bonds of this company must have been made easier by the fact that UPM's chairman at the time was a certain Björn Wahlroos. This investment in corporate bonds has already yielded a €1.5bn gain, according to the company.

As a result of these astute capital allocation decisions, the Sampo share price has comfortably outperformed its financial services peer group and has outperformed the overall European stock market by a factor of nearly 2.5 times since January 2001. The Sampo case study combines many of the key elements that we look for in management; namely, it has a chief executive who both understands and is able to drive the industry's capital cycle (the Nordic P&C consolidation story), allocates capital in a countercyclical manner (selling equities prior to the GFC), is incentivized properly (large equity stake) and takes a dispassionate approach to selling assets when someone is prepared to overpay (Finnish bank divestment). The pity is that there are so few examples of Sampo-esque management elsewhere in Europe.[6]

---

[6] Sampo's share price has continued to perform strongly, up 75 per cent in US dollars from the time this article was written to the end of 2014.

3.4   NORTHERN STARS (MARCH 2011)

The superior long-term performance of Nordic stocks reflects the quality of management

To an observer steeped in the laissez-faire tenets of Anglo-Saxon capitalism, the success of Nordic corporations presents a conundrum. Why have the quasi-socialist societies of Northern Europe, with their high taxation and comprehensive welfare systems, proved to be such successful havens of capitalist enterprise? Given our longstanding overweight position in Scandinavian stocks, we thought we might try to answer this question.

For stock market returns, Sweden ranks as the world's top performer over the course of the twentieth century, delivering annual real returns of 7.6 per cent compared with 6.7 per cent from US stocks. Compounded over a hundred years, an investor in Swedish equities would have done more than twice as well as his American counterpart. Scandinavia has also produced a number of world-beating companies across a number of different industries, including H&M and Ikea (retail), Maersk (shipping), and successful capital goods companies including Atlas Copco (compressors), Sandvik (carbide tools), and Volvo and Scania (truck manufacturers). In the technology field, Ericsson and Nokia still hold market-leading positions, despite the latter's widely publicized difficulties in recent years.

As well as benefiting from a generous endowment of natural resources, the Nordic countries have enjoyed stable legal and political structures, reinforced in the case of Sweden by the policy of neutrality in armed conflict. A Protestant work ethic, generally cooperative relations between unions and management, and a willingness to engage with the rest of the world are also factors driving success.

A Nordic capacity for hard work is combined with a geographical openness. The total population of the Scandinavian states of Sweden, Norway, Finland and Denmark, with Iceland thrown in as an honorary member, is less than 25m (Sweden with a population of 9m is the largest). As the boss of Sweden's Atlas Copco likes to point out, that is considerably less than the Chinese city of Chongqing, whose population exceeds 30m. Scandinavia's small population and limited domestic markets have forced its companies to look abroad for their living. Many have thrived in the era of globalization. China has become Atlas Copco's largest geographical market. Nordic governments have also been active in promoting the interests of companies via trade promotion and other means, unfettered by Western foreign policy agendas. Atlas Copco has been in China since the 1920s, ABB since 1907, and Ericsson can date its operation there to 1894. Scandinavian companies have been able to operate in countries which would be deemed off-limits for US or Western European firms.

Our historical tendency to be overweight the Nordic stock markets has mostly been influenced by the perceived quality of Nordic management teams. Generally speaking, Nordic managers have been able to articulate their case clearly and apply a degree of focus that is not always the case elsewhere in Europe. One can also discern a high degree of adaptability. Scandinavian companies are not just open to foreign excursions. It was striking to note on a recent trip just how many of the large and successful companies are run by foreigners. A Belgian is head of Atlas Copco, a Scot runs SKF, and Nokia and Electrolux have recently recruited American bosses. This openness to out-siders stands in contrast to recent developments in Southern Europe, where Italy and France are engaged in a race to the bottom to redefine strategic industries for protectionist purposes.

Protectionism of sorts is, nevertheless, prevalent in Scandinavia. Many of the largest companies are cossetted from the vagaries of the stock market by their ownership structures. The influence of significant shareholder group-ings is an inescapable feature of the Nordic corporate world. On a recent visit to a conference at the Grand Hotel in Stockholm (owned by the Wallenberg family since 1968), two out of three large capitalization Swedish compa-nies providing one-on-one meetings to Marathon were also Wallenberg-controlled, namely Electrolux (owned since 1956) and Atlas Copco (since the company's foundation in 1873). The third company we met, Alfa Laval, was acquired from the Wallenberg family by the Rausing family of Tetra Pak fame in 1991, after more than 50 years of Wallenberg ownership.

While one can debate the investment skills of the later generations of Wallenbergs, executives at their family-controlled companies frequently argue that the presence of a long-term shareholder with disproportionate voting rights (via A and B share structures) has provided stability and focus for their organizations. It is interesting to examine, in brief, how some of these Nordic companies got ahead of the competition.

Atlas Copco has become the global leader in compressed air equip-ment, outperforming its initially more strongly positioned competitors from the UK and US. The current chief executive puts his company's suc-cess down to a consistent long-term strategy, global reach, tradition of innovation and early exploitation of the aftermarket for its products. Alfa Laval has achieved similar success in its chosen markets of fluid handling and heat exchangers. The company's strategy of remaining focused on a limited range of growing industrial applications around the world has paid off in competitive terms.

A high level of focus combined with a global orientation is further exemplified by Assa Abloy, the world leader in the locks business and a Marathon portfolio holding. A former CEO, Carl Henric Svanberg, once stressed to us how Assa benefited from having a board which enjoyed talking exclusively about locks. One can easily imagine such a group of earnest Swedes. In recent years, the company has been relocating its manufacturing operations to low cost countries. Here they have benefited from the enlightened approach of the Nordic trade unions, whose attitude towards restructuring stands in contrast to the inflexible attitudes found in France and Belgium. According to Assa's current chief financial officer, Scandinavian unions recognize that healthy job prospects are only possible if the company has a secure future, and that this demands both continuing profitability and overcoming competitive threats, whether current or prospective.

Within Marathon's normal analytical framework, management incentives are considered of paramount importance. We want the financial interests of management to be inextricably linked with the fate of the shareholders. But this view does not fit well with Scandinavian social democracy. In many cases, Nordic companies continue to eschew stock options for management, while the tax system for such compensation is often unfavourable. The lack of enthusiasm for lavish executive pay and the uproar over relatively minor (by international standards) corporate scandals reflect Scandinavia's social-democratic norms.

That is not to say that individuals have not created large fortunes as a result of their success. The Rausing brothers at Tetra Pak, Stefan Persson at H&M, and Ingvar Kamprad of Ikea are high on the list of the world's billionaires. Even at some public companies, CEOs have built up significant wealth, although this has generally involved taking on more risk than is commonly found in the Anglo-Saxon boardroom. A prime example would be Carl-Henric Svanberg who, by borrowing $3m to acquire shares at the outset, made over $36m from his time as CEO of Assa Abloy. Svanberg also invested $12m in Ericsson when he joined in 2003, at a low point in that company's fortunes, and later realized a gain of over two and a half times his initial investment. Other CEOs who have built up significant equity exposure, having taken risks with their own money, include Björn Wahlroos at Sampo, Johan Molin, the current CEO of Assa Abloy, and Ola Rollen at Hexagon. Marathon's holdings have tended to be concentrated in such companies.

While personal taxation and disdain for conspicuous consumption are high in egalitarian Scandinavia, corporate taxation is relatively low by international standards. In Denmark, nearly half of the full-time workforce pays the top marginal tax rate of 63 per cent, while business profits are taxed at just 25 per cent. Corporation tax rates in the other Scandinavian countries range from 26 to 28 per cent. That contrasts with an effective rate of corporation tax of 43 per cent for a company based in that bastion of capitalism, New York City.

The environment for wealth generation at the company level is thus very favourable in Scandinavia despite the social egalitarianism of the region. Stability of ownership and consistent strategic focus have created a long-term competitive advantage for many Scandinavian companies. The necessity of having to look to foreign markets for growth has lately proven beneficial in a world where growth seems to reside almost exclusively in emerging markets. The sustainability of emerging market growth is probably the main threat to the now elevated stock market valuations of a number of these successful companies.

3.5   SAY ON PAY (FEBRUARY 2012)

Long-term insider ownership is the best of all imperfect solutions to the principal-agent problem

The architects of executive pay schemes at publicly-quoted companies in the UK are under increasing pressure to justify their work. This is partly cyclical. After each stock market bust, scrutiny of bonus schemes increases, particularly in relation to "rewards for failure." There is also a secular element as income inequality has risen, driven in large measure by globalization. Politicians are keen to play on public discontent. Since 1998, average CEO remuneration at FTSE 100 companies has risen by a factor of 4 times, whereas average employee earnings have gone up by 50 per cent, according to Manifest. Over the same period, the price level of the FTSE 100 Index is unchanged. We have a certain sympathy for the pay consultants. It is no easy matter to design incentives schemes which align the interests of management with those of long-term shareholders.

Increasingly, shareholders have been voting against remuneration reports at company AGMs. Marathon receives more and more visits from company chairmen and heads of remuneration committees, often accompanied by remuneration consultants, seeking to pre-empt a shareholder revolt on pay. In part, this direct contact with investors is designed to circumvent the independent proxy advisory service companies (such as ISS Governance Services and Pirc). These organizations act as a healthy counterweight to the remuneration consultants whose peer group analyses of company remuneration has acted as an upward-only ratchet on pay. We cannot recall a situation where a company proposed to reduce remuneration of top executives on the basis that it was above the peer group median.

While the increasing influence of the proxy advisory services is welcome, the prescriptive, rule-based approach of these organizations does not suit every case, particularly when it comes to executive remuneration. What is the optimal incentive scheme, then? The answer is it depends on the circumstances. Remuneration structures based on earnings per share (EPS) growth and total shareholder return (TSR) performance measures are increasingly commonplace. Yet they suffer from the problem identified long ago by the management guru, Peter Drucker, who observed that the search for the right performance measure is "not only likely to be as unproductive as the quest for the philosopher's stone; it is certain to do harm and to misdirect." This is particularly the case when pay is linked to EPS – a particular bête noire for Marathon over many years.

The earnings per share measure is prone to manipulation by unscrupulous executives; it takes no account of risk and encourages value destroying acquisitions and buybacks, especially when interest rates are low. It also encourages the quarterly EPS guessing game beloved by the sell-side. At times, it seems that meeting the EPS target has become the main strategic purpose of the company. This is regrettable. Corporate strategy should be about how best to allocate resources. If a turnaround requires a three-year investment phase, management may not pursue the optimal business plan if their compensation is linked to interim EPS results. While these inter-temporal issues can be partly resolved by phasing in performance rewards over a period of years, investor myopia and management's own interest tend to lead to an exclusive focus on the calendar year EPS, which bears no relation to long-term value creation.

Linking compensation to total shareholder return (TSR), the most common share price-based measure, is better than EPS, as it forces management to think about what drives shares prices over the medium term. Such schemes suffer from point-to-point measurement, which can be distorted if the stock price at either the start or end date is inflated by takeover speculation or by general overvaluation in the stock market. Then, there are questions over what time frame to measure the returns; also, whether the benchmark should be absolute or relative – both have their merits, neither is perfect. In the case of relative schemes, should the benchmark be provided by a peer group or by the broader market index? Sir Martin Sorrell, the head of advertising giant WPP, has become a very wealthy man thanks to his ability to outperform a small group of marketing service companies. Unfortunately, this wealth creation has not been shared with the company's owners due to the under-performance of this sector over many years.

For this reason, we normally prefer corporate incentives schemes to be benchmarked against the stock market index, in line with our own performance fees. Company managers might feel aggrieved that they have no control on performance relative to a broad index, which may be driven by moves in some heavily-weighted sector, such as mining or pharmaceuticals in the FTSE 100. Some companies have come to us seeking to switch from a relative TSR scheme to an absolute one – often after a period of relative outperformance which presumably management believes will end imminently.

As regards the time frame over which performance should be measured, here one runs into the problem of investor myopia. Since the average holding period for European shares is down to 12 months (see Chart 3.2), the "average" investor has little interest in the performance of a company over a five-year period. We prefer longer measurement periods, with multiyear phasing in of benefits to encourage long-range strategic thinking. The views of high frequency traders and investors obsessed with quarterly EPS should be given a very low weight by management. Time frames may also need to vary by sector. In the capital goods and extractive industries, project terms may be well in excess of five years (for aero engines, product life cycles can be decades).

Given that each measure has pros and cons, it is not surprising that remuneration consultants seek a compromise, bundling together a mixture of measures in the incentive scheme. But so-called "balanced" approaches, such as those which mix an EPS target with a return on capital overlay and

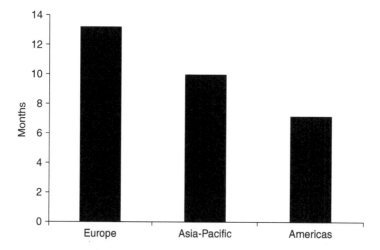

Chart 3.2   Average holding period for equities by geographic region (February 2012)
Source: World Federation of Exchanges Limited, HSBC estimates.

a TSR override, are likely to confuse both management and investors and, even worse, can encourage sophisticated gaming strategies.

Insider ownership has always seemed to us as the most direct way to deal with the principal-agent problem, which arises with the separation of corporate management from ownership. Our portfolios have tended to be skewed towards companies where successful entrepreneurs run their companies and retain sizeable shareholdings. Pleasingly, a number of companies have followed the example set by Reckitt Benckiser, where executives are required to build up significant shareholdings. Along similar lines, HSBC has recently revamped its incentives so that generous deferred share awards, which vest after five years, have to be held until retirement. Long-term share ownership is probably the best way of concentrating the minds of management on the true drivers of value. The manager's instinct for wealth protection should guard against excessive risk-taking, the unfortunate counterexample of Lehman's Dick Fuld notwithstanding.[7]

3.6   HAPPY FAMILIES (MARCH 2012)

Family control can cause problems for outside shareholders, but it can also provide an elegant solution to the agency problem

The evils which arise at joint-stock companies where management and ownership are separated are not of recent vintage. In the year of the American Revolution, Adam Smith observed what we now call principal-agent problem:

> The directors of such companies … being the managers rather of other people's money rather than of their own, it cannot well be expected that they should watch over it with the same anxious vigilance with which [they would] watch over their own … Negligence and profusion, therefore, must always prevail, more or less, in the management of the affairs of such a company. (*Wealth of Nations*, 1776)

One potential solution to this problem is to invest in companies which remain under family control. Unfortunately, this is not without its pitfalls. It's often the case that the interests of the family are elevated above outside investors. Aside from this, such businesses are often prone to nepotism and paralysing family disputes. Everyone knows the saying that rich families

---

[7]   The Lehman CEO held nearly 11m shares in the Wall Street bank. From their peak valuation to Lehman's bankruptcy in September 2009, Fuld may have suffered a paper loss of up to $931m (see Lucian Bebchuk *et al.*, "The Wages of Failure: Executive Compensation at Bear Stearns and Lehman 2000–2008," *Yale Journal on Regulation,* 2010).

go from rags to riches and back to rags in three generations. As a result, many investors prefer to stay away. That's pretty difficult, since around of a third the S&P 500 companies are under family control. Besides, this type of corporate control can also bring significant benefits to outside share-holders. There's some evidence to suggest that in the US, at least, compa-nies with large family stakes have outperformed the rest of the market (see Chart 3.3). Families which are united and committed to handing down wealth to later generations have often proven themselves to be good stew-ards of capital.

At its best, family control can be an elegant solution to the agency prob-lem. Families are better able to withstand short-term profit fluctuations and to invest for the long-term benefit of themselves and outside sharehold-ers. The Internet company, Amazon.com, which is 20 per cent-owned by founder Jeff Bezos, appears happy to endure operating margins of 4 per cent while it invests in technology and dominates competitors on price, just as Wal-Mart, another family-controlled firm, achieved in bricks and mortar retailing. The support of stable family ownership can also enable manage-ment to enter new and profitable lines of business, as was the case when a beverage and financial business acquired a shipping company (Quiñenco, Chile), a supermarket and hotel group bought an Indonesian automotive

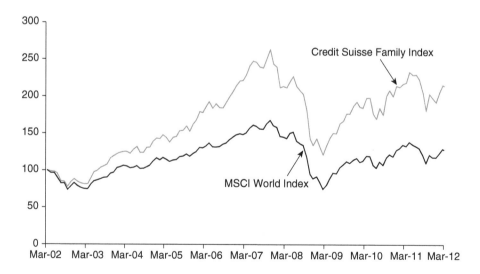

Chart 3.3   Credit Suisse Family Index
Source: Bloomberg.

producer (Jardine Matheson in Singapore), and a British food company built a successful clothing retail business (AB Foods).[8]

The problem for investors is to determine between the good and bad family stewards. Readers of a scientific bent may be aware of the Anna Karenina principle,[9] in which a deficiency in just one of a number of factors dooms an endeavour to failure. What follows is a list of common family deficiencies, any one of which is liable to undermine a company's success:

1. Lack of family unity

Family schisms and internal squabbling can do lasting damage to the interests of both family and non-family shareholders. Italy's Gucci family was too busy infighting to prepare to face competition or to professionalise management. Only after Gucci was taken over by the French luxury goods group, Pinault-Printemps-Redoute, did its fashion business revive.[10] The Mondavi family, California's great wine dynasty, suffered two generations of sibling rivalry before the business was finally sold in 2004 to beverage giant Constellation Brands. The Ambani brothers' dispute in India led to the break-up of the textiles-to-telecommunications conglomerate Reliance Group in 2005. Occasionally, however, disputes within the family or between families over control of an asset can work in minority shareholders' favour, driving large share buybacks.

Not all family businesses are unhappy ones. The Parisian luxury goods group Hermès – the last buggy whip company, as we like to call it – has enjoyed great success. Despite there being over 70 adult descendants of the Hermès founder, the family has remained unified within its shareholder group. On occasion, a particularly dominant family member has been able impose his, or her, will on the rest of the family in order to maintain the family's dominance and the long-term success of the company – one thinks of Ferdinand Piëch at Volkswagen, Gina Rinehart at Hancock Resources, and Jan Stenbeck at Investment AB Kinnevik in Sweden.

---

[8] Diversification (or "diworsification," as Peter Lynch calls it) does not always bring unalloyed benefits. Marathon itself had longstanding issues with the Keswick family's control of Jardine Matheson.

[9] The principle, widely applied from statistics to ecology, derives from Leo Tolstoy's book *Anna Karenina,* which presents an idea that for a marriage to be happy it must succeed in several key aspects, while failure on even one such aspect can produce an unhappy marriage.

[10] Gucci got into trouble in the 1980s as family disputes ran out of control. The last Gucci family member to head the company was murdered in 1995. His wife was later convicted of hiring the killers. PPR gained control of Gucci in 2003.

2. Loss of business acumen

The "Buddenbrooks' effect," named after Thomas Mann's novel of that name, describes how family businesses deteriorate over time as later generations become more interested in the trappings of wealth than its generation. The decline of US beauty company Estée Lauder shows what can happen when a controlling family becomes uninterested and ineffective. At that point, the appointment of an outside professional is key to turning around the company. The British catalogue company Littlewoods owned by the Moores family failed to prepare for Internet competition and was finally sold.

3. Self-dealing

Companies controlled by families which pay scant regard to principles of corporate governance have tended to trade on lower earnings multiples than their peer group. Actual theft is rare, but it is not uncommon to see corporate dealing between the family and the listed entity which appear to favour the former. Questions were raised, for example, when CSN, the Brazilian steel company, acquired Metalic, a steel can firm owned by the controlling family. The family, which controls Mayora Indah, an Indonesian food company, owns the distribution business outside of the listed entity. Gerdau, another Brazilian steel firm, was challenged after it made a loan to a stud farm owned by the controlling family and paid royalties to its controlling shareholders for use of the family name. Since companies which enjoy good governance tend to attract higher valuation multiples, there is an incentive for family-controlled companies to desist in self-dealing. Duratex and Embraer in Brazil, for example, improved corporate governance as they looked to reduce the agency discount embedded in their share prices.

4. Poor succession planning

Family-controlled companies must prepare to hand over the reins to the next generation. When the success of the company is not tied to the family, but to the social and political connections of the founder, minorities should brace themselves for occasional whiplash. This has been a particular feature of Asian family-owned companies whose fortunes have been built on the monopolies and concessions derived from political connections, and where a lack of succession planning by octogenarian founders has led to stock price weakness.

5. Politics of rent-seeking

While companies which rely on extracting rents can do very well, it's naïve to assume those rents will continue once the founder has departed. What is good for the family (and non-family shareholders) may not be so advantageous for the country. Close relationships with politicians and regulators appear to have allowed Carlos Slim's Telmex to maintain a near monopoly on Mexican fixed-line telephony, whose interconnection rates have been significantly higher than the OECD average. The dominance of a small number of high-profile families in the Philippines, Hong Kong, Mexico, Israel and Turkey has rewarded families and minority shareholders, but stifled competition and entrepreneurship.

Under such circumstances, there's the danger of a political backlash. Carlos Slim's American Movil received a near $1bn fine for "monopolistic practice."[11] Israel seems finally to be tackling its powerful family conglomerates, such as Delek Group and IDB Holdings. One needs only to look at the abrupt change in the fortunes of Egyptian companies close to the Mubarak regime, such as Palm Holdings and EFG Hermes, to see how quickly the tables can turn. By contrast, successful family companies – such as Koç Holding, Investor and Quiñenco – seem adept at keeping out of the direct heat of the political arena.

Family-operated businesses which are competitive and not-flagrantly rent-seeking generally turn out to be better long-term investments than those businesses whose success derives from the family's political and financial dominance. Despite the problems family control can bring, we sleep a little better at night having put some of your money to work with the Wallenbergs (Investor), Bezos (Amazon.com), Koç (Koç Holding), Lukšić (Quiñenco) and Ayala (Ayala Corporation).

3.7 THE WIT AND WISDOM OF JOHANN RUPERT (JUNE 2013)

The departing boss of Richemont is a true corporate star
Marathon looks to invest with corporate managers who know how to allocate capital effectively. This requires certain character traits in the individual, such as suspicion of investments fads (and investment bankers), and a willingness to swim against the tide. One of our more successful decisions has been to invest alongside Johann Rupert, until recently the executive chairman and CEO of Richemont, the Swiss luxury goods group in which his family owns a controlling interest. As Mr. Rupert prepares to move on,

---

[11] A couple of months after this piece was written, Mexico's Federal Competition Commission rescinded Slim's $925m fine.

we decided to look back over our meeting notes to remind us of the qualities which attracted us to this truly outstanding manager.

First, some background. Richemont has been part of Marathon European portfolios since March 2002, and its predecessor company, Vendôme, was owned from at least 1994 (when our computerized shareholding record begins) until its buyout in 1998. When the company was founded in 1988, with Mr Rupert as CEO, its main businesses were the non-South African assets of the Rembrandt Group, which had been established by Mr Rupert's father. These consisted of holdings in the Rothmans cigarette business and a collection of luxury goods brands, including Cartier, Alfred Dunhill, Chloé and Mont Blanc.

Over time, the cigarette business was expanded and eventually spun off to shareholders. After a lucky escape from the European pay TV business during the TMT bubble, Richemont has focused on luxury goods, in particular high-end Swiss watches and jewellery. Acquired brands include Vacheron Constantin, Panerai, Van Cleef & Arpels, Jaeger LeCoultre, IWC and A. Lange & Söhne. Over the 25 years since its foundation, an original investment of SF 5 is now worth SF 120, taking account of dividends and spin-offs, an annual compound return of 13.5 per cent.

Mr. Rupert has not been one to spend much time schmoozing investors – Marathon has never had a one-on-one meeting with him. Over the years, however, we have attended many group meetings and listened in on many conference calls with Richemont. We have collected below a number of throwaway comments from Mr Rupert, who speaks with a distinctive South African accent, which illustrate to our mind why he has been such a successful steward of other people's money.

On management:
"The danger sign is always when a manager does not understand the business that he or she is in."

[On relations with a dominant supplier] "Don't play cat and mouse games if you're the mouse."

"I think if you want to be successful you need a very healthy dose of paranoia that every day there's somebody out there who wants to eat your breakfast, and if you're not alert they will do."

"Don't postpone until tomorrow what you can delegate today."

"I learned many years ago – that from the day you're born until you ride the hearse, things are never so bad that they can't get worse."

"The real question is do companies redeploy free cash flow accretively, or do they waste it?"

On short-termism:

"I raised a glass of champagne when Al Dunlap fell on his chainsaw."

"So anybody who's going to ask, so what do you think the next year looks like, why don't you just not ask the question because we're not going to answer any. And it's not because we're coy or funny. We don't know."

"I'm not going to tell you what I think our third quarter XYZ is going to be."

On M&A and buybacks:

"Ultimately, if any asset is wrongly priced, it is abused."

"If you pay an excessive multiple, deals will never make it."

"No, no, no, no. I didn't lose a lot of money when I tried to sell the business. I lost the money when I bought the bloody thing. That's when you park your money, it's not when you try to find a bigger idiot than you to take it off your hands."

[On successfully exiting pay TV] "Never confuse luck with genius."

"Our job here is to create goodwill and not to pay other people for goodwill."

"[There are] three stages of [an] acquisition, which [are] euphoria and then disillusionment. And the next thing is looking for somebody to blame for buying the place."

"The grass is always greener on the other side of the fence. But you only find out when you climb over that the reason why it's greener is because of all the cow dung hidden in the grass. And as soon as you start stepping in all this stuff then you wonder why you ever crossed the fence."

"You can discount us ever using equity for acquisitions. Equity is always the most expensive way to pay."

[On share-financed takeovers during the TMT bubble] "Like a child selling his dog for $1m, only he gets paid with two severed cat's paws."

"If you talk up your share price, when the price comes down, the folks come looking for you."

"We don't talk about a load of rubbish that I also had a hand in buying."

"If you look at share buybacks, and at the prices at which companies bought their shares back, they inevitably bought the shares back at very close to the top of the market because that's when they had a lot of cash. And boy, do they regret it when two years later all hell breaks loose."

On investment bankers:

"Recessions occur because the investment bankers provide capital at too low a cost which leads to overcapacity and a slump."

"When you really need firepower, the banks are not there and the funds are gone."

On corporate governance:

"So if you want a perfect governance score, get somebody you don't know, whom you've never met, who knows nothing about your business because he's never been involved, employ him and give him a nice bonus for sitting on a committee. Then you get all the boxes ticked [by the proxy voting services]. And guess what happens? After five years, chaos. There's a direct, inverse correlation between the best corporate governance box-ticking and medium-term performance."

On the luxury business:

"The only way we know how to maintain a sustainable competitive advantage is to grow the brand equity…. because that brand equity creates demand and will result in pricing power."

"I'm just a normal business person who thinks that the luxury business is a great business to be in to create shareholder value"

[Quoting Coco Chanel] "Fashion fades, only style remains the same."

"Coco Chanel years ago said that money is money is money. It's only the pockets that change. We've got to find those pockets."

"Anniversaries, birthdays and girlfriends are always going to be there."

"If your business model, or your intellectual property, is in ones and zeros, you're going to have issues. So luckily our intellectual property resides in atoms and it's tough to wreck."

"Cartier sleeps in the vault."

[On brand integrity] "You cannot make Ferraris in Fiat factories."

On China:

"When the Chinese nouveau riche want to spend, they do not want to buy Chinese."

"In the East, authenticity, originality and history matters."

"I feel like I'm having a black-tie dinner on top of a volcano. That volcano is China…. Personally I don't think anything's going to go wrong in China, that's my view, but I know nothing and I mean it."[12]

3.8   A MEETING OF MINDS (JUNE 2014)

One can learn a lot from meeting with managers, providing the setting is right

Over the last two years, Marathon has engaged in nearly two thousand meetings with company management. This activity, along with preparation and the writing of notes, consumes most of the investment team's working hours. Yet many commentators view such meetings as a waste of time. One can see their point. Managers are now so well prepared by PR advisers that meetings can seem like a promotional exercise. Investors still turn up. But for many of them, we suspect, their purpose is to gain an informational advantage about the short-term outlook for the business – in our view, a fruitless endeavour. Given the long-term nature of our investment approach, capital allocation is of paramount importance. The prime purpose of our company meetings is to assess the skill of managers at investing money on behalf of their shareholders.

Meeting management is not a scientific process. Rather, it involves making judgements about individuals, an activity which is prone to error (witness the rate of divorce). We go into meetings looking for answers to questions such as: does the CEO think in a long-term strategic way about the business? Understand how the capital cycle operates in their industry? Seem intelligent, energetic and passionate about the business? And interact with colleagues and others in an encouraging way? Appear trustworthy and honest? Act in a shareholder-friendly way even down to the smallest detail?

To assess such questions, the format of the meeting is important. In general, the smaller the number of people in attendance the better. Having fewer attendees on both sides of the table – large meetings often include company managers, investor relations personnel, financial PR types, stock brokers,

---

[12] Mr. Rupert's departure from Richemont turned out to be short-lived. He returned to the company as chairman in September 2014.

and other hangers-on – encourages a more open and friendly dialogue. It also reduces the risk of attendants showing off, which can result in the conversation becoming hopelessly bogged down in detail. A new and dreadful manifestation of the quest for redundant detail is the "fireside-chat" format used at many sell-side conferences, which typically involves a CEO being quizzed by the specialist analyst. The conversation generally turns into a "deep dive" into factors impacting short-term earnings, which can be of no interest to long-term investors. Questions of this sort can be ludicrous. At a recent conference we attended, the boss of a major industrial firm was asked whether we could expect that same pattern of seasonality as the year before.

Large delegations from a company can be a sign that the CEO lacks confidence, resorting to a safety-in-numbers approach. This is often the case when dealing with companies in difficulty, as well as with many Japanese, Spanish and Italian firms. Contrast this with Geberit, the highly successful Swiss plumbing equipment company, whose CEO tends to arrive alone at our offices, having seemingly made his own travel arrangements, fitting us in between meetings with plumbers, architects and other customers.

When it comes to discussing a company's strategy, it is alarming how frequently one finds managers confused on the topic. Too often, the CEO mistakes a short-term target – say an earnings per share target or a return on capital threshold – with a strategy. "Our strategy is to deliver a 15 per cent return on capital," they say. Real strategy, whether military or commercial, involves an assessment of the position one finds oneself in, the threats one faces, how one plans to overcome them, and how opponents might in turn respond. During his tenure at General Electric, Jack Welch required managers of GE's divisions to prepare a few simple slides describing their operating environment in terms of: what does your global competitive environment look like? In the last three years, what have your competitors done to alter the competitive landscape? In the same period, what have you done to them? How might they attack you in the future? What are your plans to leapfrog them?

Getting CEOs to open up about their competitors can be difficult. They fear that too much openness may lead to a breach of confidentiality (professional investors are a thoroughly untrustworthy bunch) or that revelations about the firm's true market dominance might raise anti-trust issues. Besides, many managers are so fixated on growth, they fail to anticipate the likely competitor response (another example of the "insider view"). Still, on occasions something useful slips out. When a management team compliments a competitor, this can be like gold dust to investors. Learning that DMGT, the

UK media company, found it hard to compete with Rightmove, the property listings website, contributed to our decision to invest in the company.[13]

Discussing how a firm uses investment bankers and how it makes acquisitions (e.g., whether it prefers friendly negotiated deals to contested auctions) can be revealing. Unexpected diversifications into an unrelated area may suggest that something is not right in the core business. Views on share buybacks can also be highly informative. Very few CEOs see this as a legitimate investment on a par with capital expenditure or M&A decisions, presumably due to an aversion to shrinking any aspect of the company. Many fear that buybacks are an admission that the company has run out of investment ideas. On this subject, we like to hear managers justify buybacks based on an internal valuation model, as this can then lead to an interesting discussion about valuation of their business.

Forming impressions of the CEO's character, intelligence, energy and trustworthiness can be gleaned using a variety of questioning techniques. Intellectual honesty can be tested by asking the CEO to pick out what he or she thinks is important. To unsettle the more promotional CEOs, we like to ask what is not working and wait to see whether they have given the matter much thought. Sometimes the boss will seek to evade responsibility by asking a colleague to talk about a problematic area of the business. The CEO in denial often blames problems on a divisional boss and follows up by saying that management has now been changed. How the chief executive interacts with colleagues, such as the CFO or investor relations personnel, often reveals their leadership qualities. We like to see signs of individual curiosity at meetings – revealed, for instance, by their taking an interest in our own business. Signs of humility – say a recognition of past mistakes – give us some confidence that the chief executive has a grip on reality.

Appearances can also be revealing. A CEO of an industrial company who wears expensive shoes, or a snappy suit, is more likely to enjoy the expensive company of investment bankers than spend his time visiting factories and customers. Signs of vanity are generally off-putting. One CEO was spotted before a meeting carefully adjusting his elaborate bouffant hair style in our washroom. Several months later, he launched a large and foolhardy acquisition.

Meetings can also provide insights into a management's approach to costs. This frequently comes out in discussions about compensation. Learning about something as mundane as corporate travel policy can also tell us a lot. After Brazil's AmBev took over the Belgian-based Interbrew, its managers

---

[13] Rightmove has developed a lock on the market for UK residential listings, and by the end of 2014, its shares were up over 400 per cent in US dollars since floating in 2006.

told us about a new edict limiting business-class flights to those lasting six hours or more. This insight into corporate frugality was a pointer to the same management's ability to cut costs at Anheuser-Busch – which prior to the merger sported a fleet of eight Falcon executive jets – and increase the US beer company's operating margins by a massive ten percentage points (between 2005 and 2011). We were equally impressed to learn that senior executives at another company preferred the underground to chauffeured limousine when travelling around London. The number of IR representatives in attendance is a good indicator as to how carefully a company counts its pennies. Of course, we have made mistakes when assessing management teams. But, in our view, trying to spot a great manager remains a game very much worth playing.

3.9   CULTURE VULTURE (FEBRUARY 2015)

Marathon's focus on management forces us to think about corporate culture
Corporate culture is constituted by a set of shared assumptions and values that guide the actions of employees, and encourage workers to act collectively towards a specific goal. Cultures both reflect the values, and are a prime responsibility, of management. Yet strong cultures can persist long after the careers of those who put them in place. Still, sceptics might ask, why should investors bother with something so ineffable, so intangible? Well, the evidence suggests that culture pays.

Perhaps the best-known study of the subject is *Corporate Culture and Performance* by John Kotter and James Heskett. This work examines the relationship between corporate culture and company performance in over 200 firms during the 1980s. The authors asked employees their opinions of attitudes to customers and shareholders at competitor firms. Shares in companies exhibiting strong and positive cultures outperformed rivals by more than 800 per cent during the study period. Other studies which measure corporate culture according to how employees regard their own workplace have found a similar link between *esprit de corps* and stock market returns.

Kotter and Heskett's work established that strong cultures are liable to produce extreme outcomes, both exceptionally good and dreadfully bad. Positive cultures can take different forms. Perhaps the most commonly successful corporate trait is an emphasis is on cost control. Almost every firm periodically engages in bouts of cost-cutting. Exceptional firms, however, are involved in a permanent revolution against unnecessary expenses. In the early days of Admiral, the British insurance company, employees wishing to use the printer were required to do a push up in sight of the CEO. Another example of the corporate Scrooge is Fastenal, a US distributor of low-value industrial products, which boasted the "cheapest CEO in America." There are legends of Fastenal executives being required to share hotel rooms at conferences. Company offices are said to be equipped with second-hand furniture. Frugal cultures may not sound attractive to employees, but when married to decentralized profit-sharing schemes, they can work wonders. Between 1987 and 2012, Fastenal provided a return of over 38,000 per cent (excluding dividends), better than any other company in the index. Take that, Bill Gates.

Cost-cutting is not the only successful cultural model. In fact, some firms have strengthened their cultures by spending more, not less. The classic example is Costco, the North American discount retailer. Bucking the conventional retail model, Costco pays its staff more than the legal minimum wage – and far more than rivals. The average Costco employee makes in excess of $20 an hour, compared to average US national retail pay of less than $12 an hour. The company also sponsors healthcare for nearly 90 per cent of workers. Wall Street is constantly pressuring Costco to cut its wage bill, with the cacophony reaching a peak during the crisis of 2009. Instead, the company raised wages over the following three years. The return for this munificence is that Costco employees stay on longer, thus saving on training costs. Turnover for employees who have been with the company for more than one year is a paltry 5 per cent. Loyal employees are more likely to excel. Costco is regularly rated as excellent for customer service.

The point is that a strong corporate culture constitutes an intangible asset, potentially as valuable as a high-profile brand or network of customer relationships. As Warren Buffett says of Berkshire Hathaway's family of businesses:

If we are delighting customers, eliminating unnecessary costs and improving our products and services, we gain strength…. On a daily basis, the effects are imperceptible; cumulatively, though, their consequences are enormous. When our long-term competitive position improves as a result of these almost unnoticeable actions, we describe the phenomenon as "widening the moat."

On the other hand, a rotten culture can be a firm's undoing. Look no further than AIG, one of the major disasters in the recent financial meltdown. Dominated for so long by an imperial CEO, Hank Greenberg, the global insurance company developed in the words of one commentator "a culture of complicity." Unthinking obedience, the lack of an "outside view," and an obsession with growth at any cost led to riskier and riskier positioning. Even as the end grew nearer, AIG executives proved incapable of recognizing the danger the company faced. In August 2007, the head of AIG Financial

Products commented on his division's positions in the credit derivatives market: "It is hard for us, without being flippant, to even see a scenario within any kind of realm of reason that would see us losing one dollar in any of these transactions." Little more than a year later, AIG announced a quarterly loss of $11bn, which largely derived from its Financial Products division.

Just as positive cultures take a number of different forms, so too can negative ones. An obsession with growing earnings occasionally results in outright fraud. In the 1990s, during the tenure of Al "Chainsaw" Dunlap, the accounts of consumer appliance maker Sunbeam were concocted to meet aggressive earnings targets. In extreme cases, a poor corporate culture can have tragic consequences. In 2010, 29 miners were killed in an explosion at one of Massey Energy's coal mines. The US Labor Department investigation blamed a corporate culture that "valued production over safety" and fostered "fear and intimidation."

If a beneficial culture is a valuable intangible asset, and a corrosive one an existential threat, it becomes important to ask: how can an outside investor tell the difference? As with so much of investment, the process is one of piecing together incomplete and obscure pieces of evidence, gathered over time through meetings and research.

Some quantitative measures can be helpful: staff loyalty and inside share ownership are liable to be higher at firms in which employees believe in what they are doing. Corporate incentive schemes say a lot about the firm's culture. Is management being greedy? What performance metrics are valued – growth for its own sake or customer satisfaction? What do employees think? Opinions can be unearthed through websites such as glassdoor.com (a sort of TripAdvisor for companies). We are constantly looking out for signs of management extravagance and vanity. Danger signs include expensive executive travel (a corporate jet is liable to elicit groans), too numerous pictures of the CEO in the annual report, and dandyish attire.

There are numerous examples of successful cultures among our portfolio companies: the empowerment of branch managers that promotes responsible banking at Sweden's Svenska Handelsbanken, for instance. Reckitt Benckiser, another holding, fosters an entrepreneurial spirit among its senior managers. Yet even if a strong culture is instilled in a company, it can take many years for its full effects to play out. That may be beyond Wall Street's limited investment horizon. Long-term investors, however, would be wise to take heed.

PART II

BOOM, BUST, BOOM

4

ACCIDENTS IN WAITING

After the financial crisis erupted, the Queen famously asked on a visit to the London School of Economics why the problems hadn't been spotted in advance. The true answer – one which the Queen presumably was not supplied with – is that economists had developed a deeply flawed paradigm for how the economy operates. Economists posited a world of equilibrium and rationality, in which money and the operations of finance were essentially inert. This academic model turned out to be far removed from reality.

It's not true, however, to say that *nobody* in the financial world saw *it* coming. On the contrary, in the years prior to 2008 many serious investors and independent strategists were alert to the dangers posed by strong credit growth, dubious financial innovation and the appearance of various housing bubbles around the world. From its ring-side seat on the financial markets, Marathon became concerned about the risks associated with securitization and excessive credit growth from as early as 2002. Such fears were exacerbated by meetings over the years with managements at various banks which seemed to be steering their institutions at high speeds towards the rocks. The case of Anglo Irish Bank, a financial institution which came close to sinking the sovereign credit of the Irish state, is examined in detail below.

The looming financial crisis also can be understood from a capital cycle perspective. During the boom years, the banks were rapidly growing their assets (loans) and competition was increasing – as evidenced by the appearance of a shadow banking system and the decline in bank lending spreads. This outward shift in the supply side for the finance industry impacted eventually on the industry's profitability. Viewed in this way, there is nothing particularly special about the banking sector. Capital cycle analysis could also applied usefully to the housing markets in the pre-crisis world. High and

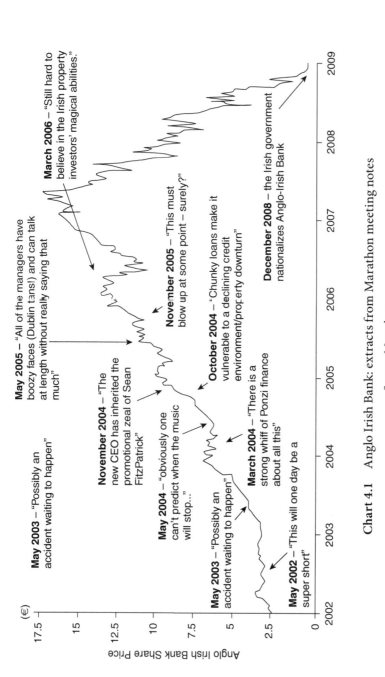

Chart 4.1   Anglo Irish Bank: extracts from Marathon meeting notes

Source: Marathon.

rising house prices in some countries elicited an enormous supply response, notably in Spain and Ireland. Those economies which experienced the most extreme capital cycle – in terms of increased stocks of credit and housing – later suffered from the most severe hangovers.

4.1 ACCIDENTS IN WAITING: MEETINGS WITH ANGLO IRISH BANK (2002–06)

In the years before the crisis, our meetings with British and Irish bank management teams created a strong sense of foreboding

Many people in the investment industry are sceptical of the value of meeting with management teams. Armchair analysts take the view that the process has become an exercise in promotion which is likely to lead an investor not nearer to but further from the truth. In his book *Behavioural Investing*, James Montier devotes an entire chapter to the topic entitled "Why Waste Your Time Listening to Company Management?" Montier argues that meetings can overload fund managers with information and are likely to confirm pre-conceptions, especially overly optimistic ones. Fund managers may also become too impressed with authority figures. Admittedly, there's a danger that the naïve will be gulled into dreadful mistakes. On the other hand, exposure to a truly terrible manager can help investors steer clear of the rocks. Marathon's own experience of avoiding some of the worst banking disasters of the credit bubble suggests that meetings can have considerable value. We keep notes of our meetings. Below are some pre-crisis observations of a banking accident waiting to happen.

Anglo Irish Bank

Meeting Date: May 2002 (Market Cap: $1,900m)

Business assessment:
Anglo Irish lends to proprietary (i.e., owner-manager) directors, primarily in the service sector in Eire, the UK and Boston. Ninety per cent of the security for this lending is property. Unashamedly, they pronounce that the cost of borrowing from Anglo Irish is higher than from a normal bank with whom a customer does his or her everyday banking business. So aren't they providing a risky, lender-of-last-resort service, asks yours truly? Why should I borrow from them when I know their rates are higher – unless I know that Lloyds won't give me the loan?

The answer given is that their loans tend to be large in size (on average €4.5m in the UK) and it will take weeks for Lloyds to give me an answer, whereas they can decide more or less on the spot. A typical loan for them is when a client comes to them to finance a €20m property purchase, but only has €5m in cash. They look at the leasing agreement with the tenant and try to understand the creditworthiness of the underlying tenant.

They claim not to care if the property market goes down, as the tenant has undertaken to pay rent on a long-term contractual basis, and so long as the tenant stays solvent, they are confident that the interest will be paid. That raises a question about repayment of the principal – but that is far enough off in the future for no one to worry for now at any rate! Surely if property prices halve, they will be paid the interest but lose a lot of the principal?

Regarding the [bank's] infrastructure, there is basically very little. The client base does not require a vast branch network. Two-thirds of the business over the last seven years has come from the existing client base, and new clients come to them by word of mouth. The result is an extremely low cost income ratio of around 30 per cent. In 1H 2002 the loan book (€18bn) grew by 12 per cent, with the UK and the US growing at 21 per cent and 26 per cent respectively. Eire represents 50 per cent of lending today compared with 80 per cent five years ago.

Overall, I find it very hard not to believe that this is an extremely risky business model built on the back of the Irish property boom and now hinged on something similar in the UK.

Management assessment:
"I am here unashamedly to sell you Anglo Irish Bank!" [says CEO Sean FitzPatrick], as if it were not obvious, so hard is the sell (one of the worst I've seen). The shares have more than doubled since last September and have risen seven-fold since 1997.

Valuation assessment:
This will one day be a super short – the problem is that FitzPatrick will captivate his audience to the extent that one can't tell whether it might not double again.

Meeting Date: May 2003 (Market Cap: $2,648m)

Management assessment:
The management are very promotion-oriented and everything appears fantastic. The CFO [William McAteer] is one of those people who immediately learns somebody's first name and uses it for the rest of the meeting. He seemed to know a lot of the audience at the [investor] conference

presentation as well, which is always worrying since it means that he has developed a close interest in investors and knows who can buy his shares. His finance junior was also overly promotional.

Valuation assessment:
The shares don't look that expensive for a return on equity of 25 per cent; however, there are risks implicit in their lending strategy and their high growth rate. One also can't help feeling uncomfortable with their demeanour. Possibly an accident waiting to happen … .

Meeting Date: March 2004 (Market Cap: $5,000m)

Business assessment:
The business model, as discussed previously, is to lend to businesses (mainly property related) in Eire and the UK (and a bit in Boston) without a branch network. The competitive advantage is the speed at which they approve loans (95 per cent of what goes to the weekly credit committee gets passed) and their flexibility and speed of execution. (Is being able to say "yes" quickly really an advantage in the banking business?) … .

Their "mission" is to make rich people richer. They rely on existing customers and word of mouth for growth and do not use brokers. Last year, net lending grew by €4.3bn or 33 per cent … There is a strong whiff of Ponzi finance about all this, since repayment of principal cannot be as secure as the interest. For instance, if I borrow £10m over ten years to finance a property purchase and McDonalds is my tenant, there should be no problem paying the interest on the loan. But when I have to pay back the £10m principal, I have to rely on the market being as buoyant ten years from now.

Because these are long-tail liabilities, they will not affect Mr. FitzPatrick in his Marbella villa, particularly after recent share sales![1] Their provisions are at 217 per cent of NPLs [non-performing loans], which compares with a European average of 80 per cent. But they would need to be higher to reflect the chunky size of the individual loans.

---

[1] Marathon's prediction that the retiring Anglo Irish chief would enjoy a prosperous retirement in the south of Spain turned out to be wide of the mark. Despite the share sales mentioned above, FitzPatrick retained nearly 5m Anglo Irish shares with a peak value of over €85m, which were rendered worthless by the bank's collapse. It transpired that FitzPatrick had also borrowed heavily from Anglo Irish. In 2010, he was declared bankrupt. Three years later, the former bank boss went on trial, accused of failing to inform auditors of loans made to himself or connected entities by the Irish Nationwide Building Society that, it was alleged, temporarily replaced loans provided by Anglo Irish, thereby avoiding accounting disclosure requirements. In 2015, The Irish Government was still struggling to secure the extradition of David Drumm, FitzPatrick's replacement as CEO, from the US to face charges of fraud.

Management assessment:
FitzPatrick mentioned in his presentation how the directors had "misread" the market with the heavy insider selling in February – presumably referring to the market reaction as opposed to their timing (the share price was then at €13). He got quite angry when I asked why directors were such enthusiastic sellers of shares. He justified his own sale of some €20m as diversification as he approached retirement. His total holding was worth €60m. The 42-year old head of the UK business [John Rowan], however, sold €3m of shares (40 per cent of his holding) at the same time and FitzPatrick appeared to suggest that this had affected his chances of succeeding him. Doesn't it show that he is a smart as FitzP., i.e., a worthy successor?

Valuation assessment:
With equity of €1bn it wouldn't take many €10m loans to wipe out the half of the equity (in fact, only 50 loans – and they are approving 20–25 loans per week). Insider selling and the long-tail liability time bomb are the really scary features of this. And it looks expensive at four times book.

Meeting Date: May 2004 (Market Cap: $5,000m)

Business assessment:
A combative presentation from the CEO of the niche lender – "We're not full service – we just ask customers to put a few eggs in our basket".... The UK and Boston are seen as "an extension of Ireland." The UK is growing faster than Ireland so now accounts for around 40 per cent of the loan book or about €8.7bn, with the average loan being €5–7m. A "large chunk" of this is investment property....

The other thing that occurs to me about the word of mouth expansion strategy is that it probably means that the company has a fairly lopsided customer exposure – all Paddy ex-pats and their mates? Anglo is also changing its strategy on provisioning. The bank currently has around €290m of bad debt provisions, or around 134 basis points of the €21bn loan book. The actual bad debt level is 66 basis points, giving a provision to non-performing loan ratio of 207 per cent, compared to a European bank average of 80 per cent, which one would imagine is appropriate given the nature of the secondary lending here. However, FitzPatrick says they have decided to add nothing to provisions until the loan book is up to €55bn, which more than halves the provisioning ratio.

Is this a vindication of their model or hubris looming?

Management assessment:
FitzPatrick glowers from the speaker's rostrum, daring anyone to disagree with his business model, which of course, this being an Irish conference, no one does. Size is clearly important – he began by boasting, "We're bigger now than Bank of Ireland was in 1998." He thinks they can double their current 14 per cent of the Irish business market within ten years, but it is hard to see how there can be 28 per cent of the market who are willing and able to pay up for Anglo type service – so presumably the niche model must be diluted to grow. He claims that 2004 and 2005 [earnings] are both "in the bag."

Valuation assessment:
It is hard to escape the conclusion that this sort of growth and profitability are unsustainable, but obviously one can't predict when the music will stop....

Meeting Date: October 2004 (Market Cap: $6,270m)

Management assessment:
The new CEO [designate David Drumm] is 37 and previously head of banking in Dublin and the US. He seemed fairly low key particularly compared with the outgoing CEO and won't one suspects be able to razz up investors in quite the same way. John Rowan is the chap who scuppered his chances of succeeding FitzPatrick by selling shares quite aggressively alongside FitzPatrick earlier in the year. He was made to look quite uncomfortable when someone in the audience asked a question about succession disruption.

Valuation assessment:
The bank trades at 4.2 times book value with a 30 per cent return on equity. Chunky loans make it vulnerable to a declining credit environment/property downturn. The bull case is based on the very rapid (+25 per cent p.a.) growth in book value.

Meeting Date: November 2004 (Market Cap: $7,580m)

Business assessment:
To recap: 80 per cent of profit comes from lending to businesses on a secured (property) basis, with half the loan book in Eire, 41 per cent in the UK and the rest in the Boston area. The UK loan book has grown faster than the Irish one over the last five years and is likely to overtake Eire soon as their largest market. This is a bit weird given that the UK is hardly immature or uncompetitive and the Irish economy has been growing at much faster rates....

On a new loan, the loan to value ratio is typically 70 per cent and usually the collateral is at the level of 35 per cent when the tenancy expires. Thus they estimate that property prices would have to fall by 65 per cent for Anglo Irish to suffer … .

I suspect that this market is highly dependent on the relationship between rental yields, lending rates and the outlook for property prices. The management team talked about the dangers of the current frenzied speculation in Irish residential property, where rental yields have collapsed and yet property prices continue to rise, Ponzi-style. One suspects that the residential and commercial markets (e.g., a dentist's surgery) are related in some ways.

Management assessment:
The new CEO has inherited the promotional zeal of Sean FitzPatrick, and it is quite hard to get one's questions in, as each answer contains another long string of bull points.

New investment and rationale:
The loan book grew by €6.3bn last year (35 per cent) which actually represented a gross increase of €9bn with €3bn of repayments. They continually make the point that they do not reach for growth (i.e., a target to increase lending year-on-year), which has the ring of "doth protest too much" about it.

Meeting Date: May 2005 (Market Cap: $8,600m)

Business assessment:
This was the first time the company has held a results meeting in London on account of the "growing interest" in the stock. As usual, the results show very strong growth with total assets up +17 per cent in 1H to €40bn on the back of a net €4bn of new loans … .

They admit that rental yields have declined in the UK (now at c.4 per cent) and Eire, but insist that their clients are not banking on capital appreciation and that their (Anglo's) repayment cover calculations are secure. But they also make the point that their clients are smart property people (i.e., they made money in the upswing!) who will benefit from a downturn as new opportunities arise. This story doesn't seem terribly consistent with 15 per cent loan growth at the top of the cycle. Nevertheless, the stock market continues to believe in the EPS growth story (+30 per cent in 1H) and the shares rose by 5–6 per cent on the day of the announcement.

Management assessment:
All of the managers have boozy faces (Dublin tans!) and can talk at length without really saying that much.

Valuation assessment:
The equity base now stands at €1.5bn (or 4.4 times book value), having doubled over the last two and a half years, and the return on equity currently stands at 33 per cent. There are lots of reasons to remain sceptical about the solidity of Anglo's business model, not least of which is how an overbanked market like the UK can really provide such a wonderful growth opportunity in commercial property lending over the next five years.

Meeting Date: November 2005 (Market Cap: $9,350m)

Business assessment:
Anglo Irish continues to deliver very strong loan growth (+40 per cent for the year ended 30 September 2005) as the Irish loan book (56 per cent of the total lending) grew at a rip-roaring 46 per cent. The UK, which represented 40 per cent of lending in 2005, grew at 27 per cent. They had previously talked about the UK being the main engine of growth, and one suspects that even they are a little surprised at the continuing buoyancy of the Irish business. Its strength is put down to the dynamism of the Irish economy. Nevertheless, their loan growth of 46 per cent is considerably higher than the market, which grew at 26–27 per cent. Gross lending during the year was an additional €10bn ... [which] actually represents 80 per cent of the loan book at the start of the year....

As before, they insist that all lending is asset (i.e., property) backed and 70 per cent is to existing customers, and they prize their ability to make fast decisions because of devolved decision-making combined with an effective credit committee....

In the UK, net new lending was €2.6bn and the gross figure was €5bn, on a starting base of €9.9bn.... Recall that the UK boss [John Rowan] left recently (having missed out on the top job), apparently forfeiting a fair fortune in stock options (1m options with a strike price of €6.3 so worth c.€8m!), which was a bit suspicious. McAteer indicated that it was at the discretion of the remuneration committee [to decide] whether Mr Rowan would be able to keep some of these options despite the fact that their first exercise date is December 2006 and the primary purpose of the options (to retain and incentivize management) could hardly be said to still apply!

New investment and rationale:
They raised €300m by way of preferred shares in 2005 as the Irish regulator deemed that their "core" Tier One ratio "was a bit tight."

Valuation assessment:
The P/E ratio has been rerated recently (from 10–11 times to the current level of 14 times) at the same time as earnings have been growing rapidly. Most brokers have buy notes on the stock and [the Irish broker] Goodbody uses a group of Eastern European bank stocks (its growth "peers") to show how cheap Anglo remains! The stock still feels like a play on Irish property bullishness – there has been strong growth in lending for Eastern European property (up to €1bn of 4 per cent of underlying assets, a growth of 66 per cent on 2004). This must blow up at some point – surely?

Meeting Date: March 2006 (Market Cap: $11,500m)

Business assessment:
The spin remains as bullish as ever. Loan assets by location are 41 per cent in Eire, whereas 56 per cent of the loan book is to Irish clients, which indicates the extent to which they fund Irish investors abroad. Total Irish lending is up 46 per cent in 2005! They are, for instance, setting up an office in Prague to service Irish property investors. They have great faith in the abilities of their clients (the Irish have bigger brains when it comes to property investing?) ... .

Since our last meeting, the bank slipped out a placing of 5 per cent [of outstanding shares], which was 4 times oversubscribed. Of course, they maintain that this [share issuance] has nothing to do with stretched capital ratios (risk-weighted assets are €40bn compared with €1.7bn of equity and Tier 1 capital is only 4 per cent). There was no EPS dilution and no immediate plan for M&A. "The market was there." In Eire, they claim not to have been affected by new entrants such as Danske and RBS.

In the UK, the emphasis is now on growing outside London in "the regions" (Manchester, Birmingham, Glasgow and Belfast). RBS is their biggest competitor in the UK commercial market, whereas in Eire it is Allied Irish. Overall, Anglo Irish has benefited from cyclical growth in commercial property, fuelled by low interest rates, increased liquidity, and exceptionally benign credit conditions. This should make the bank vulnerable in a rising rate environment.

Management assessment:
[CFO Willie] McAteer seemed more shifty than usual. The remuneration committee decided to gift one-third of the options owned by John "friend

of the bank" Rowan, even though they had not vested at the time of his departure.

Valuation assessment:
Still hard to believe in the Irish property investors' magical abilities. The business model is unlikely to be easily adaptable to a different credit environment. Corporate governance grubby too.[2]

4.2 THE BUILDERS' BANK (MAY 2004)

A pre-crisis look at the Anglo Irish can of worms

> "Time is a great story teller."
>
> Irish proverb

Anyone who thinks Europe is a mature economic region suffering from sclerosis and doomed to perpetually low rates of growth, should have attended a recent Irish equity conference in Dublin. Growth featured heavily on the menu, nowhere more so than in the presentations of Ireland's leading financial institutions. The main driver of growth is mortgage lending, which last year expanded by 26 per cent in Ireland (curiously, all of the principal banks reported that their own mortgage lending growth exceeded the national growth rate). Ireland is experiencing a housing boom, as low nominal rates of interest – in Ireland's case negative real rates thanks to the Eurozone's monetary umbrella – entice individuals to bid up property prices. The arguments for and against the sustainability of this megatrend, and its implications for banks, are well rehearsed.[3] What is perhaps more instructive is to observe the case of an especially successful Irish banking story, namely that of Anglo Irish Bank, and to imagine what lies in store.

---

[2] *Postscript:* Anglo's former CEO Sean FitzPatrick resigned as chairman in December 2008 amid mounting revelations of hidden loans at the bank. The scandal led to the collapse in the company's share price and subsequent nationalization in January 2009. Total losses sustained by the Irish state from assuming Anglo's liabilities have been estimated at over €30bn.

[3] Capital cycle footnote: Unlike in the United Kingdom, high Irish property prices provoked a boom in new supply. In 2003, 69,000 homes were built in the Irish Republic, which had a population of 4m. This compares with 180,000 new homes in the UK, with a population of around 60m, a housing supply differential of nearly 6 times on a per capita basis. This huge difference in relative housing supply explains why the UK housing market and UK homebuilders weathered the global financial crisis far better than their Irish counterparts.

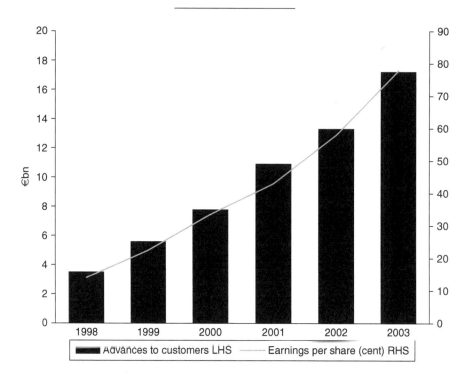

Chart 4.2   Anglo Irish Bank EPS growth and customer advances
Source: Anglo Irish.

Anglo Irish has grown from a small finance business, with a market capitalization of €8m in 1986 and an asset base of €138m, into a large bank with a market capitalization of €4.3bn and assets of €25.5bn. The bank's growth has been fuelled by lending against property in the booming Irish economy, and it has expanded into the UK and Boston markets. Currently 90 per cent of the loan book is secured against property. Rather than individual mortgages, however, Anglo Irish generally lends to small businesses that either wish to expand their property base, acquire premises that had previously been leased, or are borrowing against property to release capital.

The bank's success has been achieved without a branch network. Although this deprives it of low cost deposits, not having a branch network also means lower overheads. Anglo Irish boasts an impressive cost-to-income ratio of only 30 per cent. Average loan size is €4.5–5.5m in Ireland (€7–8m in the UK), reflecting the fact that the bank is not significantly involved with residential mortgages. In the UK, which now accounts for €7bn of the total loan book of €17bn, a greater proportion of lending is for investment property, where the borrower finances the purchase of a property (often a shop or a warehouse) which is then let to tenants on long-term lease arrangements.

Provisions against non-performing loans are 217 per cent, compared with a European average of 80 per cent. As for valuation, the bank earns a return on equity of 32 per cent, trades at 4.2 times book value and offers a yield of 1.6 per cent. Earnings per share grew at 34 per cent last year, having compounded by 41 per cent annually since 1998.

A central feature of the business model appears to be the relationship between Anglo Irish and its property-owning customers. Chief executive Sean FitzPatrick, who has run the bank since 1986, suggests that its competitive advantage is based on the speed with which they approve loans compared with bureaucratically-challenged peers. At the weekly credit committee meetings, up to 25 loans are approved with an approval rate of 95 per cent. The bank's publicly professed mission is to "make our customers richer."

Management presents Anglo Irish's credit risk in terms of current debt-servicing, but this overlooks potential repayment risk. Even though interest payments may be secure in a falling property market – assuming that tenants stay solvent, under such circumstances there must be a large question mark over property developers' ability to repay the loan principal. To use the terminology of the maverick American economist Hyman Minsky, it appears that Anglo Irish is engaging in "speculative finance" whereby borrowers are only able to cover their interest payments from earnings, as opposed to the more prudent "hedge finance" whereby borrowers can meet all their liabilities, including interest and principal payments, from current cash flows. We are not yet at the point of Minsky's "Ponzi finance," which describes the situation when borrowers are unable to fund even interest payments from current cash flow.

The bank's business model works particularly well in a falling interest rate environment. On the cost side, the bank's cost of funding in the wholesale loan market declines in line with EURIBOR rates. On the revenue side, lower interest rates have made mortgages more affordable, leading to higher property values, and strong credit growth. As Irish rents have so far moved in step with values, leveraged property developers have more income to meet lower interest payments.

If rates were to increase, however, this virtuous cycle could turn vicious. Without a deposit base, Anglo Irish's cost of funds would rise quickly. On the revenue side, declining property values would make capital repayments on existing loans problematic, raising default risk. In other words, Anglo Irish is a wonderful money-making machine when interest rates are declining, but not one to invest in under different circumstances. Not many €10m loans would have to turn sour before Anglo Irish's €1bn equity base was seriously compromised.

It might be argued that management has anticipated these risks and prepared for longer-term contingencies. The trouble is that the equity-based incentives paid to senior executives favour growth in the near-term, while bad debt problems are likely to have a very long tail. The bank has issued stock options for over 6.2m shares (2 per cent of the total share capital), with strike prices of between €1.09 and €6.70 compared with the current market price of €13. Management have responded to the enormous rise in the share price – which fails to discount what a myopic stock market cannot see – by selling vast numbers of shares. Mr. FitzPatrick, who is retiring at the tender age of 55, recently sold half of his holding for around €20m, and the 46-year old boss of the UK business has disposed of 40 per cent of his holding.

Charles T. Munger is fond of saying that there are "more banks than bankers." A competitive advantage based on a willingness to make loans in an instant would be anathema to old-fashioned bankers. Of particular concern to us is the extent to which Irish bankers engage in the hard-sell to investors. One of them declared at the conference we recently attended: "I am here unashamedly to sell you X bank!" This rather goes against our preference for bankers as cautious individuals, obsessed with long-term downside risks. As we have seen in many other businesses, an obsession with growth, combined with overpromotion, is likely to end in tears. As to when this will happen, we must wait for time, Ireland's proverbial story teller.

4.3   INSECURITIZATION (NOVEMBER 2002)

Securitization has flooded certain sectors with too much cheap capital

Marathon's investment methodology is based on the tendency for returns on capital for any particular company, or industry, to trend towards a normal level over time. Depending on how quickly this evolution takes place, relative to the market's expectations, an investment opportunity may arise. For this process to work, however, poor and failing businesses must be deprived of cheap funding. Yet the securitization process now supplies capital at an abnormally low cost to inherently risky activities, delaying the normalisation of profits and storing up losses for the future. This has capital cycle implications. Shareholder returns in industries funded with easy money from securitizations are likely to oscillate around the low marginal cost of funding.

For those unfamiliar with the practice, it may be useful to describe briefly the mechanics of a typical asset securitization. In the airline industry, for example, the process begins with a purchase order from the aircraft manufacturer at a significant, bulk discount to list price. Upon delivery, this asset is sold by the airline to a newly established securitization vehicle at a price closer to list price, and subsequently leased back for the life of the aircraft. The vehicle issues Enhanced Equipment Trust Certificates (EETC) to investors. Lease payments are tranched, with investors who take on the greatest default risk (junior note holders) receiving more and those who take on the least risk (senior tranches) getting less. Compared to a conventional debt instrument, what makes securitization so attractive is the fact that the airline often retains the junior tranches. These become an asset on its balance sheet. Any discount associated with the low credit rating of these layers is more than offset by the discount on the purchase of the aircraft, thereby creating an immediate profit and cash inflow on delivery of the aircraft. Such are the wonders of modern financial alchemy.

Under good, even normal, business conditions, the airline makes lease payments to the securitization vehicle. But in a recession or a bankruptcy filing, when payments are suspended, the owners of the senior strata are able to seize the collateral. The junior participants in the securitization have no rights, and any such assets on the airline's balance sheet must be written down to zero, further increasing the airline's losses. By this clever piece of financial engineering, the airline gets shiny new planes for an extremely low cost of funds – recently as low as 6 per cent – while equity shareholders carry nearly all of the business risk. That an industry which has rarely earned an acceptable return on capital should have access to such cheap capital is quite astonishing.

Similar feats of financial engineering, facilitated by securitization, are apparent in a backwater of the US mortgage market. GreenPoint Financial originates through a broker network mortgages that fail to meet mortgage standards set by Fannie Mae and Freddie Mac. These risky loans, known as Alt-A mortgages, generate on average a yield of about 100 basis points above the typical conforming mortgage. A casual observer might assume that this yield pick-up was a commensurate compensation for the increase in credit risk. So we were amazed to learn that GreenPoint are able to sell these loans whole, retaining absolutely no credit risk, while keeping 95 basis points of the yield premium over the agency rate as a one-off gain on sale.

According to GreenPoint, this windfall is possible because the buyers, usually investment banks or specialists in mortgage servicing, take the loans and repackage them as securitizations attracting what GreenPoint describes as money that "doesn't care a hoot" about the underlying economics of the mortgage. By keying off recent default statistics which are unbelievably benign (at less than 5bps of losses annually), the buyers of the senior tranches have been lulled into thinking the risk-reward characteristics are in their favour and accept a tiny spread over the rate available from a conforming loan. Those buying the more risky junior notes are happy to earn a significant yield premium while putting off the (inevitable?) write down of this highly leveraged instrument. GreenPoint has taken full advantage of this market madness by doubling the volume of mortgage originations and whole loan sales over the past couple of years.

The eagerness of aircraft and Alt-A securitization buyers to accept a "reliable" stream of income, while deferring possible losses, is not surprising in this age of financial myopia. Securitizations have been an effective way of obscuring the real economics of these activities, while facilitating the inflow of more and more capital.[4] As for the airlines, only when managements' growth ambitions are restricted by greater rationing of finance will the industry's returns on capital move towards a more acceptable level.[5]

4.4   CARRY ON PRIVATE EQUITY (DECEMBER 2004)

The buyout boom has entered a bubble phase
Paul Achleitner, investment director at Allianz, recently commented that: "The traditional strategy of buying and holding [listed investments] worked well for decades but it doesn't work in a modern regulatory environment.... Private equity holdings don't swing about in value like publicly listed companies."
He is not alone in his enthusiasm. Europe is now the world's largest private equity market by transactions, accounting for some 60 per cent of global private equity M&A activity, according to various industry estimates. In the UK, one fifth of the UK private sector workforce is reportedly employed by private equity firms. In the month of November, four major European private equity bids with a total transaction value of $20bn were announced, including a possible $14bn bid by a consortium of private equity firms for Auna, Spain's number three mobile phone operator. If successful, this latter bid would constitute the largest ever private equity deal in Europe. Private equity firms are doing more deals with more debt and have come to resemble

---

[4] Losses on Alt-A mortgages after the Global Financial Crisis were estimated by Goldman Sachs to be $600bn on a total stock of $1.3tn (*The Economist*, February 2009.) In February 2004, GreenPoint Financial was acquired by North Fork Bancorporation for $6.3bn. In December 2006, Capital One acquired North Fork. A year later, Capital One shut down GreenPoint, after suffering losses on its mortgage book.

[5] Since this piece appeared, there has been a spate of North American airline bankruptcies, including United Airlines (December 2002), Air Canada (April 2003), US Airways (September 2004), Northwest (September 2005), Delta (September 2005) and American Airlines (November 2011).

the 1960s conglomerates like LTV, Litton and ITT in the breadth of their activities. So will today's private equity firms suffer the same fate as the conglomerates of the past, or are they here to stay, playing an essential role that cannot be fulfiled by public capital markets?

There are a host of factors working in favour of private equity. In an age obsessed with quarterly earnings, ownership of unlisted assets allows private equity firms to take longer-term decisions than would be acceptable to stock market "investors." Corporate restructuring under private equity ownership is also probably easier to achieve. Consider how difficult it is for Siemens to reduce the workforce at any of its 900 consolidated subsidiaries. Managers in private equity firms are not encumbered by the increasing bureaucracy for listed firms, called forth by the Sarbanes-Oxley legislation. Furthermore, management compensation escapes the public prurience associated with executive pay at public firms. In theory, the principal-agent problem is reduced via greater control by owners (whereas in practice, buyouts bring with them a host of new fee-hungry agents).

We have a number of concerns, however, about the current private equity boom. For a start:

1. The boom appears to be fuelled by the willingness of banks and other financial institutions to fund deals on more lax terms to private equity firms. The ratio of net debt to earnings before interest, tax, depreciation and amortization (EBITDA) – a cash flow measure of how much debt banks are willing to lend for a corporate acquisition – has been rising. Deals with multiples of 6–7 times EBITDA are now not uncommon. "Seven is the new five," as one observer put it, raising the spectre of a credit bubble. Banks, awash with capital, justify their enthusiasm for private equity deals on the grounds that interest rates are low and that there have been few defaults on historical private equity loans (a "driving-via-the-rear-view-mirror" argument). We also sense that slippage is occurring with regard to the security and loan covenants demanded by creditors. Lax lending encourages private equity to take on more leverage. Given that buyout loans are non-recourse to the private equity sponsor, the risk is less with private equity firms and more with the suppliers of debt – namely, the banks or whoever has acquired the loans from the banks. However, increased debt capacity increases the probability that private equity deals will be overpriced.

2. Higher levels of debt could be justified if the underlying busi-
    nesses have sufficiently predictable cash flows to support higher
    leverage. Yet in a number of recent cases, large amounts of debt
    are being applied to highly cyclical businesses. In the case of
    Rexel, a French distributor of electrical parts, the €3.7bn buy-
    out has been funded on a debt to EBITDA multiple of almost
    7 times. Or take the case of Celanese, a bulk chemical com-
    pany, where the $1.2bn purchase was funded on a multiple of
    5.5 times.[6]
3. The private equity firms themselves are awash with cash. There
    are now said to be over 100 buyout firms with funds of more
    than $1bn. According to the British venture capital firm 3i, three-
    quarters of all capital ever raised by private equity firms has been
    raised in the last five years. With so much money to invest in a
    relatively short time (most funds seek to be fully invested within
    three years of capital raising), competition among private equity
    firms, skilfully stoked up by investment bankers in auctions, may
    become excessive.
4. There are reasons to be sceptical about the private equity indus-
    try's ability to replicate historical returns achieved during the
    long bull market. David Swensen, the manager of Yale's endow-
    ment, pointed out in his book, *Pioneering Portfolio Management*,
    that private equity funds produced annual returns of 48 per cent
    between 1987 and 1998, compared with the annualized 17 per
    cent return of the S&P 500 over the same period. This appears
    impressive. But, as Swensen points out, if an investment in the
    S&P had employed the same leverage as private equity, then
    annual returns would have compounded at 86 per cent.
5. Private equity firms are outbidding trade buyers. This is now a
    very frequent complaint at our meetings with companies. At a
    recent meeting with Associated British Foods, the CFO com-
    plained about the difficulty of competing for deals with private
    equity firms. For instance, Hicks Muse recently paid 16 times
    operating profits to acquire the venerable Weetabix breakfast
    cereal business. (In this particular case, there may be syner-
    gies with Hicks Muse's other food businesses.) When asked
    how they could afford to pay more than trade buyers, a senior

---

[6] Celanese had an initial public offering in January 2005, and its private equity sponsor,
Blackstone, reportedly made five times its investment in the US chemical company.

figure at 3i recently commented that they were "smarter" than corporate buyers and did "more work" on deals. Not terribly convincing.

6. The lack of transparency in the private equity world, frequently cited as a significant benefit, is double-edged. After all, it is easy to forget that demands for increased transparency in public markets arose from a reaction to specific cases of corporate malfeasance. If such behaviour goes "under cover" in the private equity arena, the problem does not go away. Raiding a pension fund or overstating the value of assets or any other dubious practice seems to us much more likely to occur in the private equity world than in public markets where the spotlight of regulation shines far brighter.

7. There are anecdotal signs of a private equity bubble, including the entry of hedge funds into the private equity field, the obsession with EBITDA valuation measures (which remind us of the mania for "pro forma" earnings during the tech bubble) and the proliferation of complex finance structures, including the use of "special purpose vehicles." Private equity has become one of the most sought after career options for MBA graduates – a reliable contrarian indicator.

8. Given the lacklustre market for IPOs, private equity firms have been looking for other more incestuous exit routes. There's been a spate of "secondary buyouts" – the practice of one private equity firm selling its investee company to another buyout firm. It is hard to see that the new owner can generate huge gains if the previous owner, who presumably thinks in a similar way, has exploited all the value creation opportunities. An alternative exit is provided by leveraged re-capitalizations in which equity is returned through special dividends funded with debt. If things go bad, this risk is more likely to land up with the banks than with the private equity sponsors.

9. Private equity firms generate billions of dollars of fees for investment and lending banks, lawyers, accountants, and sundry other hangers-on in the world of finance. In the world of "integrated" corporate finance, we see the potential for conflicts of interest. One obvious potential conflict comes from a bank's desire to generate transaction fees (advisory, origination, etc.) and its need to ensure the security of the loan principal. We suppose the transaction-hungry investment bankers have the upper

hand over the traditionally more sober-minded lending officers. One dubious new practice is "staple lending," whereby the bank advising the vendor on the sale offers a loan to the purchaser, "stapled" to the purchase and sale agreement. This occurred in the sale of VNU's directories business in which Goldman and CSFB both advised the bidder and provided finance to the acquirer. As adviser, one would expect the banks to seek the highest price, but would it not be reasonable for the bank as lender to want the lowest price?

10. Finally, Allianz's bullishness about private equity should be enough to make the most determined optimist shudder. When it comes to capital allocation, Allianz deserves a special booby prize. One thinks back to the German insurer's 2001 acquisition of 80 per cent of Dresdner Bank for €25bn or its sale of €12bn of equities near the market trough in late 2002! That a director of investment at Allianz cannot tell the difference between price and value does little to inspire confidence (hint: the latter doesn't fluctuate with the daily moods of the market). In short, there is a good chance that the capital cycle in private equity, as in hedge funds, is about to turn nasty.[7]

4.5 BLOWING BUBBLES (MAY 2006)

Several indicators of speculative activity suggest a market peak has been reached

"I'm forever blowing bubbles, pretty bubbles in the air,
They fly so high, nearly reach the sky,
Then like my dreams they fade and die,
Fortune's always hiding, I've looked everywhere,
I'm forever blowing bubbles, pretty bubbles in the air."

                                    Chant of West Ham football supporters

The recent crack in the markets had to some extent been foreshadowed in recent months by signs of excessively confident behaviour from market

---

[7] In retrospect, Marathon failed to anticipate the extent to which private equity firms would be bailed out by unconventional monetary policies following the financial crisis. They remain some of the largest and least deserving beneficiaries of ultra-low interest rates and quantitative easing.

participants. Given the capital cycle focus of our firm, we have always had a strong interest in identifying bubbles. Recent speculative activity in commodities, emerging markets, hedge funds, IPOs and, of course, private equity all suggest a market peak has been reached. Current evidence of market froth can be found in:

1. Commodity bubbles

The gold price has recently touched a 25-year high, while the prices of copper, zinc and other base metals have all risen vertically for several months. Most recently, however, commodity prices seem to have gone into overdrive as natural strong user demand (mostly from China) has been exacerbated by speculative demand from financial market participants. Copper is trading at a premium to the face value of the coinage. It now pays to melt down pre-1992 British pennies, as well as US cents and nickels. The steep rises in commodity prices in recent weeks remind us of the intraday spikes in Internet stocks in the last few weeks of the 2000 tech bubble. It is rather ominous that the pink paper launched a new supplement, entitled "FT Copper," on May 10, two days before copper touched an all-time high only to plummet subsequently by 14 per cent.

2. Private equity mania (I)

In the last few months, some large and well-established private equity groups – namely KKR and Apollo – have taken advantage of abundant market liquidity and the allure of their own historical track records to list funds that invest in their own funds. Needless to say, these funds charge management fees on top of the fees already charged by the underlying funds. KKR initially aimed to raise $1.5bn, but interest was so strong they increased the amount to $5bn. After Citigroup and other bankers took $270m (5.5 per cent of net asset value) for placing fees, KKR's fund is now trading at a discount to the issue price. Nice money if you can get it! Incidentally the Apollo fund is set to pay away 6 per cent in fees to Goldman Sachs and friends.

3. Private equity mania (II)

A few weeks ago, Blackstone, one of the world's largest private equity groups, invested €2.7bn for a 4.5 per cent stake in Deutsche Telekom, the German telephone operator. Deutsche Telekom is a publicly traded company that index funds (no fee) and many long-only (low fee) managers are free to invest in. Yet

Blackstone paid a 2.6 per cent premium for its stake and has agreed to be locked up for two years – its consolation prize being the possibility of getting a board seat on a 20-person German board. The shares are trading 11 per cent below Blackstone's purchase price. This is by far the largest investment made by a private equity outfit in a listed equity. Why their private equity clients should pay exorbitant fees for this kind of investment is difficult to comprehend. To us, the DT deal suggests that buyout groups now have more money than ideas.

4. IPO frenzy

The IPO calendar has suddenly exploded. Marathon's proprietary IPO indicator – namely the size of the pile of issue prospectuses by our desks – which worked so well in the TMT bubble, is flashing a strong warning sign. Interestingly the industry composition of the IPOs has shifted markedly from the last bubble, and now the main areas of capital raising include the energy, commodity, utility and specialist financials industries.

In the case of the latter, specialist fund management groups and fund of fund managers are opportunistically raising money or selling out. One listing last March that caught our interest was that of a Swiss-based entity, called Partners Group, which manages funds of funds in private equity and hedge funds. At the year end, Partners had assets under management (AUM) of SFr 11bn and 2005 revenues of SFr 125m. After the first day's trading, in which the shares popped 25 per cent, Partners was valued at SFr 2.1bn, a staggering 19 per cent of AUM and nearly 17 times revenue.

At around the same date, Charlemagne Capital went public on the London Stock Exchange. This fund management business was founded by some of those who had been behind the Regent Pacific group and the now defunct Regent Eastern European leveraged debt fund. Charlemagne specializes in investing in the hot Eastern European emerging markets. Its AUM has grown from $250m in 2000 to $5bn today. The current share price values the fund manager at some 10 per cent of AUM. Two-thirds of last year's profits came from performance fees. The IPO provided the opportunity for insiders and directors to sell between 25 per cent and 33 per cent of their holdings in the company. Following the emerging market turbulence of the last few days, Charlemagne's stock is down 32 per cent in the seven weeks since listing.

5. M&A Mania (I)

Another indication of market froth is the return of animal spirits in the mergers and acquisition world, where activity has moved back up to levels last experienced in the 1999–2000 technology bubble. According to Thomson Financial, announced M&A volumes in Europe in Q1 2006 amounted to some $437bn, which is 240 per cent above the same period last year. It is conventional wisdom that M&A destroys value over the long-term, which is why the share price of an acquiring company normally falls when a deal is announced. Yet we've recently observed several cases when the acquirer's stock has climbed on the announcement of a bid, even it is paying a large premium for the target company. For instance, when Ferrovial, a Spanish infrastructure group, announced it was buying the somewhat larger British airports group, BAA, at a 28 per cent premium to the undisturbed share price, Ferrovial's own share price climbed by nearly 6 per cent. Likewise when Mittal Steel announced a bid for rival steelmaker Arcelor, its shares rose by 14 per cent over a 48-hour period.

6. M&A Mania (II)

M&A deals devoid of strategic logic or potential cost savings is a strongly developing theme. We have recently witnessed an Australian infrastructure fund buying a national telecom operator in Ireland and a similar Singapore entity buying a UK ports operator in combination with the private equity arm of an investment bank. In both cases, large acquisition premiums were paid, despite the absence of synergies. The tax savings from leveraging these companies after they've been taken private can hardly justify these hefty takeover premiums.

7. Retail exuberance

No discussion of stock market excess would be complete without reference to the antics of the retail investor. After the debacle of their day-trading experiences at the turn of the century, retail investors have finally recovered their appetite for equities, their spirits lifted by US house prices at record levels and an equity market that has been rising steadily for over 18 months. In the US, Charles Schwab recorded triple the commission income in February versus three years ago. The retail crowd is currently behind some 60 per cent of option trades on the NYSE, where turnover has been rocketing. It comes as no surprise that emerging markets have caught the eye of Main Street, given emerging's strength over the last few years (from its low in 2003 to the recent peak, the MSCI Emerging Index rose by 240 per cent, while S&P 500 is up only 63 per cent from its 2003 trough). In the first ten weeks of this year, emerging market funds attracted more in-flows from US investors than for the whole of 2005, which itself was a record year.

8. Insiders out

Directors' dealings have also been sending some strong signals of late. The level of insider selling has risen steadily over the last several months. The most recent monthly statistics for the UK show that directors sold 16 times as many shares as they bought in April. This compares with a ratio of lower than four times a year ago. Although the ratio of insiders' purchases to sales is almost always skewed towards selling, as directors tend to accumulate free or cheap shares from options and incentive plans over the years, the current level of insiders exiting is pronounced.

All of the above, combined with the usual anecdotal signals transmitted in meetings with companies and sell-side practitioners, suggests that May 2006 has represented something of a market peak.[8] It is always difficult to predict market turns, but the signs of excessive and hubristic behaviour should serve as a warning. The period of easy money which has fuelled much of this speculative activity may be coming to an end, and if easy money continues it will probably be for bad reasons.

4.6   PASS THE PARCEL (FEBRUARY 2007)

The securitized debt markets are responsible for the private equity mania
Rarely a day goes by without some rumour of an imminent private equity bid. The size of the prey has risen to include companies which are perceived as national institutions (in the UK, they include BAA, the airports group, and Boots, the high street chemist). This has led to public complaints against asset stripping and tax evasion by private equity "locusts." In the UK, ire is now being directed at the principals of the private equity firms, who, being rich and foreign, make perfect scapegoats.

We suspect, however, that the real villain of the piece, if there has to be one, is the debt market. Debt provides most of the firepower for buyouts. Lower spreads and more lax lending terms are the magic inputs that make the high projected returns in private equity deals still materialize despite ever giddier transaction prices. In short, the key to understanding the private equity business lies in what is going on in the credit world.

First, credit spreads have compressed. This is a global rather than European phenomenon, which a senior Moody's analyst at a recent

---

[8] Calling stock market peaks is a perilous activity. As it turned out, the S&P 500 continued to climb until October 2007, at which point the S&P 500 was some 22 per cent higher than its level at the time of writing.

conference ascribed to the "savings glut" coming out of Asia and the Middle East. Too much money has been chasing too few "quality" financial assets. In the European credit markets, there has also been a decline in the proportion of buyout finance provided by commercial banks. The banks' share of leveraged loans has declined from over 90 per cent at the start of the decade to less than 60 per cent today. In place of banks, a growing share of the European buyout debt market has been taken by the securitized credit vehicles – namely, collateralized debt obligations (CDOs) and collateralized loan obligations (CLOs) – and by hedge funds. This development in the credit markets occurred in the US many years earlier. In Europe, the recent trend has been more exaggerated in the riskier tranches of acquisition finance where traditional bank lenders have largely disappeared over the past 18 months.

Gone are the days when European banks hung onto loans because they prized the associated corporate relationships, not to mention the net interest income. There are a number of implications to these developments. First, there is the moral hazard aspect. As banks hold on to less of the debt that they originate, they are bound to have less concern about longer-term credit quality. A recent survey by the UK's Financial Services Authority found that, on average, banks distribute 81 per cent of their exposure to their largest buyout transactions within 120 days of finalizing the deal. Anecdotal evidence suggests to us that this originate-then-distribute model is leading to a decline in the quality of lending.

For instance, Svenska Handelsbanken, a prudent institution and the only Swedish bank to come through the early 1990s banking crisis unscathed, is currently experiencing a loss of market share in the corporate loan market in Sweden. The bank has a policy of not entering into a loan agreement unless it is prepared to keep the loan on its books. It is tempting to conclude that its recent loss of market share is due to competing banks adopting the "pass-the-parcel" business model and the resultant lowering of credit standards. We've noted elsewhere the appearance of off-the-shelf loan packages to fund private equity deals offered by fee-hungry investment banks. Staple finance is no doubt used to extract the highest possible price from potential bidders. One can have little doubt that the investment banks which provide such debt don't hold on to it for long.

More evidence of declining credit standards was provided by a recent article in the *Financial Times*, where a City lawyer bemoaned that nowadays no one seems to be negotiating over intercreditor arrangements relating to potential corporate defaults. After sending out a draft agreement on a loan to some 50 funds, the lawyer received no comments on the terms of the default arrangements. In the past there would have been a tussle over every clause. A recent survey undertaken by Standard & Poor's, the credit ratings agency, found that the proportion of senior corporate debt being fully amortized had fallen from 41 per cent in 2002 to 25 per cent in 2006. Another finding was that the proportion of excess cash flow swept into debt amortization for LBO firms has declined, leaving more money available for dividends to buyout sponsors.

For the banks engaging in this pass-the-parcel game, there is always the risk of being caught at the point when the credit market turns. Furthermore, it may be that the banks have not been as clever as they claim in getting rid of potentially toxic credit risks. Once offloaded, the securitized debt may end up back at the same bank's proprietary trading desk. A recent FSA survey of banks found that only 50 per cent of respondents were able to provide an indication of where they believed the debt had been distributed to. Andy Hornby, chief executive of HBOS, has said that the matter of where leveraged lending risk ends up is one of the biggest issues currently facing UK banks.[9]

For private equity players, the attitude of making hay while the sun shines seems wholly appropriate, although a scenario of rising defaults is unlikely to leave them unscathed. From the standpoint of an investor in listed equities, however, it appears sensible to maintain a cautious stance towards the European financial sector. Bank assets continue to reach new highs despite the widespread adoption of originate-then-distribute banking practices. Passing on risk, however, may prove easier than passing on blame.

4.7   PROPERTY FIESTA (FEBRUARY 2007)

Over the past few years the Spanish have gone property mad

"A tree that grows crooked will never straighten its trunk"

Spanish proverb

Our attention was drawn recently to Astroc Mediterraneo, a Spanish real estate developer, which IPO'd in the early part of last year to little fanfare. Even by the standards of the current bull market in Spanish equities, the share price performance of Astroc has been nothing less than spectacular. Its stock has climbed more than tenfold since flotation, giving the company a market capitalisation

---

[9] Hornby might have spent his time looking for risks closer to home. HBOS eventually failed as a result of "reckless lending policies pursued by HBOS Corporate Division," according to a UK Parliamentary Report.

of some €8–9bn, which makes it the fifth largest property company in Europe by value. Chairman and founder Enrique Banuelos, who has a 51 per cent stake, has suddenly become one of the richest men in Spain. Management is taking advantage of this strong market performance to issue another €2bn of shares.

Other Spanish property companies are similarly hot. Metrovacesa, Europe's largest office landlord, currently trades at 100 per cent premium to its net asset value – a pretty hefty premium to other European property companies, although one partly explained by a battle for control of the company between its two largest shareholders. Rising share prices in the sector have attracted new capital. There were four IPOs of the Spanish property companies last year, which equals the total number of listings in the sector over the previous four years.

These stories illustrate a feature of Spain which will be obvious to any recent visitor – over the past few years the country appears to have gone property mad. Cranes abound and every major city centre has turned into a huge building site. Depending on which estimate one believes, construction comprises between 15 per cent and 20 per cent of Spain's economic output, compared to a European average of well below 10 per cent. And though it has less than 15 per cent of Western Europe's population, Spain now accounts for fully half of the Continent's annual cement consumption.

One reason for the construction frenzy is that Spain has been the grateful recipient of some two-thirds of the Cohesion Funds doled out by the European Union over the past few years, alongside smaller economies such as Greece, Portugal and Ireland. This money has been spent on roads, bridges, airports and other big ticket infrastructure projects. As the Spanish share of the EU funds begins to wind down in favour of worthier recipients, the Spanish government plans to increase its own infrastructure budget to take up some of the slack.

Then there's the booming market for residential construction. The sheer scale of building in Spain is fairly breathtaking: some 800,000 housing starts a year accounting for around one-third of the new houses being built across Europe. The Spanish housing stock has doubled since 1997. This partly reflects external demand, notably the number of second homes purchased by Britons, Germans, and Scandinavians, and strong immigration. Spain's economic boom has attracted large numbers of workers from outside the EU, and immigrants have risen from 2 per cent of the population in 2000 to over 9 per cent today.[10]

---

[10] As it turned out, much of this immigration was related to Spain's housing boom. After the bubble burst, this migration trend reversed course and in 2013 more than half a million foreigners left the country.

With confidence high and immigrants still flooding across the borders, is there any reason to believe the boom cannot continue? For a start, the house price inflation seems to be slowing. Household debt has reached 130 per cent of disposable income, up nearly 50 percentage points since 2001, and one of the highest levels in Europe. Since Spain is locked into the euro, interest rates are well below what would appear appropriate for such a strongly growing economy. While debt service costs remain relatively affordable, there comes a point when households simply do not want to take on any more debt. Another concern is that Spanish property is no longer such good value for foreigners looking to buy holiday homes – many might prefer cheaper alternatives in the Mediterranean, as can be found in Greece, Turkey and Croatia.

A slower pace of housing construction would be bad news for many of Spain's municipalities, which derive a significant chunk of income (no one seems to know quite how much) from selling building permits to eager developers. While most of this is above board, this is big business with some murky dealings – when a scandal broke over illegal development in the southern city of Marbella a couple of years back, the authorities' investigation ended with the arrest of the mayor. A country in which it seems difficult to get anyone to accept a €50 or €100 note is said to host around quarter of the entire €500 note issue. No doubt most of this cash is floating around the construction industry in one way or another.[11]

Spain's economy has become dependent on the construction industry, which employs around 22 per cent of the workforce. Unlike Ireland, the other formerly peripheral European economy which has seen very strong growth for the past few years, Spain hasn't enjoyed anything like the same productivity gains. While immigration has kept a lid on wage rises to some extent, unit labour costs are still climbing at twice the Eurozone average,

---

[11] The collapse of Spain's property boom has opened a can of worms, which have writhed for several years under an increasingly hostile public glare. Several corruption scandals came to light in October 2014. That month, Spain's bank bail out fund approached prosecutors regarding €1.5bn worth of apparently irregular real estate and debt operations at two local savings banks (known as "cajas"). At around the same time, dozens of persons were arrested across Spain following an investigation into local government corruption involving councillors, civil servants, builders and sundry others. Adding to an already turbulent month, a former chairman of Bankia (a financial conglomerate created in 2010 out of several failed savings banks) and a former CEO of one of the cajas folded into Bankia were summoned before a judge to answer questions about a scandal involving dozens of Bankia executives – all political appointees of local parties and trade unions – who had allegedly spent millions of euros of the bank's money, using so-called "black credit cards." Public disgust with corruption in Spain has contributed to the rise of the radical left-wing party, Podemos.

which is making Spain an increasingly uncompetitive place, especially given the lack of productivity growth. One indication of this is the fact that foreign direct investment has more than halved from 4 per cent of GDP in 2000 to less than 2 per cent in 2005, as foreign companies look for more competitive places to invest. If Spain had a floating currency, one would expect this combination of relatively high inflation and low productivity growth to be offset by a decline in the exchange rate. Spain, of course, is stuck in the euro and can't devalue to restore its lost competitiveness.

While Spain's economy continues to grow at well above the European average, increasingly the growth has been funded by borrowing on the part of both corporations and households. The effect of this is that Spain's current account deficit – which measures the amount an economy consumes and invests relative to what it produces and saves – has ballooned, reaching a fairly remarkable 8.8 per cent of GDP at the end of 2006, higher even than the US in percentage terms (the US current account deficit is 6.8 per cent). In absolute dollar terms, Spain's current account deficit is the second largest in the world, worsted only by that of the US.

As European interest rates edge upwards, servicing Spain's debt burden is becoming more painful. It is difficult to see how it is sustainable. A soft landing scenario is possible, but that would require a long period of below average inflation and wage growth without overly damaging consumer and business confidence, a combination which is difficult to envisage. It may well be that much tougher times lie ahead for the Spanish economy, and indeed for Señor Banuelos.[12]

4.8   CONDUIT STREET (AUGUST 2007)

The fragmented nature of the German banking system makes it especially accident prone

There is a rather weary inevitability in the fact that the two primary European casualties (so far) of the current turmoil in the credit markets have been German banks, and mid-sized ones at that. Both IKB Deutsche Industriebank, a listed specialist lender to the mid-market corporate segment, and Sachsen LB, one of Germany's accident-prone Landesbanken, have had to be bailed out by a combination of the larger German banks and state institutions. The fault

---

[12] Shortly after this article appeared, shares in Astroc Mediterraneo plunged by 70 per cent in a week following an auditor's report which suggested that Mr Banuelos had purchased property from his own company equivalent to 65 per cent of annual turnover (Reuters, 26 July 2007).

lines of German banking appear to lie in the fragmented nature of the industry, together with the tendency of German bankers to be duped by City slickers.

At the beginning of the decade, several German banks faced substantial losses on their property lending. Only a few years before that, one of the largest Landesbanken, WestLB, was forced to write down its private equity investments. This time around, the problems are related to investment vehicles called conduits, which sat mostly off the banks' balance sheets. Here's how they got into trouble. IKB and Sachsen financed their conduits in the asset-backed commercial paper market. Such funding is usually cheap and short-term, typically 90 to 180 days maturity. The loan proceeds are then invested in higher-yielding, longer-term assets, such as collateralized debt obligations or asset-backed securities, with the sponsoring bank only having to post a small amount of collateral to repay the commercial paper holders in case of problems. So as long the commercial paper could be rolled over at a cost of funding below the income generated from the longer-term assets, these conduits generated sizable profits for the banks.

Over the past four to five years, a number of European banks have been very active in this market, with some $510bn of asset-backed commercial paper sitting in European conduits, up from only $200bn five years ago and accounting for nearly half of the $1.2tr asset-backed commercial paper market. Sachsen and IKB were enthusiastic adopters of the conduit model. IKB's conduit, Rhineland Funding, started in 2002 and was expanded rapidly, reaching €14bn in assets by the middle of this year. At this point, IKB's own exposure to Rhineland was €8bn, compared to its combined Tier 1 and 2 capital of only €4bn and a peak market capitalisation of less than €3bn. The story was similar at Sachsen, whose Ormond Quay conduit, originated in 2004, grew to €17bn or a quarter of the bank's total assets of €68bn and as much as 11 times their equity capital.

While things were going well, this level of exposure didn't seem problematic. The credit merry-go-round, however, stopped abruptly a few weeks ago when concerns surfaced about just how much of the "investment grade" securities held in the conduits had exposure to the US subprime mortgages, which themselves might not be quite as secure as their ratings suggested. Suddenly the renewal of funding in the commercial paper market became impossible and, with liabilities many times what they could afford to pay, both banks would have defaulted on the spot had it not been for the hastily-arranged bail-outs.

Although IKB and Sachsen LB are the most extreme examples, they are by no means isolated cases in Germany. Indeed the German state banks appear to have taken the conduit model particularly to heart. None of the eight largest Landesbanken is among the 30 largest banks in Europe, yet they all figure in the top 30 when it comes to the use of conduits. Sachsen LB's Ormond Quay was one of the largest European conduits of all, which is astonishing given that Sachsen is a small bank even by German, let alone European, standards.

So what is it about the German market structure which makes it susceptible to these pitfalls? Part of the problem lies with the fragmented nature of the German banking system. Unlike most other European markets, where a small number of highly profitable nationwide banks have emerged, in Germany even the largest private sector banks have only single digit market shares. The ability to compete in corporate lending became harder for the regional Landesbanken after the ending of state guarantees which allowed them to borrow more cheaply in the wholesale markets and undercut private sector banks when lending to corporations. The European Union put a stop to this in 2005, squeezing margins.

Sachsen, the only Landesbank in former East Germany, has had a particularly tough task trying to grow a lending business in what is still a depressed region. Growing the loan book in other parts of Germany, as well as an aggressive expansion into investment products, such as conduits, may have seemed like a sensible solution. Similarly, IKB's growth was constrained by the willingness of its 38 per cent shareholder, the state-owned bank KfW, to stump up additional funds for conventional expansion. Instead, it turned to growth through off-balance sheet vehicles which was not supervised by domestic regulators and required little capital apart from a small back-stop loan facility (which itself could be syndicated).

German banks are also exposed to moral hazard – the ability to take risk at other people's expense. This may explain why they continue to make such gross blunders. It must have been very tempting for the Landesbanken and other public sector banks, such as IKB, to take on substantial risks, knowing that the German state, which is concerned about availability of credit for Mittelstand businesses, would never have allowed them to fail.

Furthermore, managers had little or no equity stake in their banks. Management incentives at IKB were geared around an annual return on equity target. This only increased the attraction of conduits which could manufacture profits using only small amounts of bank capital. In its most recent financial year, over 40 per cent of IKB's profits came from its Structured Finance Division which, among other things, contained conduit activities as well as assets in structured investment vehicles (SIVs) that are constructed along much the same lines as the conduits. The profitability of this arm of the bank was more than twice that of its other banking lines.

Nor must we overlook the possibility that German bankers were simply ignorant – they did not understand the complex risks that they were taking on. In the case of IKB, which had been securitizing and selling on books of their loans to the Mittelstand companies since the end of the 1990s, the conduit business must have seemed familiar. This bank actually prided itself on its risk management – 25 pages of its most recent annual report are dedicated to showing how various risk committees supervised banking activities to ensure that risk was minimised and much was made of their expertise in the area of securitized finance.

The perception that the risk was being tightly controlled was doubtless encouraged by the investment banks, which generated substantial fees constructing products to put into Rhineland, Ormond Quay and its other conduits. Our suspicions in this respect have been alerted by the curious names of some of the German conduits. For example, one goes by the rather dubious title of "Poseidon." Did someone think this vehicle might end up underwater? Another conduit at the Landesbank Berlin rejoices in the name of "Check Point Charlie." To our mind, these suspect names appear to have been conjured up by some Canary Wharf wit, rather than originating in Hamburg or Berlin.

While some might argue that German banks have improved in recent years, (none of the largest listed banks so far seem to have been seriously caught up in the mess this time around), as long as the industry structure remains fragmented, it seems that German bankers are destined to play the role of the patsies in the sharpers' game of global finance.

4.9   ON THE ROCKS (SEPTEMBER 2007)

Northern Rock's fickle funding source made the UK bank vulnerable to a credit crunch

A run on a large Western European bank is not a usual occurrence – the last one in the UK happened in 1866. So it seems a subject worthy of review both from the perspective of the Northern Rock organization itself (what drove people to do what they did?), and also in the context of Marathon's long-standing underweight in European financial stocks.[13] Our banking exposure currently stands at 14 per cent of the portfolio versus a sector weighting of 29 per cent in the index benchmark.

Our meetings with Northern Rock over the years had left us baffled, rather than particularly apprehensive about the sustainability of its business

---

[13] In September 2007, Northern Rock suffered a bank run and was forced to turn to the Bank of England for liquidity. The following February, Northern Rock was nationalised.

model. No investment was ever made in the company. The fact that the bank was borrowing short and lending long and exploiting the latest financial innovations (a.k.a. pass-the-hot-potato) did not strike us as particularly abnormal in the context of current banking norms. Innovation in capital markets and the pursuit of fee-driven approaches which shift risk to those least capable of evaluating it is a widespread phenomenon, not one isolated to a North of England mortgage originator.

Consider that Deutsche Bank generates almost 80 per cent of its income from non-interest sources, compared with a figure of 49 per cent 12 years ago. Our meeting note from the October 2006 Deutsche Bank annual investor day recorded the opinion that "any blow up in CDOs, securitization, distributed debt (the areas where they claim to have a competitive advantage) is likely to be extremely damaging from a credit and ongoing fee generation perspective, since the bank appears to be positioned as the scrum half in the pass-the-hospital-pass game of modern debt markets."

What did strike us in our meetings with Northern Rock was how atypical the young, shaven-headed CEO [Adam Applegarth] was compared with one's image of a traditional banker. After a one-on-one meeting, the writer of our meeting note mused that the "main fear is that he is a

Illustration 4.1   Northern Rock headquarters
Source: Getty Images International.

bit too clever by half." The alarm bells might also have been set off had we seen plans of the company's new £35m head office. Perhaps a photograph of every company's HQ should be studied before making an investment to see how it compares with the high-water mark set by Tesco's shabby HQ in suburban Cheshunt, England. One could also point to what are nowadays politely described as governance issues – for example, the fact that the chairman of Northern Rock is best known as writer of popular science books.

With hindsight, the extreme dependence on a fickle source of funding and lack of business diversification made Northern Rock vulnerable to the new scenario which played out in August 2007. There are a number of financial institutions which have stayed on the sidelines during the period of credit excess and now stand to benefit from current market conditions. This is particularly true for European regional retail banks, like Svenska Handelsbanken, which has been losing market share in corporate lending. Other possible winners are companies whose business models in some way resemble that of Northern Rock and are currently being unfairly marked down by association. An example of this, in our view, is Provident Financial, the dominant player in the UK home credit market. The company is tainted in the first instance with the subprime moniker and by virtue of the fact that its funding profile is relatively short duration. The reality is of a reverse carry trade, in the sense that Provident's lending profile is very short-term compared with its borrowing profile, the exact opposite of the Northern Rock case.[14]

While there are some individual instances worthy of attention, our overall sense is that underweighting of the financial sector is the correct position to maintain at this point in time. A number of commentators have drawn the distinction between liquidity risk (lack of wholesale funding) and solvency or the credit quality of the underlying collateral (whether the mortgage is ever repaid). The current crisis is limited to liquidity risk, so the argument goes, and one has nothing to fear regarding the asset side of banks' balance sheets. Yet the correlation between ever more abundant liquidity and asset price appreciation over the past decade suggests to us that asset prices are vulnerable in the absence of generous support from lenders. From this perspective, it is better to wait for the rise in non-performing loans and asset write-downs, before raising our exposure.

---

[14] From September 2007 to December 2014, Provident Financial's share price rose by 109 per cent in US dollars, while the MSCI Europe Banks Index declined by 64 per cent.

4.10   SEVEN DEADLY SINS (NOVEMBER 2009)

How a Swedish bank sailed through the financial crisis unscathed

"Money, money, money, must be funny, in the rich man's world," chanted Abba. Besides this famous band, Sweden has given the world that deadly combination – dynamite and the safety match. Sweden even managed to detonate its own banking system in the early 1990s. One large European financial institution, however, which didn't blow up during the Global Financial Crisis is Svenska Handelsbanken, Sweden's largest bank and a long-term Marathon holding. Over the years we have gotten to know the bank quite well. Our meetings with management have often provided timely insights into the folly of their European banking competitors. A recently published book about the bank, entitled *A Blueprint for Better Banking,* by Niels Kroner, describes the history and culture of the bank and, as the title suggests, argues that many of the recent problems of the financial system could have been avoided if other banks were run in the "Handelsbanken way."

Handelsbanken is a very conservatively run, branch-based retail bank which was the only major Swedish bank not to break in the Nordic banking crisis of the early 1990s. This time around, Handelsbanken has pulled through yet again, avoiding the need to raise fresh capital or receive government support. That puts it on a short list of only three major European banks. Handelsbanken's decentralised business model encourages branch managers to make loans based on local, face-to-face knowledge of customers rather than relying on centralised credit scoring techniques, as their competitors do. The bank consistently has the best customer service ratings in the industry and the lowest costs (as demonstrated by a low cost to income ratio compared with other banks). A few years ago, we asked management why (as we had been told) there were holes in the carpets at many of its branches. "Carpets don't make money," was the reply.

Having avoided the disasters of its peers, since the beginning of 2007 Handelsbanken shares have outperformed those of all other major European banks. According to Niels Kroner, Handelsbanken has succeeded by not committing what he calls the *Seven Deadly Sins of Banking.* These are as follows:

First deadly sin: Imprudent asset-liability mismatches on the balance sheet

Obviously there are many cases around the world of how borrowing short and lending long can go wrong for banks. Recent examples in Europe include Northern Rock in the UK and the Irish banks. During the boom years, the Irish banks financed household mortgages that had a contractual maturity of two decades or more, with commercial paper of less than one year's duration. Handelsbanken is acutely conscious of the risks posed by asset-liability mismatches. The bank uses a central treasury function to match and price deposits and loans according to their respective maturities. In this way, branches cannot report a profit by simply engaging in maturity transformation.

Second deadly sin: Supporting asset-liability mismatches by clients

The classic example here is foreign currency lending to households in Central European countries. Not long ago, European banks were providing low interest euro and Swiss franc mortgages to Hungarian and Latvian consumers. It was unlikely these customers understood the foreign exchange risk they were running. Handelsbanken does not engage in such lending, mainly because the primary incentive of the branch managers is to eliminate default risk. The worst thing a branch manager can do is to run up bad loans. Internally, branches are ranked on this measure to shame the underperformers.

Third deadly sin: Lending to "Can't Pay, Won't Pay" types

Here one immediately thinks of banks lending to subprime borrowers and private equity firms. Handelsbanken's approach is rather to "lend to people with money." Theirs is a niche lending approach rather than a mass market one. In company research meetings over the years, Handelsbanken told us that the banking industry had become obsessed with earning a few extra basis points of spread each quarter, while losing sight of credit risk, namely the chance that borrowers might never be in a position to repay the principal.

Fourth deadly sin: Reaching for growth in unfamiliar areas

A number of European banks have lost billions investing in US subprime CDOs (UBS has blown some $40bn in this manner), having foolishly relied on "experts" who told them that these were riskless AAA rated credits, i.e., they outsourced the underwriting decision. In Scandinavia, many banks pursued growth in the Baltic states and have suffered as GDP in the region has contracted by 15–20 per cent this year (house prices in Latvia are now down 70 per cent from the peak). Handelsbanken's approach to foreign expansion, by contrast, has always been one of cautious "organic incrementalism," as they describe it. The bank largely eschewed the Baltic states as too risky. Instead, Handelsbanken expanded its branch network in a number of mature Western European markets – including UK, Germany, and Norway – where it has been easy to recruit good branch managers among those who have grown disillusioned with the centralising tendencies at their old banks.

In the UK, Handelsbanken hired local branch managers who brought with them their best clients and most highly regarded colleagues.

Fifth deadly sin: Engaging in off-balance sheet lending

Recent examples of the cardinal banking sin of off-balance sheet lending include the use of conduits and SIVs by European banks. By contrast, Handelsbanken's approach is to accept only risks which it is prepared to hold on its balance sheet until maturity and not to lend money to those that are in the business of lending money themselves. Incidentally this principle also restrained the bank from engaging in pass-the-parcel securitization schemes which have had such a damaging effect on underwriting standards across the European banking system.

Sixth deadly sin: Getting sucked into virtuous/vicious cycle dynamics

The sixth deadly sin is to be seduced by what might be termed Ponzi economics. Lending by Scandinavian banks in the Baltic states seemed like a good idea for a long time partly because GDP was growing rapidly. The strong economic growth, however, was a function of rapidly growing credit supplied by the banks themselves. The fact that every bank was lending in the same market made it feel safe, and for a while the virtuous cycle continued. Real estate markets around the world were similarly characterised by the notion that asset quality was independent of credit conditions. Handelsbanken prides itself on its contrarian streak. It is less prone to high level "strategic" moves (which normally entail engaging in happy groupthink) because of its reliance on the branch network. The branches have a fairly consistent risk appetite through the cycle and so tend to lose market share in frothy times (e.g., during the 2006–08 period) and gain share when others are unwilling or unable to lend.

Seventh deadly sin: Relying on the rearview mirror

A recent expression of this common financial vice includes the widespread use of value-at-risk models. Such models tend to be based on a limited amount of historic data, which in the years before the crisis were relatively benign. True risk was understated. In its 2007 annual report, Merrill Lynch reported a total risk exposure – based on "a 95 per cent confidence interval and a one day holding period" – of $157m. A year later, the Thundering Herd stumbled into a $30bn loss! After house prices have risen by 85 per cent in ten years, as they had in the United States, was it realistic to expect a maximum decline of 13.4 per cent (Freddie Mac's worst case scenario)? Handelsbanken determined its capital requirements based on more pessimistic crisis scenarios, such as a repeat of the Swedish banking crisis.

There are many other ways in which Handelsbanken is different from its peers. In its dialogue with investors, bank representatives refuse to engage in the game of trying to estimate this year's profit number. They have no other choice, since divisional budgets were abolished in 1972. If managers have budget targets, so the thinking goes, it becomes more difficult to stay out of the market when pricing is unfavourable.

Management incentives are also unusual. The bank funds an employee profit-sharing scheme called the Oktogonen Foundation, which receives allocations when the group's return on equity exceeds the weighted average of a group of other Nordic and British banks. If this criterion is satisfied, and it usually is, except at the peak of the cycle, one-third of the extra profits can be allocated to Oktogonen subject to a limit of 15 per cent of the dividend to shareholders. If the Handelsbanken lowers the dividend paid out to its shareholders, no allocation is made to the profit-sharing foundation.

The foundation channels a large part of its resources into Handelsbanken stock and currently holds 11 per cent of the bank's equity. All employees receive an equal part of the allocated amount (without the traditional skew towards the upper echelons), and the scheme includes all staff in the Nordic countries and, since 2004, in Great Britain. Disbursements are only made once a member of staff has reached the age of 60. Employees who have been working for Handelsbanken since 1973 have around $600,000 – which turns out to be roughly half the value of a Nobel prize – due to them at retirement, regardless of whether they have worked as the CEO or as a security guard. The system undoubtedly contributes to the bank's tribal culture and aligns employee interests with shareholders.

Ultimately, Handelsbanken is a wonderful example of a bank with a strong culture and management team that allocates capital in an intelligent way, with the right incentives and a long-term approach. All of these qualities appeal to Marathon's investment philosophy. The valuation remains attractive, trading at 1.4 times book value, a P/E of 14 times and a dividend yield of 3 per cent. If only more banks were built this way.[15]

---

[15] Handelsbanken's share price rose by 87 per cent in SEK from the date of this article to 31 December 2014.

5

THE LIVING DEAD

Capital cycle analysis is strongly influenced by J.A. Schumpeter's notion of creative destruction, namely that competition and innovation produce a constantly evolving economy and spur improvements in productivity. From this perspective, an economic recession serves a useful function as – to use a rather hackneyed image – the forest fire burns away the dead wood and weaker trees, allowing healthy young plants to grow and prosper.

The decline in equity prices following the global financial crisis presented a variety of investment opportunities. Some of the best appeared in industries where capital was rapidly withdrawn after the bust and consolidation took place. The experience of Ireland's banking sector described below is a good example of the capital cycle moving into a benign phase. It has not been all good news, unfortunately. Several of the pieces in this chapter comment on how European policymakers have prevented various industries – in particular the employment-heavy auto sector and the politically sensitive Continental banking sector – from consolidating. As a result, the operation of the capital cycle has been arrested. This is bad news for investors as the problems of excess capacity and weak profitability have not been addressed. It also augurs ill for the eurozone economy, which appears doomed to low productivity and weak economic growth. These problems have been exacerbated by the post-crisis policy of ultra-low interest rates which, by lowering funding costs, have allowed weak businesses – the corporate zombies – to continue limping along.

5.1   RIGHT TO BUY (NOVEMBER 2008)

Now that signs of speculative excess have been dispelled, the markets look attractive again

The stock market is in a very different place than it was back in May 2006 [see "Blowing bubbles"], when we observed clear signs of excess. Most of the bubble indicators we pointed to then have now turned positive. In addition, market valuations suggest that equities are very attractively priced for long-term investors.

The inversion of the earlier bubble signs include:

1. *Commodity price declines*: Commodity prices have witnessed a dramatic decline which will have beneficial effects on inflation. At the company level, commodity-related firms are rapidly shelving plans to expand capacity. For instance, ArcelorMittal has announced significant cuts in output with the aim of stabilising steel prices as demand evaporates.

2. *Private equity valuations collapse*: During the boom period, Apollo, KKR and Blackstone all took advantage of record valuation levels to launch their own private equity IPOs. How the mighty titans of finance have fallen! Blackstone shares are down 81 per cent from the June 2007 IPO. KKR Private Equity Investors is down around 90 per cent since listing in April 2006, in line with the Apollo fund (AP Alternative Assets LP has declined 86 per cent since May 2006). The Lehman Private Equity Fund, which listed in July 2007, has fallen by 80 per cent.

3. *Private equity losses*: Back in May 2006, we questioned the wisdom of Blackstone's purchase of a 4.5 per cent stake in Deutsche Telekom. That stake is now registering a loss of around 20 per cent on the purchase price (excluding any magnifying effect of leverage). The collapse of Washington Mutual cost the TPG buyout group some $7bn in just over five months (of which the TPG fund itself lost $1.2bn).

4. *Sunken flotations*: Activity in the IPO market has sunk to multiyear lows, although there has been significant distressed capital issuance, most notably from the financial sector. Flotations which epitomised the late market excesses have been particularly hard hit: Partners Group, a Swiss-listed fund of funds group, has fallen by 60 per cent since its peak, while Charlemagne Capital, an emerging market manager, is down 89 per cent.

5. *M&A doldrums:* M&A behaviour was another excess indicator back in the heady days of 2006, when animal spirits ran wild. We noted back then that Ferrovial's share price had actually climbed on the announcement of its leveraged bid for BAA. Ferrovial's stock has since slumped by 77 per cent, as access to credit is cut off and the true cost of overpaying for assets is revealed. A recent major reversal in the M&A world is the withdrawal of BHP Billiton's bid for Rio Tinto.

   We also complained that many mergers in 2006 produced no cost saving but rather appeared to be driven by leverage. We now note that Babcock & Brown, the Australian infrastructure company, which purchased shares in Eircom from investors, including Marathon, has put that investment up for sale less than three years after the acquisition at a minimum 40 per cent loss. Babcock & Brown's share price is down 76 per cent, as the market has lost confidence in leveraged infrastructure funds.

6. *Directors' dealings:* In the UK, insider purchases were running at less than 10 per cent of sellers in April 2006. That has now reversed dramatically. Directors' share purchases in October 2008 exceeded sales by two to one.

7. *Retail investors burnt:* Retail investors injected record sums into mutual funds in 2005 and 2006, with a bias towards emerging market funds. Emerging markets have not "decoupled" and are now 63 per cent lower than the October 2007 peak. Once bitten, twice shy. On the retail side, there is a record $4tn reportedly parked in money market funds.

Aside from the disappearance of earlier signs of market excess, market valuations are now compelling. For the first time in 50 years, the yield on US Treasuries has fallen below the dividend yield of the S&P 500. The price of European equities relative to their ten-year average earnings (a measure known as the Graham and Dodd or Shiller P/E ratio) is close to a long-term trough. Market liquidity has evaporated. There is a significant shortage of buyers (aside from insider buying). Hedge funds face redemptions amounting to perhaps one-third of their total assets. In anticipation, many hedge funds have been selling assets to raise liquidity. At the corporate level, share buybacks, which were running at record levels in 2007, have virtually ceased. Even companies with apparently sound balance sheets are suspending their programmes, due to the difficulty of accessing funds from banks and the closure of the debt markets.

Markets are now restrained by fear and conservatism. Tight liquidity is producing great pricing anomalies. Although the macroeconomic outlook is bleak, this is clearly discounted in equity prices and there would have to be a significant shock to jolt markets further. There have not been such compelling valuations for equities in a generation. From such a low base, it is difficult to believe that investors will not make good returns over any reasonable investment time frame.[1]

5.2 SPANISH DECONSTRUCTION (NOVEMBER 2010)

Now that the empire-building antics of Spanish construction firms are over, investment opportunities are appearing

Arriving at Terminal 4 of the Madrid-Barajas airport, a one-kilometre-long building with a bamboo-lined gull wing roof and floors of limestone, one gets one's first view of the infrastructure boom enjoyed by Spanish construction companies during the "magical years" of economic growth. Finally completed by Ferrovial in 2006, the terminal cost of €6.1bn was €2bn over budget. The design team of Antonio Lamela and Richard Rogers spared no expense, their stylish touches putting in mind the adage about the quality of airport buildings being inversely proportional to the economic development of a country.

The boom in expensive civil works has now ended. The Spanish government has finally yielded to pressure to make cuts in its infrastructure budget. European Union funding has more or less dried up. Most of the construction firms had foreseen the domestic slowdown and had spent a number of years diversifying their activities and expanding abroad. Unfortunately, the results have been woeful for investors. Share prices in the sector remain depressed – in some cases, over 80 per cent below the peak levels. As deep pessimism about all things Spanish now prevails, could there be some value in the rubble from Spain's construction bubble?

Fomento de Construcciones y Contratas (FCC) was one of the first companies to diversify by assembling a large portfolio of street-cleaning contracts. Others followed in more capital-intensive service activities, such as car parks, water treatment and baggage handling. A number of companies built up significant toll road businesses around the world (OHL, Ferrovial, and FCC). Others invested in renewable energy (Acciona, ACS, and Abengoa). Instead of selling the energy assets at completion, however, the construction

---

[1] The stock market continued falling until March 2009, bottoming out around 20 per cent lower than at the end of November 2008. By the end of 2014, however, the S&P 500 was roughly 136 per cent higher than at the time of writing. A case of short-term pains, long-term gains.

firms chose to operate them. They funded this activity largely through debt. In fact, during the boom years, Spain's construction companies became a funding source for the government to build roads, airports and energy infrastructure. They began to resemble banks, just at the time when Spanish banks, with their expanding mortgage books and increasing exposure to property developers, were looking more like property companies.

The ease with which projects could be funded encouraged many construction companies to make overpriced acquisitions. The Spanish government encouraged the folly by allowing firms to deduct goodwill amortization from their taxable profits. A number of firms made spectacularly bad acquisitions at the top of the cycle, including Ferrovial's £10.5bn acquisition of BAA, owner of London's Heathrow airport, at a price of 1.3 times the regulated asset base. Ferrovial today still has debt of €19.5bn, 70 per cent of which relates to BAA, and the company's share price trades 41 per cent below its peak. Acciona, a Marathon portfolio holding, entered the bidding war for Endesa, Spain's largest electricity generator, acquiring a 25 per cent stake and increasing its debt burden from €8.9bn to €18bn. Fortunately, it was able to sell the stake to Enel for a healthy profit, with part of the consideration in the form of Endesa renewable assets. Acciona's share price is nevertheless down by 78 per cent from the peak.

As they diversified and expanded, Spain's construction companies accumulated vast quantities of debt, justified on the basis that the companies and concessions being acquired were stable enough to bear massive leverage. While this may have been true in the early stages of the cycle, such was the combination of debt and lofty valuations in later deals that only a small decline in operating performance had catastrophic consequences for the equity position. When the global financial crisis struck, the construction companies' projections for steadily increasing toll and airport passenger traffic looked optimistic. In some cases, the regulatory environment became distinctly less benign: Ferrovial, acquirer of BAA, was forced to sell Gatwick airport at the market trough, due to competition concerns.

Other acquisitions were of a more cyclical nature and have suffered accordingly. Here, the booby prize is hotly contested. FCC's €1.09bn purchase of a majority stake in Barcelona cement company Uniland, increasing its exposure to cement in Spain shortly before the implosion of the property market, looks hard to beat. FCC's share price has declined by 78 per cent from the peak in 2007. Sacyr Vallehermoso upped its bet on Spanish property rather late in the day and then sought to diversify into concessions and services, with its Itinere subsidiary making ludicrous bids at the wrong time in the cycle. Its share price is down by 91 per cent.

Now that these empire-building antics are well and truly over, the main objective of most Spanish construction companies is to deleverage their balance sheets. So far, some have been more successful than others. Ferrovial has reduced its parent company debts (i.e., those debts which are non-recourse) from €3bn to virtually zero via the sale of toll roads, car parks and airport activities. These disposals have been achieved at prices comparable with market valuations in June 2007, although one should probably not take this to mean that retained assets are also worth peak levels, given that a certain amount of cherry-picking of the most saleable assets has taken place. Others have been slow to make disposals, hoping perhaps that an economic recovery will improve their chances of getting a more reasonable sale price. Since management change has not been a big theme at these often family-controlled companies, one suspects that there is an element of denial at work. After all, crystallising losses is an admission of failure which is easier to achieve if the architects of failure are no longer in their posts.

From an investment perspective, the sector now warrants close scrutiny. Take the case of Acciona. The company has nearly €8bn of debt, of which just over half is non-recourse, being tied to wind energy projects. In total, Acciona has 8,000 MW of installed renewable capacity. Management believes that this is worth between €1.5m and €1.8m per MW, implying a value for this business of €12bn to €14bn. Not only does this comfortably exceed Acciona's debt level, but it is also significantly above the company's enterprise value of €11.4bn. If this figure is correct, then the rest of the group's portfolio – including the core construction business; a Mediterranean ferry operation thought to be worth up to €650m; motorway and other concessions with invested capital of €1.3bn; a water treatment business; and a fund management company with €5bn of funds under management – has a negative market valuation.

Despite this apparent wealth of assets, the company is not without issues. It has some €800m tied up in Spanish land for development, which is probably unsellable in the current property environment. There is also the thorny problem of €1.5bn of Endesa-related debt needing to be refinanced in the short-term, which is likely to prove expensive in the current febrile climate. Still, Spain's real estate collapse appears to have created a significant investment opportunity. Taking a three- to five-year view, the likelihood is that Acciona and other Spanish construction firms will be able to work through their current difficulties, implying attractive valuation upside.[2]

---

[2] From the time of writing to 31 December 2014, Acciona shares rose by 4.5 per cent in US dollars, underperforming the MSCI Europe Index. The company was negatively affected

5.3 PIIGS CAN FLY (NOVEMBER 2011)

In the wake of the financial crisis, the capital cycle has entered a positive phase for certain Irish businesses

Marathon recently received a phone call from a Dublin-based broker, seeking feedback on behalf of Irish corporate clients as to whether we believed that being listed in Ireland was depressing the valuation of certain companies and, if so, whether they should relocate to bump up their rating. Shortly after this conversation, Ireland's largest public company, the building materials supplier CRH, announced that it was moving its primary listing to London. This move was ostensibly for liquidity reasons – the shares already traded over half their volume on the LSE – but one suspects that they also wanted to remove the "Irish discount" being applied to a business which generated only a small proportion of its sales in the Emerald Isle.

For many investors, Ireland has become a no-go. In the fixed income world, we are told, managers are having their investment guidelines redrawn by clients to prevent them investing in "peripheral" (PIIGS being too politically incorrect) Europe. Capital flight from Ireland, whether semi-symbolic in the case of CRH or even actual in the case of some fixed income investor mandates, is interesting in the context of two of our more recent European investments, Bank of Ireland and Irish Continental Group. It would take a name change for these companies to hide their Celtic origins.

Marathon was always very suspicious of the property-fuelled Irish economic boom, in particular the incredible growth of that aggressive corporate and property development lender Anglo Irish [see above]. Anglo prided itself on its high margin, mostly wholesale-funded, lending model and its close relationships with key property developers. The buoyant market conditions also benefited the two largest Irish lenders, Bank of Ireland and Allied Irish, which traditionally had pursued a more conservative approach than the young upstart but found themselves tempted into riskier lending as the cycle progressed. In his entertaining book, *Anglo Republic: Inside The Bank that Broke Ireland*, journalist Simon Carswell describes how the two Irish banking majors initially ignored the competition, but once Anglo had got beyond nuisance value, sometime around the turn of the century, they established "win back" teams for key accounts. In retrospect, this was at exactly the moment when the banks should have been ratcheting down their Irish property exposure.

---

by changes to Spain's wind farm subsidy regime. The position was sold in 2015. Marathon would have been better off investing in Ferrovial whose shares rose by 108 per cent in US dollars from the date of this article to the end of 2014.

The strong demand for credit also attracted foreign lenders, notably RBS, through its Ulster Bank subsidiary, and HBOS (now owned by Lloyds), whose Irish business Bank of Scotland Ireland (BOSI) really took off in earnest after the acquisition of a state-owned lender in 2000. The last to the party was Danske Bank, which in late 2004 acquired the Irish operations of National Australia Bank, and proceeded to triple the loan book over the following three years. So at the peak of the cycle, six players each had a market share of around 10 per cent share, with Danske playing catch up.

Since those giddy days, the Irish property bubble has collapsed, taking down the economy with it. The situation in Ireland's credit markets could scarcely be more different. After heavy losses, foreign banks have lost their appetite for lending in Ireland, with Danske shuttering half its Irish branches and Lloyds putting BOSI – which has written down an incredible 32 per cent of its loan book – into run-off mode. The domestic banks have not fared much better – Anglo Irish is also in run-off after 50 per cent of its loan book was written off. Allied Irish has been all but nationalised, as the government now owns a 99 per cent shareholding.

That leaves Bank of Ireland, where large losses also obliged the Irish state to come to the rescue. Following a capital-raising last summer, in which a group of foreign investors (including Fairfax Financial and Wilbur Ross) acquired a 35 per cent holding, the government's stake is down to 15 per cent. Marathon also participated in the share issue, since it seemed to us that the depressed state of Irish banking had the makings for a decent capital cycle upturn.

It is not yet clear what the competitive landscape will look like once the dust has settled, but it certainly will not be anything like the situation before

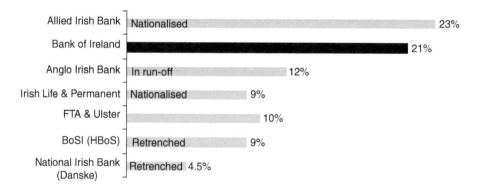

Chart 5.1   Irish bank's lending share (October 2011)

Source: Central Bank of Ireland.

the crisis. The Irish government plans to run with a "two-pillar" bank system, one of these pillars being Bank of Ireland and the other Allied Irish, now merged with the EBS building society. The state-controlled Irish bad bank (NAMA) has taken many of the problem development loans off the banks' balance sheets, leaving Bank of Ireland with a loan book of some €107bn, of which just over half are mortgage loans in the UK and Ireland, with most of the rest non-property related SME and corporate lending. Unlike with most other European banks, the loan book has been independently stress-tested under tough conditions to ensure that it has sufficient capital. Bank of Ireland now boasts a core Tier 1 ratio of 15 per cent, which is among the highest in Europe.

In the short-term, the outlook for the Irish economy remains difficult. House prices are still falling, although at a much reduced rate, unemployment remains high, and consumer confidence is weak. Further out, however, it seems reasonable to assume that the pricing power afforded to Bank of Ireland as the dominant institution in a far less competitive banking system should enable it once again to earn a double-digit return on equity. That makes the current valuation of less than 0.4 times book value appear very attractive.

The situation at Irish Continental Group (ICG) is similar from a capital cycle perspective. This firm operates as Irish Ferries between Holyhead–Dublin and Pembroke–Rosslare, the shortest sea routes between Ireland and the UK. The crossing is quick enough for the operator to be able to offer a daytime return service for passengers and a nighttime one for freight to maximize the utilisation of the ships. The only other competitor on these routes is the privately owned Stena Line, as capacity constraints at the harbours mean that there is no room for a third operator. Despite the disadvantages of long-sea routes, the expansion in Irish trade over the last couple of decades encouraged additional capacity on the freight side, in particular, with the likes of P&O and the Danish conglomerate AP Moeller/Maersk (what is it about the Danes and Ireland?) among those adding long-sea capacity in freight. Following the downturn in the Irish economy, freight volumes dropped 4 per cent in 2008 and a further 14 per cent in 2009. Capacity on these longer routes which use more fuel and attract less premium freight has shrunk in response to losses.

The downturn has also affected ICG, with freight roughly halving from a peak of 55 per cent of ferry revenues in 2007. Still, the company's outsourced crewing arrangements give it a lower cost base, and volumes may be boosted as some of the loss-making ferry capacity is taken out and Ireland's export-led economy begins to grow again. On the passenger side, where 60 per cent of the car traffic comes from UK passengers visiting Ireland, ICG saw only a small reduction in volumes last year, offset by higher yields. They should benefit from Ireland's newfound competitiveness as a tourist destination (there is plenty of oversupply in the hotel market), as well as from a reduction in airline capacity: both Ryanair and Aer Lingus have scaled back capacity growth plans.

ICG's current fleet does not need renewing for another five to ten years, so any pick-up in activity should flow straight through to cash flow. In the meantime, ICG's valuation looks extremely attractive, given its free cash flow yield of 10 per cent, while the chief executive's 16 per cent stake in the business aligns the interests of management with shareholders. Roll on Ireland.[3]

5.4   BROKEN BANKS (SEPTEMBER 2012)

The necessary cleansing process for the European banking sector is being thwarted by politicians

Marathon looks to invest in sectors where competition is declining and capital has been withdrawn, and where depressed investor expectations produce attractive valuations. At first glance, the European banking sector would appear to fit the bill. Competition and capital are seemingly in retreat, and credit is being repriced. Investors have been put off by impenetrable balance sheets and by the complexity of new banking regulations (Basel III runs to thousands of pages). Then there's sovereign default risk to worry about. European banks are trading at a discount to tangible book, making them considerably cheaper than their US counterparts. Yet from a capital cycle perspective, the investment case for European banks is not clear-cut.

First, take the question of whether capital is really in retreat. During the boom years, banks gorged on cheap capital to fund asset growth. Since 1998, eurozone bank assets relative to GDP have climbed from 2.2 times to 3.5 times (by the first quarter 2012). European bank assets have always been higher than in the US, since mortgages are generally kept on their balance sheets and European companies have limited access to the corporate bond market. Yet despite all recent talk of deleveraging, the ratio of bank assets to GDP hasn't fallen. This is thanks largely to life support

---

[3] From the date of this article to the end of 2014, the share prices of the Bank of Ireland and Irish Continental Group increased by 203 per cent and by 106 per cent respectively in US dollars.

from the official sector, notably the European Central Bank. In fact, in the 12 months to 31 July 2012, eurozone banks actually increased their assets by €34bn. In short, European banks have accumulated a huge mountain of debt, and so far little has been done to reduce it.

The banks are also short of capital. So far, banks have engaged in some of the easier deleveraging, withdrawing capital from abroad and retreating to home markets. As senior unsecured debt funding has diminished, so ECB short-term funding has taken its place. This form of funding, along with covered bonds, consumes a large amount of collateral. To attract new, senior unsecured funding (a requirement of Basel III), European banks will need to have more equity capital. McKinsey has estimated they will need to raise €1.1tn by 2021 to meet all the new regulatory requirements. One of the lessons from (bitter) experience of investing in banks in the US and UK is that when something as fundamental as the ultimate share count remains uncertain, the investment outcome is unpredictable.

Another contributor to improved returns in bombed-out industries is consolidation, either through mergers & acquisitions, or through the failure of weak firms. Outside of Spain and Ireland, however, the Continental European banking sector seems incapable of rationalising. One story illustrates this point. After the rogue trader, Jérôme Kerviel, lost Société Générale some €4.9bn in 2008, the incumbent French finance minister, Christine Lagarde, was asked whether SocGen could now become a takeover target. She responded simply, "Ce n'est pas possible." This attitude is symptomatic of the unwillingness of Europe's national authorities to allow takeovers of the weak by the strong, especially if the latter are foreign. Many markets remain plagued by excessive numbers of banks – there are over 6,800 banks in Europe – and anachronistic structures. Even in Germany, that paragon of economic virtue, the banking landscape is littered with hundreds of unlisted local cooperative banks, savings banks (Sparkassen) and wholesale Landesbanken. As a result of this fragmentation, the German banking system generates little by way of profits.

In essence, the capital cycle is not working in the banking sector in Europe, because the creative destruction that is required is politically unacceptable. Under the cover that the banks face liquidity problems and not a solvency crisis, eurozone governments are propping up their banks and are likely to continue doing so for years to come. For investors in banks with stronger balance sheets, returns are likely to be restrained by weak lending growth and excessive competition. Schizophrenic policymakers, who on the one hand exhort banks to lend more and on the other hand restrict lending capacity via onerous capital and liquidity requirements, make matters even worse. The threat of abrupt deleveraging in Europe has been replaced by the prospect of many years of slow and painful adjustment.[4]

5.5   TWILIGHT ZONE (NOVEMBER 2012)

Low interest rates are slowing the process of creative destruction
Media coverage of the European economy remains trapped in the horror genre, as fatigue over the long-running euro crisis has given way to an equally depressing sequel about lost decades and Japan-style ossification. Such reports are not limited to the eurozone periphery. News that 10 per cent of British businesses are "zombies," kept alive by ultra-loose monetary policy and the reluctance of lenders to write off bad loans, coincided with a report from the Bank of England suggesting that 5–7 per cent of outstanding mortgage debt was in various forms of forbearance. One of the striking takeaways of our conversations with European business managers in recent years is that excess capacity built up during the credit boom has yet to be purged to a significant extent. This is particularly apparent in the more capital-intensive and cyclical industries.

When credit was cheap and animal spirits ebullient, the desire to press "go" on new capital projects was hard to resist, particularly when peers were engaged in the same race and the stock market was rewarding growth. Unfortunately, such "malinvestments" as were made during boom times have proved hard to eradicate in a period when interest rates have remained low, banks have been reluctant to call in bad debts to avoid losses, and politicians across the eurozone have done their utmost to prevent unemployment moving even higher.

The poster child of this failure is the European auto industry, which appears incapable of reducing its capacity despite weak demand and dwindling exports to emerging markets (which have been busy boosting their own car production). The low equity market valuations of French car makers – Peugeot trades at a tenth of book value – have limited appeal in the light of political resistance to plant closures. Nor can the European automakers resist new investment. Volkswagen has recently announced it will spend €50bn over the next three years on capex! Given the limited options available, it is hardly surprising that auto managers resort to price cuts aimed at raising capacity utilisation at the expense of profitability.

---

[4] The MSCI Europe Bank Index underperformed its US counterpart by 20 percentage points from the date of this article to the end of December 2014.

The situation in the European steel industry mirrors that of automakers. Demand for steel in Europe remains 20 per cent below the (inflated) peak, and a trade body estimates surplus capacity at 30–40m tonnes, enough to make 25 million cars a year or nearly twice current European auto demand. ArcelorMittal, in which Marathon has an investment, described to us how ten of its 32 European blast furnaces are temporarily shut, with staff under contract but working shorter hours. Attempts to close two further blast furnaces at its French site in Florange, with the loss of 629 workers (3 per cent of the company's French workforce), have been met with a threat from the left-wing industry minister of expulsion from the country due to the company's failure to "respect France," as reported by the *Financial Times*. Arnaud Montebourg, the anti-globalization industry minister, has also accused the company, one of France's largest industrial investors, of resorting to "blackmail and threats" in relation to the Florange plant, something which the company denies. With the freedom of managers to manage capacity so severely constrained, the outlook for ArcelorMittal's European business (40 per cent of the firm's total output) appears much less attractive than its operations in other parts of the world.

The problems of European auto- and steelmakers relate primarily to a fall in demand as opposed to any recent overbuilding of domestic capacity in more favourable macroeconomic conditions. Other industries have suffered from disruptive new technologies or business models which have left legacy companies struggling to cope. Flag-carrier airlines, saddled with outdated employment contracts and national champion status, have suffered greatly from the growth of unencumbered low cost carriers. The CEO of struggling SAS in Scandinavia recently bemoaned the lack of a Chapter 11 process in Europe. Perhaps he is jealous of a system which in the US has led to the anti-Darwinian outcome of the survival of the least fit!

Other European industries have built up export capacity only to find that their putative export markets have developed their own domestic supply which threatens one day to lead to imports into Europe. Here one thinks of the European paper and aluminium industries, besides the aforementioned auto sector. A recent article in the *Financial Times* described how China has gone from producing just under 3m tonnes of aluminium in 2000 to nearly 18m tonnes in 2011, or 40 per cent of world output. This has led to a surplus of 10m tonnes of aluminium stacked up in warehouses around the world, enough to make more than 150,000 Boeing 747s or 750bn soda cans.

From a capital cycle perspective, the above situations only become attractive when stock market valuations fall to a fraction of replacement cost *and* a path opens up for dealing with the excess capacity. While the first condition is close to being met in many European sectors, the prospects for the second appears dim. In previous downturns, capacity adjustment has come as a result of interest rates rising to choke off inflation, leading to widespread bankruptcies and industry consolidation. In the early 1990s, for example, our portfolios benefited from UK investments which survived the shake-out and prospered in the subsequent recovery, among them homebuilders (Taylor Woodrow), conglomerates (Trafalgar House) and advertisers (WPP).

With interest rates low and set to remain so, and banks prepared to prop up weak businesses for fear of crystallising losses, monetary policy looks very unlikely to precipitate a major reallocation of resources. Indeed, it appears designed to head-off such a denouement. Under such circumstances, supply side restructuring via industry consolidation also looks like a long-shot, especially as many European industries are already quite consolidated and face anti-trust barriers.

While the outlook from a shareholder perspective looks grim for those sectors discussed above suffering from excess capacity, the situation facing many businesses with higher returns on equity is much more promising, particularly as their valuations are tarnished by excessive Euro-pessimism. Our European portfolios have undergone a gradual shift towards higher return on equity businesses over the last ten years or so. Although valuations are at a premium to less profitable businesses, their potential to deliver shareholder value appears far more promising.

5.6   CAPITAL PUNISHMENT (MARCH 2013)

The capital cycle ceases to function properly when politicians protect underperforming industries

The credit boom created excess capacity in a wide array of global industries. If the capital cycle had been operating smoothly, the subsequent collapse in share prices and demand ought to have led to consolidation and capital withdrawal. This has not always been the case, despite notable exceptions in certain industries (e.g., US homebuilders). Errors of capital cycle analysis can lead to mistaken share purchases. Still, they help us adapt and evolve our investment discipline. With hindsight, our capital cycle approach has failed at times when we have underestimated the impact on industries of political and legal interference, disruptive technologies and globalisation.

To this list of external factors, one can add the self-inflicted wounds of mismanagement. The most common problem is the failure of capital to exit industries with unacceptably poor returns. In the latest cycle, the forces of creative destruction have been moderated by aggressive monetary easing and low interest rates. This has allowed weak firms to continue in business, servicing what are likely to prove unsustainable debt levels. This situation contrasts with the end of previous economic cycles when interest rates have risen to stave off inflationary pressures leading to mass bankruptcy. The effect has been exacerbated in a number of territories (notably Europe) by forbearance on the part of banks whose appetite for further write-downs is already constrained in an environment of rising regulatory capital requirements.

Matters tend to get worse when politicians enter the picture. Jobs in manufacturing, unlike financial services, hold a particular allure for the political classes in many developed economies. Lack of growth and over-capacity in mature industries would ordinarily require restructuring and consolidation, particularly as off-shoring is more prevalent in more basic, labour-intensive industries. Nostalgia for a past golden age of "honest" jobs and the politicians' hunger for votes fuel protectionist instincts. Nowhere is this more apparent than in Europe, where nationalistic urges are irresistible.

Managers in politically sensitive industries struggling with excess capacity can face a prisoner's dilemma. Why should a French automotive manufacturer shut capacity when the benefits accrue disproportionately to its Italian competitor? Or, the Swedish paper company draw back to the advantage of its Finnish rival? Why not wait for others to deal with the capacity problem? In the emerging markets, the identification of "strategic industries" by Chinese politicians has led to excess capacity in various sectors, as diverse as solar and wind power, stainless steel, shipbuilding and telecommunications equipment. As a result, certain markets in the developed world, where competition was seen as regional in nature, have suddenly become global. Because of the difficulty of assessing what motivates competitors under conditions of state capitalism, capital cycle analysis tends to be more effectively applied to industries which are largely domestic in nature or where the dominant players are inclined to Anglo-Saxon style capitalism (as is the case in the global beer industry).

New technologies often interfere with the smooth operation of the capital cycle. The Internet has wreaked havoc on many industries, including music, regional newspapers, book retailing and travel agencies. Marathon has suffered in a number of cases where the benefits of supply side consolidation in distressed sectors was insufficient to offset a secular decline in demand.[5] Fortunately, the capital cycle approach is well attuned to identifying superior

---

[5] An allusion to Marathon's unsuccessful investments in companies with strong incumbent positions but whose business models did not survive into the digital age. They include a

Internet business models which can sustain high returns of capital.[6] An understanding of the power of network and scale effects that protect companies from the chill winds of competition has led to successful investments in a number of Internet businesses including Amazon, Priceline and Rightmove. (Although, to date Amazon has proven better at destroying profits in other businesses than in generating any for itself.)

In recent years, capital cycle analysis has been more useful at picking stocks in companies which can maintain high returns than in finding opportunities among bombed-out industries recovering (or not) after a supply side restructuring. For the former, the investment case rests on whether competing capital can enter the sector and boost supply, eventually driving down industry returns. What we have seen in a number of cases is that dominant businesses often become more powerful when they have well managed, proprietary assets. Examples here include Nestlé, Unilever, and McDonald's. It has helped that the durable cash flows generated by such businesses have the bond-like characteristics investors crave in the current environment of low interest rates.

In short, the great strength of the capital cycle approach lies in its adaptability. The basic insight doesn't change. Namely, both high and low returns are likely to revert to the mean as valuation influences corporate behaviour and brings about shifts in the supply side. In Marathon's early years, our discipline was focused on finding stocks where the supply conditions were changing. More recently, the emphasis has shifted to identifying sectors and companies where the forces of competition are blunted and the process of mean reversion is drawn out.

5.7   LIVING DEAD (NOVEMBER 2013)

Extraordinary monetary policy should be seen as a negative rather than positive sign by investors

As 2013 draws to a close, the MSCI World Index is up over 20 per cent year-to-date and 130 per cent since March 2009. One oft-cited contributing factor to the equity market's strength is the unprecedented monetary loosening undertaken since the financial crisis struck. When it comes to quantitative easing, the markets are being moved by two sets of beliefs. Firstly, there's the view that monetary policy is going to stimulate the economy, which should

---

CD retailer (HMV), a photo equipment manufacturer (Eastman Kodak), a video rental firm (Blockbuster) and a music business (EMI).

   [6] See above, 2.4 "Digital moats."

help corporate profits. Secondly, low interest rates make equities look rela-tively more attractive than cash and fixed income. The trouble is that there is not much empirical nor theoretical support for either of these views.

The verdict has yet to be returned on what lasting impact recent extraordinary monetary measures have had on the real economy. What's clear, however, is that the recovery in developed economies has been muted. The size of the European economy remains 2 per cent below its level of 2007; Japan is a paltry 1 per cent ahead; and the US national out-put is only 6 per cent higher. Even for the outperforming US economy, this is a markedly subpar performance relative to previous recoveries (see Chart 5.2). Corporate earnings have fared little better. Profits growth during the recent recovery has lagged significantly behind past upturns. Global earnings have not grown in nearly three years – and are still below their 2007 peak.

High levels of indebtedness in both the private and public sector are partly to blame for the weak economies and lacklustre earnings growth. Households are less likely to borrow when their stock of debt is elevated. Under such circumstances, even an extended period of very low interest rates and an increasing monetary base cannot stimulate private loan growth, the broader money supply or inflation. Central banks find themselves push-ing on Keynes's famous piece of string. Despite ultra-low interest rates with

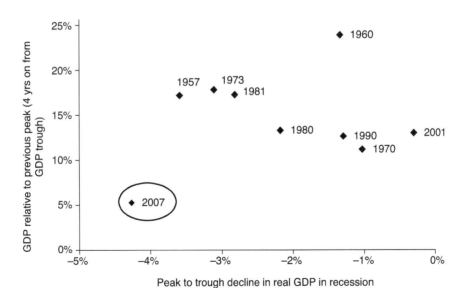

Chart 5.2   US GDP recoveries after recessions

Source: Credit Suisse.

lashings of quantitative easing, since 2009, US private sector leverage has fallen from 168 per cent of GDP to 156 per cent (as of June 2013). Deleveraging has served as a drag on growth.

To some extent this headwind has been offset by larger government deficits. But public spending adds less zip to the economy (in Keynesian terminology, the multiplier is lower). Furthermore, large government borrowing can undermine public confidence. That's what happens when households, fearing that one day they will be called upon with higher taxes to bail out the public sector, restrict current spending in the face of continuing fiscal deficits (what economists call Ricardian equivalence).

While seemingly supportive of the economy in the short-term, artificially low interest rates distort incentives and hence outcomes in the economy. So-called "zombie" firms are allowed to live on, while a low cost of funding means lower hurdle rates for new investment. Over time, if capital is not flowing freely to its most productive use, aggregate returns on capital and economic growth will decline.

The Japanese experience, since the early 1990s, is worrying in this respect. After the bubble economy collapsed and the private sector went into deleveraging mode, low interest rates have prevailed. During Japan's two lost decades, returns on equity have been persistently lower than in Europe or the US – they currently average around 8 per cent compared to 12 per cent and 15 per cent respectively, albeit with lower gearing. Despite Japan introducing the world to ZIRP (the zero-interest rate policy), the country's nominal GDP per capita remains below the 1991 level. Rather like the current Western experience, the decline in private sector leverage has been replaced by rising public sector debt – which is now over 200 per cent of GDP, up from around 50 per cent in the early 1990s. Total debt, both public and private, is greater today, relative to Japan's economy, than in 1990. In short, Japan's long experiment with low rates has hardly been a positive one, with respect to either corporate profitability or the country's ability to outgrow its debt burden.

If the argument that quantitative easing benefits the economy is without much foundation, what about the notion that lower interest rates support higher equity valuations? In a world where debt yields little, equities at first glance appear relatively more attractive. In finance theory, a lower risk-free rate implies a lower cost of capital (unless the equity risk premium rises to offset this). And a lower cost of capital means a higher market P/E is justified. But it's naïve to forget the reason why interest rates are so low in the first place, namely a weak economy, high leverage and the memory of a near catastrophic financial collapse in the rearview mirror. These factors might be expected to increase investors' cost of equity assumptions warranting a lower P/E multiple.[7]

Overall, the continuation of extraordinary monetary policies should be a negative signal for equity holders. It implies that the real economy remains challenged and unable to withstand normal monetary conditions. This, in turn, suggests it is unlikely that the economy will be able to grow fast enough to reduce aggregate leverage to a more sustainable level. Furthermore, the increasing leverage of the public sector raises the risk of another debt crisis – this time a sovereign one – at some future stage. Finally, the longer interest rates remain suppressed, the greater the risk of distorted economic outcomes as falling hurdle rates for investment impact on aggregate returns on capital. The danger is clear – we face a lost decade of growth, this time in the Western world.

5.8   RELAX, MR. PIKETTY (AUGUST 2014)

Ultra-low rates are enticing investors into risky assets with the prospect of future losses

Thomas Piketty in his unlikely bestseller, *Capital in the Twenty-First Century*, opines that the growing gap between rich and poor should be closed through the imposition of a global wealth tax. The likelihood of such a coordinated assault on the rich must be slim. Nevertheless, Mr. Piketty can take heart from the recent behaviour of many investors. Their hunger for yield and accompanying disregard for safety is set to reduce wealth disparities far more effectively than any new taxes. As J.K. Galbraith posited in *The Age of Uncertainty*: "The privileged have regularly invited their own destruction with their greed."

Marathon recently hosted a meeting with a company, a constituent of the S&P 500, whose history might politely be described as chequered. The sum of its efforts over the last two decades has been a net loss. This was not the result of one exceptionally bad year. On the contrary, the business has been profitable in barely half of the last two decades. Long-term debt has quadrupled

---

[7] Whether a higher cost of capital is warranted in the post-Lehman era is moot. Still, it's clear that the dividend discount model (aka Gordon growth model) doesn't justify a higher valuation for equities in the face of low interest rates. In this model, stock prices are derived from the flow of future dividends discounted back to the present, with the discount rate largely determined by the interest rate. From the monetary policymaker's perspective, low interest rates can only be justified if growth rates are also lower. However, if earnings growth and discount rates decline in tandem, then equity valuations should be unchanged (assuming that current dividends are also unchanged).

during the last ten years. Additional funding has been provided through a steadily rising share count (at the latest reading, 70 per cent higher than a decade earlier). Last May, this perennial underperformer issued an eight-year callable bond that is currently priced to yield just 4.7 per cent to maturity, a modest 2.3 per cent premium to US Treasuries. S&P rated the issuer BB-, indicating that the company "faces major ongoing uncertainties and exposure to adverse business, financial, or economic conditions, which could lead to the obligor's inadequate capacity to meet its financial commitments."

Nor is this an isolated example. Barclays High Yield Index shows the ten-year non-investment grade spread reaching an all-time low of 2.4 per cent at the end of the last quarter. This compares with an average spread of 5.2 per cent over the past two decades, and a peak spread of nearly 19 per cent in late 2008. Spreads have been following default rates lower. Moody's calculates a trailing 12-month default rate of 2.3 per cent compared to a long-term average of 4.7 per cent.

Mr. Piketty identifies the "central contradiction of capitalism" in the fact that the average rate of return on capital has tended to exceed the pace of output growth. "Once constituted, capital reproduces itself faster than output increases." In layman's terms, the rich get richer.[8] At the time of writing, the Federal Funds Target Rate is a mere 0.25 per cent, substantially below the nominal rate of US economic growth. In order to achieve higher returns, investors must take on a variety of additional risks. Treasuries with longer maturities come with interest rate and inflation risk. By shifting from Treasuries into higher-yielding corporate bonds, investors are also assuming credit risk. These risks are not independent, as interest rates and credit spreads generally rise together.

True, investors can earn 4.7 per cent on "high yield" corporate bonds, roughly a percentage point above nominal US GDP growth, which might appear to support the French economist's argument. But this compares with an average historic yield on sub-investment grade issues of nearly 9 per cent. A return to "normal" conditions in the bond market would thus produce a capital loss in the region of 25 per cent. In the case of high inflation or particularly stressed market conditions, yields could rise to twice this level, in which case the bonds would halve in value.

---

[8] There are numerous problems with Piketty's argument. For a start, he assumes that the owners of capital reinvest their returns rather than consume them, an option which is not open everyone. Besides, as noted above (1.9 Growth paradox), earnings per share growth for the US stock market has historically lagged GDP growth (this discrepancy being even more pronounced abroad).

In addition, there are currency and liquidity risks to consider. Reports abound of investors enthusiastically leaping into the global carry trade, encouraged by new lows in foreign exchange volatility (which, as measured by JP Morgan, has been running at half the long-term average). As for liquidity, in less favourable market conditions, the actual sale price would inevitably be below those quoted. This risk may be even more acute than in the past. Owing to stricter capital regulations, investment banks have considerably reduced the scope of their market-making. According to Federal Reserve data, primary dealers hold only $5bn net in high yield bonds, less than 0.5 per cent of the total market.

The wisdom of buying non-investment grade bonds at current yields can be gauged from the zeal of the issuers. Between 2003 and 2007, US high yield bond issuance totalled between $100bn and $150bn a year. In 2013, junk bonds with a face value of more than $300bn came to market, with a further $182bn of high yield issuance during the first half of this year. Nearly half of the $2tn of debt included in Bank of America's High Yield Index has been issued in the last 18 months. Recent low volatility in the bond market has fostered a feeling of security among investors. Last June, the Bank of America's MOVE Index (a measure of Treasury option volatility) was close to record lows.

Banks have joined the party. US leveraged loan issuance, which peaked in 2007 just shy of $900bn, exceeded $1tn in 2013. According to the Bank for International Settlements (BIS), over 40 per cent of syndicated lending is now to non-investment grade borrowers, again above the 2007 peak. Bankers can also celebrate the return of the type of structured products that were so discredited during the 2008 crisis. Issuance of collateralised loan obligations (known by the acronym, CLOs) reached $82bn in 2013 and is forecast to rise above $100bn this year, beyond pre-crisis highs.

At the same time, covenants are weakening. Dealogic calculates that loans of the "cov-lite" variety – so-called because they lack the traditional covenants protecting creditors – rose 40 per cent in the year to June and now represent more than half of all lending. In another seemingly forgotten lesson from the crisis, bank loans are being purchased by mutual funds and even ETFs. According to Morningstar, bank-loan funds attracted a record $61bn in 2013. This poses the risk of future liquidity problems, as funds can be sold faster than their underlying assets are redeemed.

In a doom-laden introduction to its latest annual report, the BIS warns that "a powerful and pervasive search for yield has gathered pace." The central bankers' central bank adds further words of caution: "The benefits of unusually easy monetary policies may appear quite tangible, especially if judged by the response of financial markets; the costs, unfortunately, will become apparent only over time and with hindsight." In the US, the Federal Reserve Chair Janet Yellen recently noted that: "We're seeing a deterioration in lending standards and we are attentive to risks that can develop in this environment." The Fed offered assurance that it is working with other regulators to "enhance compliance with previous guidance on issuance, pricing and underwriting standards."

These recent developments in the credit markets should not come as a complete surprise to Dr Yellen and colleagues. After all, the Fed has driven down rates with the intention of encouraging investors to take on more risk. Yet those who embrace low yields, poor credits, thin liquidity and even currency mismatches today may discover, when market conditions deteriorate, that the modest yield pick-up proves poor compensation for future losses. Mr. Piketty can rest easy. In an age when risk-free assets yield little or nothing, the determination of the wealthy to earn somewhat more will, in due course, do more to restore equality than his proposed taxes. A free market solution to a political problem – who says capitalism is failing?

6

CHINA SYNDROME

Given the importance Marathon attaches to rational capital allocation and the need for supply-side discipline, it is not surprising that very few investments have been made in mainland Chinese equities over the years. Many of these firms are state-controlled. As a result, the efficiency of capital allocation and the interest of outside shareholders (particularly foreigners) tends to be subordinate to the state's policy objectives.

From both a top-down and bottom-up perspective, China can be understood by applying capital cycle analysis. At the macro level, the People's Republic has pushed investment (as a share of GDP) to a higher level than ever seen before, even among former Asian high-flyers, such as South Korea and Japan. The result of rising inputs has predictably been a fall in factor productivity. This longstanding problem has been exacerbated by Beijing's decision, taken in the heat of the Global Financial Crisis, to keep the economy growing by taking fixed asset investment to an even higher level. China also suffers from the ill effects of low interest rates which have resulted in the misallocation of capital, in particular among asset intensive industries. The result has been excess capacity and low returns in a number of different sectors ranging from steel manufacturing to shipbuilding.

China's combination of cheap capital, excess investment and the failure of capital to exit low return industries has rendered the Middle Kingdom something of a no-go area for capital cycle investors, such as Marathon. The same confluence of factors helps explain why shareholder returns in China have been so disappointing despite strong economic growth (although at the time of writing, the Chinese market is in a bubble, with the result that historic returns are temporarily elevated). To make matters worse, many of the Chinese companies which come to the market have dubious accounts and concocted operating histories. A number of questionable Chinese IPOs are examined critically in this chapter. Caveat investor!

To justify its underweight position, Marathon has occasionally reported on some of the more curious practices of Chinese capitalism. A selection of these essays appears here.

6.1   ORIENTAL TRICKS (FEBRUARY 2003)

Earnings manipulation around Chinese IPOs has become the norm

"My heart is filled with pride…
I long to tell you how deep my love for Wal-Mart is…"

> Excerpt from the company song at Wal-Mart's store
> in Shenzhen, China

Where once Chinese workers sang the praises of Chairman Mao, now those voices are raised to the legacy of Sam Walton. The success of Wal-Mart, one of many foreign direct investors which are seeing tangible signs of progress in their Chinese operations, and the noticeable shift in the attitude of the Chinese authorities towards the market economy, has led to almost unanimous optimism surrounding investment in China. This chorus of bullishness is, no doubt, being orchestrated by investment bankers eager to extract fees from all those China-related IPOs. For our part, we do not doubt that the Chinese are eager to consume Western goods, are open to capitalism, and are hard-working. We are also aware that the population of the People's Republic somewhat exceeds one billion souls, which makes for a potentially vast market. What is not clear to us is whether this economic miracle will benefit foreign shareholders in Chinese equities.

To date, investors in listed Chinese state-owned enterprises have fared abysmally (see Table 6.1). This table measures the performance of past equity

Table 6.1   Performance of Chinese government-sponsored equity issues (1993–2003)

All issues	
Capital raised ($bn)	38.2
Current value ($bn)	37.1
Cumulative gain (loss)	(2.9%)
Annualized gain (loss)	(0.6%)

Source: Marathon.

issues, but are future prospects any better? Despite investors' euphoria for all things Chinese, the signs are ugly. Up until now, subtle accounting nuances have been used to overstate corporate profitability and asset values for Chinese listed companies. Regulation has been slow to catch up. Far from matters improving, we have lately observed a growing impudence on the part of IPO promoters.

A particularly egregious example is the recent flotation of China Telecom, the dominant fixed-line operator, on the Hong Kong Stock Exchange. At first sight, the shares appeared cheap (with a 4 per cent dividend yield and on 8 times free cash flow). Still, China Telecom received a cool reception on its global road show, partly due to the general weakness of global stock markets. What is fascinating is the government's response to what might have turned into a high-profile flop. Overnight, the telecommunication sector regulator (government-controlled, of course) raised the cost of completing a Hong Kong-originated international telephone call by a factor of 8 times. This move alone added 12.5 per cent to China Telecom's net profit per share.

Designed to show government support for the company, this was such an obvious piece of earnings manipulation that we assumed it would mark a watershed in the relationship between the Chinese privatization programme and the foreign investment community. We plainly overestimated the backbone of our peers who, encouraged by China Tel's likely inclusion in the regional MSCI index, supported the issue to the point where it was eventually oversubscribed, helped no doubt by the eleventh-hour subscription by Hong Kong super-tycoon Li Ka-shing.

We are depressed by the thought that the institutional buyers of the China Tel IPO believe that the government's meddling with a listed company's operations will only ever be to the advantage of shareholders. This strikes us as particularly foolish, considering how Beijing made life tougher for China Mobile and Petrochina within months of their significant capital raisings. These businesses, like China Telecom, depend on government largesse to maintain their profitability. In our view, their intrinsic valuation is so uncertain that owning the shares is pure speculation.

Earnings manipulation around Chinese IPOs is the norm. Research published by Credit Suisse points out that nearly every mainland-listed company saw its return on capital peak in the year before listing. The investment bank also found that Hong Kong-listed Chinese companies saw their net income margins fall by an average of 40 per cent in the four years after listing, with returns on capital sinking in tandem. As the investment audience is obsessed with China's macroeconomic story, this analysis is likely to fall on deaf ears. A recent survey by the Hong Kong Stock Exchange shows the remarkable complacency of foreign fund managers about the quality of Chinese IPOs. The majority of respondents saw the financial performance of Chinese businesses as "acceptable or better," while only 10 per cent thought that shareholder rights were being widely abused.

While such attitudes prevail, we should expect the quality of Chinese listings to remain low, if not deteriorate. Take, for instance, the case of Sinotrans, China's largest logistics company (lacking specialist industry knowledge, we are unable to fathom what distinguishes "logistics" from trucking and warehousing). Attending the firm's recent IPO presentation, the audience of potential buyers seemed captivated by charts proudly boasting margins and returns on capital rising steadily for the past three years.

Buried deep in the IPO prospectus, however, is the story that the "company" about to be listed had been created only two weeks previously through a carve-out of assets, contracts, territories and employees from a much larger, state-owned entity. Furthermore, the prospectus reveals that almost two-thirds of Sinotrans' operating assets are to be leased from government-owned companies. How the promoters of this issue managed to unpick retrospectively the financial statements of the two entities and allocate assets, costs and revenues appropriately is anyone's guess. With such accounting leeway, one can see how easy it might be to conjure up attractive historical profits. Buyers into the IPO were also offered the carrot of an "injection" of assets from the company parent at a later date – at price that we were assured would be advantageous to minority shareholders. As with many business arrangements with the Chinese government, this injection may turn out to be more bruising than foreign investors are currently expecting.[1]

The part played by the foreign investment community in facilitating these scandalous Chinese IPOs is regrettable. Until our industry starts paying more attention to the protection of our clients' capital, the emergence of one billion consumers is unlikely to deliver a positive investment return.

---

[1] In Hong Kong dollar terms, Sinotrans generated a total return of 85 per cent between November 2003 and the end of 2014, while China Telecom climbed by 134 per cent – both underperforming the Shanghai Stock Market Composite which was up 285 per cent over the same period.

6.2   DRESSED TO IMPRESS (NOVEMBER 2003)

Investors transfixed by China's growth prospects are buying flaky businesses

Over the past year Marathon's meetings with clients and consultants have often touched on the thorny issue of our lack of exposure to Chinese equities. The issue has become topical after the recent pick-up in Chinese stocks, which has whetted the appetites of other foreign investors. Our position is that we see Chinese equities – by this we mean those readily accessed by foreign investors on the Hong Kong Stock Exchange – as unattractive and very probably in the midst of a speculative bubble.

"When the ducks quack feed them," is an old saying on Wall Street. Investment bankers have been busy dusting off plans for long-postponed Chinese listings. There are numerous tricks used by promoters to get investors to part with their money or, to be strictly accurate, with their clients' money. Some of these have become standard practice. In the case of the "carve-out," for instance, we are unable to find a 2003 vintage Chinese government-sponsored listing that did not involve a corporate entity created especially for the purposes of an IPO. The high profile, foreign industry partner is now *de rigueur*, allowing IPO buyers to dream that they are getting in at the ground floor, on similar terms to the smart money. Finally, a liberal sprinkling of government regulation and intervention is all that's needed to either goose near-term profits and generate the required headline valuation or to give buyers an unrealistic sense of the robustness of the business.

All of these ingredients have come together in the recent $600m IPO of China's leading property and casualty insurer, PICC. The PICC prospectus, unlike earlier, murkier disclosures, is very up-front with the revelation that the company has been created out of a pre-IPO carve-out. We are also told that 12 per cent of the original insurance assets and liabilities have been retained by the unlisted parent company in a classic good bank/bad bank structure (or in this case, good insurer/bad insurer). Although the "missing" insurance contracts are disclosed as loss-making (in combined ratio terms), there is no detail on the size of these losses or to what extent they were a recurring feature. Any prospective buyers, who may be worried by the sustainability of the much trumpeted five-year underwriting profit record (which places PICC ahead of insurance legends such as GEICO, Progressive and White Mountains), are assured that the offending lines of business have been discontinued. The problem is that the management team on whose watch these loss-making insurance contracts were written is still firmly at the helm.

We have been told privately by Chinese financial sector analysts that the good bank/bad bank strategy, combined with selective disclosure, is a central feature of the financial sector privatisation policy. Our view is that the recent insurance sector IPOs are an appetiser to the main course, namely the Chinese government's plans to float its large public banks. Four years ago, the largest Chinese banks burdened with bad debts of up to 40 per cent of the loan book hived off their non-performing assets into asset management companies. The fresh new face of the Chinese banking sector is the one likely to be presented to institutional investors in next year's IPOs. But as with PICC, there has been little change in senior management or in lending policies. We are concerned that unless there is a sea change in the attitude of institutional buyers, the same inadequate level of scrutiny that has been applied to PICC, in our view a highly speculative proposition, will allow the recapitalisation of the Chinese banking sector on unfavourable terms to outside investors.

The restructuring and recapitalisation of the banks, according to the stated aim of central government, will allow them to continue funding China's industrial development. Any IPO windfalls are likely to be frittered away in lending practices similar to those which led to the very bad debt problems now being resolved. The source of these problems lies in very low interest rates and the availability of cheap capital in China, which result in supply side excesses. As we observed in South East Asia prior to 1997, the "beneficiaries" of cheap and plentiful liquidity tend to be asset-heavy businesses, ranging from retail stores to basic industrials. This has not gone unnoticed in China, where policymakers are looking for the means by which growth in the classic non-productive sectors, such as property, can be reined in. Even in the productive sectors, however, Chinese listed companies are facing a deterioration in business returns, owing to the availability of very cheap capital. This is evident in China's fast-growing auto industry, where supply continues to exceed demand. Marathon's capital cycle alarm bells are ringing.

Two recent company meetings brought home to us the extent of this problem. The first was an organic agricultural firm, Chaoda (pronounced "chowder") Modern, whose business model balances low farm labourer wages against relatively high retail prices for fresh vegetables. This is fine as far as it goes, but Chaoda, encouraged by regular cash injections from the stock market, is investing heavily in 30-year agricultural land leases, paying large up-front fees to local governments. With the profitability of its core business likely to fall over time as the Chinese distribution system becomes more efficient, Chaoda is being encouraged by local governments to commit ever larger funds to this asset-heavy strategy. The result has been declining margins offset by higher volumes and lashings of capital. Were the supply of capital to dry up or its cost to rise, the impact on the value of this business would be dramatic.

In another example Comba Telecom, China's leading manufacturer of cellular network coverage equipment, has resorted to an IPO to finance growth in a business which, on the face of it, generates enough profit to fund its own expansion. The trouble is that Comba's customers aren't paying their bills on time. These customers are none other than the state-controlled publicly listed mobile telephone companies which, according to Comba's executives, prefer to spend their money on buying assets from the government. Comba is hoping to grow its market share by offering easier payment terms to one particularly tardy payer, and intends to fund this expansion with its IPO proceeds. At no point were R&D spending, marketing or distribution seen as competitive weapons in the fight for market share. In the end, the health of Comba's business boils down to how cheaply, and for how long, it can obtain new capital to finance lengthening receivables.

These recent examples from the Chinese stock market remind us of schemes which came to market at the height of the technology bubble in the late 1990s. At the time, investors were so enamoured with the undoubted potential of the Internet (now China) that they overpaid for flaky businesses with no hope of sustained profitability and whose very future, in many cases, depended on the continuation of the bubble (as they needed the stock market to raise more capital). When viewed at the corporate level, the situation in China is quite similar. The top-down picture remains very robust, which suggests this bubble has further to inflate. Our strategy is to wait for the inevitable hangover from the binge on cheap capital, then look to buy strong business franchises at reasonable prices.[2]

6.3   GAME OF LOANS (MARCH 2005)

Despite strong economic growth, Chinese equities have delivered appalling returns

The industrialisation of the People's Republic of China (PRC), which has been underway for 25 years, is probably the defining business event in the careers of most folks in the capital markets today. Yet Marathon, not normally slow

---

[2] Marathon's bearish prognostications on PICC were not borne out. From November 2003 to the end of 2014, the Chinese insurer generated a total return of 637 per cent. Comba delivered a total return of 57 per cent over the same period. By the end of 2011, Chaoda had declined by 46 per cent from its IPO price and was subsequently delisted. Chaoda eventually relisted in January 2015, after producing accounts which were qualified by the auditor on the basis that they were "unable to observe the physical counting and inspection of the Group's property, plant and equipment...." Between listings, Chaoda's revenues mysteriously declined by 84 per cent.

to venture into the unknown, has yet to make any material investments in the country. This hasn't hurt our clients, since, despite the country's rapid economic growth, China pickings for portfolio investors have been slim. A dollar invested in the Hang Seng China Enterprises Index in 1993 with dividends reinvested would now be worth 35 cents, according to the *China Economic Quarterly*. How is it that China had delivered superior economic growth with ghastly investment returns?

Government-directed economic growth, as is the case with China, is not unfamiliar to investors in Asia. In countries like Singapore, for example, the result has often been an inadequate focus on efficient capital allocation and, as a consequence, low corporate returns on assets. China's version of the Asian growth model is quite complex. Some 600 central state-owned enterprises (SOEs) work with provincial and municipal governments to pursue the national development agenda: either alone or in competition with one another, and sometimes with joint venture partners or via listed private sector subsidiaries. China's state capitalism model has two further characteristics, both of which are unique. First, the bulk of corporate capital is raised via the domestic banking system, with long experience suggesting that repayment of the loans is optional. The lifeline provided by debt forgiveness allows businesses with ultra-low returns to survive. Second, centuries of municipal and provincial rivalry stimulate copycat projects across the country. The nine hundred breweries in China are partly the result of this provincial rivalry – indeed, in some parts of the country beer is cheaper than water.

Government-sponsored debt forgiveness partly explains why China's experience with listed equity has been so unsuccessful (for outside investors, at least). Equity might seem like an ideal alternative mechanism for a country addicted to bad lending, as it is the one form of corporate liability that doesn't have to be repaid. However, while listed companies don't have to redeem their equity, they do have to fulfil their debt obligations to the capital markets. Whereas unlisted SOEs can avoid debt repayment, the listed version cannot renege on its debts and carry on as if nothing has happened. Thus, the listed subsidiaries of SOEs are caught between the requirement to meet their liabilities and poor systemic profitability. As a result, the shareholders' stake in the business gradually dwindles over time.

It might appear that there is nothing much wrong with Chinese macroeconomic performance – if its sustained record of 10 per cent economic growth is anything to go by. Yet this growth appears to be resulting from increased inputs rather than improved productivity. The inefficiency of what economists call factor-use is becoming serious. For instance, at the current rate of growth, China's power industry requires that the equivalent of the entire UK-generating capacity be installed every year. Applying ever more factors of production allows China to meet the 10 per cent economic growth target, despite declining returns on assets. If China's productivity improved, the same level of growth could be delivered with fewer resources. For example, the Tsing Tao Brewery company asserts that by shortening its production cycle, it could raise annual output by no less than 20 per cent.

More than 40 per cent of China's economy is powered by investment spending (all those power stations, for instance), a level which surpasses even the investment-driven Korean experience in the 1960s. This over-investment brings with it diminishing corporate returns. The result is a squeeze on margins. In sector after sector, cost push pressures cannot be passed on because of excess capacity or price regulation. One example is the real estate sector, where the problem of oversupply has been exacerbated by a decision in 2004 to auction all land, driving up the cost of developers' land banks.

Although China's A share market has been falling for four years, it would be brave to call a turn. Indeed, all the signs from the real economy are consistent with end-of-cycle excess. It is almost as if Chinese companies were trying to offset the effects of their profits squeeze with rapid volume growth. The political incentive to delay the end of the cycle is substantial, most notably until after the 2008 Beijing Olympics. Therefore, it is likely

Chart 6.1   China's investment share of GDP

Source: Deutsche Bank.

that the economic juggernaut will keep on motoring, whatever the cost for investors in Chinese equities.[3]

6.4   WHAT LIES BENEATH (FEBRUARY 2014)

The prospectus of a Chinese asset management company reveals troubling exposures

We have long been sceptics of China's banking system. This view appears rather commonplace nowadays, judging by the languishing valuation multiples for the "Big Four" banks. It seems likely that the very investors who are avoiding China's banks are the same ones lining up to buy shares in Cinda Asset Management, one of the country's leading distressed debt investors. They believe that Cinda is a hedge on exposure to China's precarious financial system. On closer inspection, however, this asset manager is little more than a leveraged play on China's overblown property market and overinvested coal industry, propped up by cheap short-term funding provided by the banks from which Cinda acquires its assets.

In the late 1990s, the Chinese financial system was groaning under the weight of non-performing loans (NPLs), caused by lax lending and the spillover from the Asian crisis. In order to address the issue, the government set up four asset management companies (AMCs) or "bad banks." Cinda was set up to shepherd the non-performing loans of China Construction Bank and is the first of these state-owned AMCs to come to market. Before last Christmas, Marathon was invited to attend the IPO road show for Cinda. The venue chosen to add some Old World gravitas to the proceedings was the Great Hall of the Worshipful Company of Butchers in the City of London. The event opened with a ten-minute video, complete with American voiceover in deep baritone reminiscent of a Hollywood blockbuster trailer, detailing the history of the industry and the prospects of Cinda. From time to time, the audience was treated to library footage of employees collectively high-fiving.

---

[3] From March 2004 to October 2007, the Shanghai Stock Market Composite Index generated a total return of 485 per cent, compounding at annual rate of nearly 100 per cent. After the bubble burst in late 2007, the market declined by 68 per cent. Lately, Chinese stocks have been bubbling again – in the twelve months from June 2014, the Shanghai Composite rose by over 130 per cent. Margin debt in China climbed fivefold over this period to reach $325bn by mid-2015, representing more than 6 per cent of the market's capitalisation. As China's economic growth miracle fades, Chinese equities trading on 75 times earnings appear more detached from reality than ever.

In a rare demonstration of cooperation, the regional heads from two competing investment banks took it in turn to highlight the merits of the investment on offer. Chief among these, apparently, was the opportunity for investors to gain exposure to that sexiest of investment classes, distressed assets. It was implied that a position in Cinda would put investors on the right side of the impending explosion of Chinese indebtedness. At first glance, the economics look attractive. Cinda's return on equity in 2012 was 15.8 per cent, and growth was all but assured because of its dominant position: yours today for a modest multiple of 2.4 times book value. Favourable comparisons were drawn by the bankers between Cinda and one of the most respected of distressed asset investors, Oaktree Capital, itself a cornerstone investor to the offer (that is, if you regard a 0.39 per cent holding as "cornerstone").

As it turned out, we were not alone in receiving an invitation to meet the company. There were approximately 50 other investors and numerous representatives from the 18 participating underwriters. The excitement was too much for one attendant, who was seen collaring the nearest investment banker to ensure her order was filled – rumour had it that the book was ten times oversubscribed (according to the *Wall Street Journal*, the retail book ended up 160 times oversubscribed). With eight buys and four holds from the 12 analysts who cover the company and the endorsement of the numerous underwriters, the message is clear: only a fool would miss out on this opportunity.

As we often find in China, appearance and reality in Cinda's case are far apart. From the three years of data disclosed, it seems that the main driver of Cinda's return on equity has been leverage. The reported return on equity for 2012 was 15.8 per cent, yet the corresponding return on assets was just 3.4 per cent (down from 6.3 per cent in 2010). This implies that the leverage was 4.7 times (up from 4 times in 2010). Successful distressed investors tend to eschew leverage because of the uncertainty in magnitude and timing of returns. They typically have a preference for permanent capital. Being free of debt themselves, distressed debt investors can deploy capital at attractive returns in bad times when leveraged folk have run into trouble. Besides, distressed opportunities generally come with a significant degree of embedded leverage of their own.

A look at the origins of this asset manager's leverage is instructive. At the end of June 2013, the balance sheet of Cinda showed RMB 220bn in total liabilities. The two biggest and most important line items were RMB 33.5bn provided by the ministry of finance, and RMB 104bn coming from "market-orientated sources." The cost of funding for the finance ministry liabilities is difficult to determine, but we calculate it at approximately 2.25 per cent per year. The "market-orientated sources" funding comes from the inter-bank market, in other words the very same banks from which many of the distressed assets originate. This cost of funding appears to be around 4.4 per cent, not the lowest funding rate we have encountered in China by any stretch, but well below the 5.8 per cent prime rate currently being quoted by the largest banks. In short, Cinda's funding costs are artificially low, possibly unsustainable, and given the company's high leverage, the impact on profits of any normalisation of interest rates is likely to be significant.

A close reading of the voluminous offering documents also reveals the rather skewed nature of Cinda's asset book. This comprises two core ele-ments. The first is the distressed debt book, which amounts to RMB 86bn and consists primarily of unpaid receivables that have been acquired from financial and non-financial institutions. A footnote in the prospectus states that: "As at June 30, 2013 the gross amount of our distressed debt assets classified as receivables attributable (i) real estate ... [and] (iv) construction industries represents 60.4 per cent ... and 4.5 per cent of our total distressed assets classified as receivables, respectively." In other words, two-thirds of Cinda's distressed book is exposed to Chinese real estate.

The second largest element of Cinda's book is holdings of debt-to-equity swaps (DES), which amount to RMB 44bn in assets, relating primarily to interests in medium and large state-owned enterprises which have lost their way. Of the top 20 unlisted distressed assets in the portfolio, some 13 are coal mining companies, with the balance being a mix of chemical and manufac-turing businesses. Another footnote reveals that the coal miners account for some 61.5 per cent of Cinda's DES assets. The document goes on to highlight that "in 2011, the production volume of the aforementioned 21 DES compa-nies in the coal industry in which we directly held equity interests or held equity interest in their subsidiaries totalled 1,605m tonnes of coal, represent-ing 45.6 per cent of national output."

Even the ugliest of assets purchased at the right price can make for a great investment. And many of Cinda's assets were acquired at a steep discount to their original face value (often 20 to 30 per cent of the claim amount, according to the company). Yet much of this discount disappears once Cinda's valuation is taken into account. Put simply, if a company buys assets at 0.3 times book value and an investor buys the same company at 2.4 times (Cinda's price-to-book), the effect is the same as paying 0.7 times book for the original assets.

We are not criticising the authorities for attempting to restructure China's overleveraged and underperforming corporate sector. This is neces-sary. Indeed, the creation of asset management companies, like Cinda, and the tapping of external sources of capital to help deal with the rotten assets represents an encouraging, if rather small, recapitalisation of the China's credit system. What's plain wrong is the IPO marketing story that an investment in Cinda is a hedge on problems in China's financial system. Cinda's fate is entwined with that of the banks that provide the funding to buy their underperforming assets; after all, Cinda did not spring up to take advantage of the system, it was born of it. We suspect that many investors who rushed to get their Cinda order filled believed they were buying a broadly diversified distressed asset manager. They may wake up one day unhappy to discover they have leveraged long exposures to the Chinese property and coal industries, and to the increasingly fragile Chinese financial system.[4]

6.5 VALUE TRAPS (SEPTEMBER 2014)

Chinese banks are highly leveraged and poorly positioned in the capital cycle

For the contrarian investor in emerging markets, one sector appears to offer outstanding value. The four largest companies in this group generated an average return on equity of 20 per cent in 2013, and averaged 21 per cent over the previous five years. They have grown their profits at a compound rate of 18 per cent since 2008, achieving last year a respectable 12 per cent increase. Investors who crave liquidity have nothing to fear; the aggregate market capitalisation of these companies is greater than $650bn. Their stocks are unloved and can be purchased in the market for around book value.

The four companies in question are the "Big Four" Chinese banks. Conventional wisdom suggests that the financial system of the People's Republic is rotten to the core. Yet in the past, Marathon has made decent money in banks in the face of conventional wisdom. The Asian financial crisis, for instance, provided a wonderful opportunity to earn significant returns from cheap financials. Given that Chinese banks are today's pariahs, might they not provide a similar money-making opportunity?

The short answer is no – at least, in our opinion. A longer answer is best divided into two parts. The first part involves trying to determine the Chinese

---

⁴ While perhaps no hedge against a future banking crisis in China, Cinda has so far fulfilled its roadshow promise by trading inversely with the Chinese banks. To wit, from its IPO in February 2014 to the end of the year, Cinda's share price declined by nearly 20 per cent during which time the MSCI China Banks Index was up 36 per cent. Over the course of 2014, Cinda's total assets grew by 42 per cent, while implied leverage marched upwards (to 5.1 times).

banks' true profitability, and the second to where exactly these banks stand in the capital cycle. Let's start by deconstructing the banks' profitability. Take the largest of them, the Industrial and Commercial Bank of China (ICBC), which boasts a return on equity of 20.8 per cent. This derives from a return on assets of 1.4 per cent, magnified nearly 15 times by leverage. The first question is whether credit risk – that is, provisions for non-performing loans on its books – has been adequately accounted. Chart 6.2 compares the loan growth and the cost of risk over the last decade for ICBC and Bank of America, one of the largest US banks. You will notice that ICBC's credit costs have been consistently low over the past few years, during which loan growth has remained at elevated levels. The left-hand chart reveals that Bank of America had similarly low credit costs and strong loan growth in the years leading up to the Lehman crisis, when the proverbial chickens came home to roost.

A bank's reported return on capital is very sensitive to credit costs. For instance, if ICBC's cost of risk were to rise to an unremarkable 1 per cent, its return on equity would drop by nearly a fifth, from 20.6 per cent to 16.8 per cent. When considering a bank's true profitability it's also necessary to normalise the level of leverage. At ICBC, every renminbi of equity supports nearly RMB 15 of debt. Yet just as leverage magnifies profits, it can also magnify losses. The average level of leverage for an emerging market bank is around 10 times. Bank of America's balance sheet is leveraged by the same amount. Assuming credit costs of 1 per cent of total loans and leverage of 10 times, ICBC's return on equity would fall to 11.3 per cent. This figure seems to us is closer to ICBC's sustainable profitability. We reach this conclusion

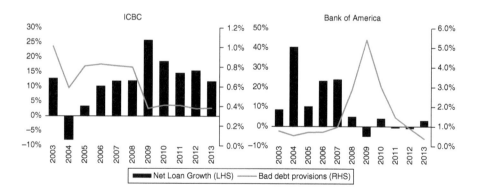

Chart 6.2   Bank of America and ICBC: loan growth and credit costs

Source: S&P Capital IQ.

without factoring in concerns about the integrity of the bank's balance sheet or systemic threats to China's financial system.

It's not just that credit costs are low and leverage is high for China banks. They also seem poorly positioned in the capital cycle. In the textbook example of a capital cycle, new capital is attracted into sectors with outsized profits. Eventually, this influx of capital causes capacity to overshoot, which hurts industry profitability and shareholder returns. This process is most marked in commodity businesses, whose products are undifferentiated. The opportunity to make really good investments tends to occur only after a turn in the cycle; that is, when capital begins to exit.

Given that credit is a commodity, capital cycle analysis is as relevant for banks as it is for any other commodity business. There are, however, some differences. Because credit has no physical constraints, its increase is limited only by the amount of equity a bank can accumulate and the amount of leverage it can assume. This makes it easier for management to get carried away in the upward phase of the cycle. When the banking cycle turns, there needs to be a catch-up charge for the unrecognised sins of the past – that is, a spike in credit costs. Capacity also needs to exit through deleveraging; this comes in the form of shrinking balance sheets and mergers.

In the case of the Chinese banks, these symptoms have yet to present themselves, which means that from an investor's perspective they are not yet in the right part of the capital cycle. Credit costs have remained eerily low and although we have seen some capital-raising, this has been done to sustain growth rather than to deleverage. How this plays out is difficult to determine. China's credit denouement may occur in a rapid (and cathartic) fashion in the mode of the Asian crisis, or be more drawn out, Japanese-style – but happen it must.

6.6 DEVIL TAKE THE HINDMOST (MAY 2015)

Chinese equities are showing every sign of speculative excess

Chinese stocks have been building up steam over the last year. In the twelve months to April, the mainland Chinese equity markets have risen by 120 per cent. Market commentators appear reluctant to call time on the Chinese bubble. A recent *Financial Times* editorial opined that even though "Chinese stocks are plainly overvalued ... [they] can go higher." That's indisputable. Goldman Sachs pronounces: the market is "certainly getting frothy" amid "very frenetic retail activity," but "is it a bubble that will crash the system? The answer is not yet." Gavekal, a Hong Kong-based strategy outfit, warns that "wallflower investors who continue to hang back may soon be in danger of missing the party." Some parties, however, leave rather heavy hangovers.

On the face of it, China's equities should be of considerable interest to Marathon. Some industries appear to have arrived at a low point in their capital cycle. Equity valuations – at least a few months ago – appeared reasonable. Beijing had announced its intention to tackle massive industrial excess capacity. All this should make for a sympathetic starting point from an investor's perspective. Yet valuations are not as compelling as they seem (lowly aggregate market valuations are influenced heavily by the troubled banks). Furthermore, the legacy of China's massive overinvestment is severe and likely to persist.

The Shanghai index is now valued at 21.7 times earnings; excluding banks, however, this multiple rises to 37 times earnings. The Shenzhen exchange, which is not weighed down by the banks and has more exposure to the frothy technology sector, is currently valued at over 57 times earnings. That three of the four largest companies on the Shenzhen exchange are retail stock brokers is troubling.

The equity market's latest rise has coincided with (yet) another substantial monetary easing policy – this time known as "pledged supplementary lending," which, commencing in the early summer of 2014, has allowed financial institutions access to RMB 1tn in short- to medium-term liquidity. Following the implementation of these monetary operations, the seven-day repo rate declined from over 5 per cent to 3 per cent by last September. Around the same time, the government cut trading fees, increased the number of brokerage accounts allowed per person from one to 20 (who could need so many?) and relaxed restrictions on margin lending. Beijing appears to have deliberately inflated this bubble.

The state media also began providing explicit support by publishing numerous articles which hyped the virtues of stock market investing. The results of these interventions are hidden in plain sight. Take the case of Beijing Baofeng Technology, an online video services provider. As of mid-May, the company had been listed for 39 days on the Shenzhen Stock Exchange. For 36 of those days, its shares have risen by the daily allowable limit of 10 per cent. Through the magic of compounding, the stock is up by over 2,500 per cent in a little over a month and a half. The company, with just $3m in operating profits, now boasts a hefty $4bn market capitalization. Beijing Baofeng is but one of the 225 IPOs launched this year – 223 of those were limit-up on their first day of trading, with the mean performance since IPO being over 400 per cent.

Margin lending is one of the fastest growing areas for retail brokers. Lending volumes are up 80 per cent so far this year and have more than quintupled since the beginning of 2014. Margin lending was first permitted in China in 2010 and has gone on to fund over 8 per cent of the free-float adjusted market capitalization – by contrast, margin lending on the Big Board is around 2 per cent of market value. Readers of J.K. Galbraith's *The Great Crash* may recall his view that margin loans were a key component of the 1929 crash, after reaching 10 per cent of market capitalization. Contemporary speculators in Chinese equities are even more leveraged than their Jazz Age forerunners. The French bank BNP believes that around 20 per cent of incremental volume traded on the Shanghai Stock Exchange is funded with margin loans.

Some of this liquidity has found its way to the Hong Kong Stock Exchange, thanks to the "Stock Connect" program, which allows mainland investors to access Chinese shares traded in the former British territory. Chinese stocks listed in Hong Kong have been trading at an average discount of 30 per cent to their mainland equivalents. The bulls hope to profit from a narrowing of this discount as Hong Kong shares rise to Shanghai valuations.

Shanghai Electric, a large industrial company with listings in Shanghai and Hong Kong, is a good example of the current market madness. In China, the company has an implied market capitalisation of $41bn, a price-earnings multiple of almost 100 times, and a price-to-book multiple of over six times (for a 10 per cent RoE). In Hong Kong, investors are valuing the same company at $13.3bn of implied market capitalisation, with a price-earnings multiple of 33 times and a price-to-book multiple of 2.3 times. Compared with the China price, the Hong Kong line may look a bargain. But in our view, both valuations are unjustifiable.

Investors appear so transfixed by the relative cheapness in Hong Kong that they are paying no attention to absolute value. The argument that Hong Kong valuations should move upwards to the bubble levels found in Shanghai and not vice versa may convince some of Gavekal's "wallflowers." But not us. Marathon is more inclined to trust the stock prices determined by worldly (if occasionally excitable) Hong Kong investors over their mainland counterparts, whose money, trapped within the People's Republic by capital controls, fuels one speculative excess after another.[5]

---

[5] Between the date of this article and mid-September 2015, the Shanghai Stock Exchange Composite Index declined by 32 per cent. Over the same period, Beijing Baofeng Technology declined by 69 per cent.

7

INSIDE THE MIND OF
WALL STREET

"Never trust the bankers"

Sir Winston Churchill

Marathon's capital cycle approach leads to a natural wariness of investment bankers. After all, Wall Street is in the business of supplying capital to hot areas of the stock market and generating fees from dubious financial engineering. Both these activities have always struck us as inimical to the interests of long-term shareholders. From the perspective of a bemused buy-side onlooker, it was clear to us that the typical Wall Street banker during the early years of the new millennium had little interest in protecting the interests of clients. Rather, the game of banking had become all about fee generation, regardless of the consequences. A whole chapter in Marathon's previous publication, *Capital Account* (2005), was devoted to investment bank antics.[1]

Writing to clients back in September 2000, Marathon predicted that "the next round of excesses will be worse than the last. When large investment banks cannot be penalised for their greed and mistakes – because they are too large and too well connected to fail – it is only a matter of time before they challenge the system itself." Unfortunately, these dark forebodings were realized eight years later when Lehman Brothers collapsed.

In order to keep our clients abreast of the dangers posed by investment bankers, we decided to write every year, as Christmas approached, a satirical piece based on a fictional investment bank, Greedspin, and its lead banker,

---

[1] See *Capital Account*, Chapter 6 'The Croupier's Take.'

"And so, while the end-of-the-world scenario will be rife with unimaginable horrors, we believe that the pre-end period will be filled with unprecedented opportunities for profit."

Illustration 7.1   A Churn's-eye view of the World

Source: New Yorker.

Stanley Churn. This practice began in December 2002 with a piece about the botched merger of an imaginary technology company with an "old economy" business, General Chocolate, which was published in *Capital Account*. The following pieces chart the career progression of the irrepressible Churn since that date.

7.1   A COMPLAINT (DECEMBER 2003)

A satirical take on promotional corporate management

Marathon occasionally receives letters of complaint from the managers of companies whom we have interviewed as part of the investment process. We recently received the following letter from the chief executive of General Chocolate (formerly, albeit briefly, known as Momentum Technologies):-

Dear Marathon Partners,

I am writing to express my disappointment about the experience my team and I had at a recent meeting with investment analysts at Marathon. Your corporate brochure states that "Marathon is an independent investment firm with a high level of professionalism, innovation and flair." However, the impression that we were left with after the meeting was not a reflection of these qualities.

The meeting was one of a series of meetings arranged by Greedspin Partners as part of our "non-deal" road show, as we relaunch General Chocolate following the difficulties experienced under the previous management after the acquisition growth phase of the late 1990s. We came with a detailed presentation pack of our new "We have Lift-Off" strategy, which is the product of a great deal of work by McTavish, our strategic consulting adviser. I am particularly pleased with our China strategy based around the "chocolate chip for every China-man" concept. The slides are complex – indeed, I have spent many hours grasping their full meaning – and require a detailed understanding of certain technical terms. Most of the analysts we met that day had taken the trouble to become fully conversant with our new corporate language. Imagine my dismay, therefore, when your analysts insisted on pursuing a quite different course during the meeting.

First your team questioned the very idea that we should grow. This is very demotivating for my team, as you can imagine. That growth is good in itself should be self-evident. Your analysts, however, appeared to be suggesting that we shrink our operations back to a profitable core and, by buying back shares, maximize the return on capital employed. There are several reasons why this is patent nonsense. Our major institutional shareholders – whose feedback we receive via our investment bank, Greedspin – want us to expand. They have considerable funds to invest and are not interested in firms with a market capitalisation of less than $10bn. Unlike yourselves, these serious investors have armies of analysts to consider the merits of our growth strategy, in addition to having the financial firepower to acquire the stock we issue to fund our acquisitions.

Shrinking the business, as Marathon suggests, would represent a failure of management imagination. Our bankers at Greedspin, who currently have a host of acquisition ideas, have never suggested downsizing. Growth is also essential if we are to achieve our career goals. Bigger companies are able to reward top talent and we need to get onto a level playing field. Buying back shares would reduce liquidity and make the investor's job more difficult. Surely you can see that. We are very proud of the fact that 10 per cent of General Chocolate's stock is now traded each month. Yet still we think we can increase this level by improving the news flow. We are currently considering offering a new "instant guidance" service for shareholders that will be automatically triggered with every percentage point movement in the cocoa price.

Even in the non-controversial area of cost control, there was no meeting of minds. Your colleagues suggested that we should raise costs in areas such as marketing and research. Yet such an action would have a negative impact on our quarterly earnings per share, hardly something we could present to our institutional shareholders. While the front cover of our annual report does indeed state that people are "our most important asset" we must weigh this against the productivity-enhancing redundancy program that specifically targets non-customer facing, non-measurable, up-front expenses with uncertain and distant pay-offs. This cost-focussed strategy improves visibility and is immediately EPS accretive.

It soon became clear that your colleagues had limited familiarity with the confectionery sector. This was a complete contrast to our meeting earlier in the day with Lobster Pot Asset Management whose analysts were fully immersed in the chocolate industry. They were able to place General Chocolate firmly in the context of its two global peers and examine all comparable metrics in considerable detail. We had a particularly fruitful discussion of the new C-WONK chocolate whipple technology. This specialization is fully in accord with the new General Chocolate shareholder agenda – the distractions of Momentum Technologies are behind us and there is little point in crying over spilt milk.

Your analysts, by contrast, insisted on pursuing ridiculous and irrelevant questions about our largest shareholder, Duo-Pump Enterprises, headed as you know by Mr. Peccavi (Senior), our former Chairman. Your colleagues questioned the validity of the 20 per cent economic interest combined with 51 per cent "turbo" voting rights. They seemed to overlook the benefits we receive from Duo-Pump. After all, Duo-Pump has a good handle on the company having seen good and bad times. I can tell you that our major institutional shareholders were relieved when Duo-Pump was prepared to buy shares after the price fell during the Iraq conflict earlier this year and sell them back later. As for the non-compete fees paid to our former Chairman, these are standard practice in the industry and are immaterial when compared to our turnover figure. They certainly do not merit the prurient and cynical questions of your analysts.

Attention then turned to my own incentive arrangements. May I say first of all that I find it embarrassing to have to discuss these matters in front of colleagues. Secondly, may I assure you that there is no link whatsoever between the date of the pricing of my personal share options and the announcement of our Year Zero asset write down (what McTavish called "Operation Kitchen Sink"). Besides, the exercise price for the options was set at the market price at the time, which, according to the efficient market theory, reflected the underlying value of the company at that time.

As far as we are concerned, these questions are far beyond the scope of information reasonably required to make an investment decision. Adding to our frustrations, the meeting ended with absurd comments from your analysts regarding the Peccavi family's influence on General Chocolate's operations. Remarks such as these are not only unacceptable but grossly inappropriate. In addition to the family members, the board includes distinguished figures such as General Manuel Tapioca, who brings a distinguished military and diplomatic record, and my father's second wife, who has a wealth of experience in the couture fashion business.

I am informed by our bankers, who employ hundreds of analysts, that the main job of an analyst is to understand the growth prospects of the business in order to forecast accurately the earnings numbers over the coming months. We are perfectly prepared to have a discussion with your team along such lines. Finally, over the years I have found it convenient for our major US-based shareholders to finish meetings by 4 p.m. I understand that fund managers need to get back to their desks to carry out trades before it is too late in the day. Because of this deadline we have fixed our executive jet departure schedule so that we finish all investor meetings at 4 p.m. throughout the world. It is therefore extremely inconvenient to have to answer irrelevant questions from corporate governance zealots on the minutiae of our major shareholder's ownership structure well beyond that time. We trust it will not happen again.

Yours faithfully
For and on behalf of
General Chocolate
Gervais Peccavi
Chief Executive

cc: Stanley Churn – Head of Sales, Greedspin Partners

7.2   PRIVATE PARTY (DECEMBER 2005)

Marathon's fictional banker, Stanley Churn, is excited by fee prospects in the private equity world

Memo to:	RearView Capital General Partners
From:	Stanley H. Churn – Senior Chairman
Date:	12 December 2005
Subject:	The Year Ahead

We're now coming to the end of another outstanding year (my first as Chairman since my move from Greedspin), and I wanted to take this opportunity to share with the team my thoughts on the year ahead. My message to you is straightforward. We must act quickly to grasp a once-in-a-lifetime fee generation opportunity in the private equity industry – an opportunity which I believe is greater even than that available in my old field of investment banking. My reasons for optimism are straightforward.

- The banking sector is truly hot to trot. We are being offered money to do deals on extraordinary terms. Just look at what we were offered on Merry Muffin. When our bankers said nine times EBITDA, I thought they were talking about the deal multiple not the amount of money they'd lend us! Talking to our lead banks, it's clear that they're not really in the credit business anymore – all Norman Broadshanks at Regal Bank talks about these days is syndication and up-front fees. So long as he can pass the debt bomb to the next man, he's happy to lend as much as he can in order to meet his growth targets. Indeed, Broadshanks and his ilk are bringing us not just the finance but the deals themselves these days. And remember, just because borrowing for LBOs in Europe doubled in 2005 doesn't mean it can't double again.
- Our clients are increasingly desperate to invest with us. They're all juiced up by our past returns. Just think – our industry will have raised $250bn worldwide this year. The tsunami of inflows means we can run larger funds, do larger deals and earn larger fees all round. We no longer even have to worry about exiting into the public markets or finding a penny-pinching trade buyer. With the growth in LBO-to-LBO, we can exploit daisy chain economics to our advantage further down the track. We can also go

back to Broadshanks and do leveraged recaps or reverse flexes. So let's get on with investing the remainder of RearView VI and accelerate capital raising for RearView VII SuperSize.

- The fund management industry still doesn't "geddit." The new leverage paradigm has passed most of these guys by and they're still using ridiculous cost of capital metrics and debt structures left over from the past. Don't they understand what little you need to do to enhance earnings per share? Just add debt! And the buy-side fools so confuse value and price, that when we say "20 per cent premium," they scream "deal!" Their pockets are ripe for picking!

- Managements can see where their bread is buttered. The real money is on the private side of the fence, and they're fed up with all the pesky regulation on the public side. We just need to bring them on board and reload their incentives. With the C-Suite in our pockets, we can get the pre-deal earnings disappointments and all the board recommendations we need. The principal-agent conflict isn't our problem – it's our solution.

- The scale of the Supersize fee opportunity is compelling. Consider that Vertigo Partners are taking in $10bn for their latest fund. The 1.5 per cent management fee earns $150m p.a. which, over the six-year life, is worth $900m, shared largely between the 12 partners. That's nearly a bar each. With that kind of security, you can afford to really wing it on the deals! And that's on just a single fund….

Of course, there's a risk that the window may close in the next couple of years. Think:

- At some point, the institutions which invest with us might wake up to the fact that we are taking businesses they already own (and on which they pay fees of around 50 basis points to long-only fund managers), introducing leverage (something management could do without our help) and moving the equity sliver to a high fee model (1.5 per cent annually + 20 per cent carried interest). The buyout debt then gets recycled back to them via Broadbanks, so our investors end up where they started minus this fee leakage. Truly, this is one of the biggest wealth transfers from principals to agents in history.

- We take advantage of the fact that interest payments are tax-deductible. The tax man might realize that one of the reasons he's out of pocket is because of the leverage game we're playing. In the

UK, private equity employs up to 20 per cent of the private sector workforce and so we could attract unwelcome attention.

- These wretched pension regulators are onto us. They worry some buyout buccaneer will plunder the pensions pot à la Maxwell. Next they'll be asking for personal guarantees!
- The hedge fund world and his wife are gate-crashing our party, and corporate buyers are starting to get frisky again after a long spell in the doghouse.
- The era of easy money must end at some point. If the macro side turns nasty, we need to be as closed as a clam.

What we need now is action.

- Hurry up and invest RearView VI.
- Don't spend so much time worrying about realization.
- Spend at least half of your time marketing RearView VII SuperSize.
- Get closer to our friends in the investment banks. Not long ago, we would let them entertain us. Right now we should be entertaining them. We simply can't afford to miss out on deal flow. We have to be present in all the large auctions. Forget about poor old Warren Buffett's rule for auctions ("Don't go!"). Auctions are our business – "Go!"
- On the subject of investment banks, there was a time when I worried about conflicts of interest as they tried to lend us money at the same time as providing us with advice. Phooey! If Greedspin want to staple finance onto a deal, who are we to say no? We should also be open to the bankers' triple play (advise, finance and co-invest). As to advisers generally, we can share the fruits of our success with many intermediaries and professional firms – there's plenty of gravy to go round.
- Start to think big on where we can invest RearView VII and VIII thereafter. Large-cap conglomerates are sitting ducks if only we can persuade management to play ball. Although in the US less than 20 per cent of companies in the S&P 500 have more than two lines of business, in Europe the figure is still well over half. If we can team up with our peers in consortium bids, that's great, as we can cut down on nasty bidding wars.
- Recruit more washed-up politicians – you never know when we'll need them!

So the message is simple. Go to it guys and gals – the grass has never been greener!

S.H.C.

12.12.05
f:/rearview/confidential/fees/outlook/2006

7.3 CHRISTMAS CHEER (DECEMBER 2008)

Stanley Churn envisages a profitable future for Wall Street in the aftermath of the Lehman bust

Chalet Geldchurn
Fortresstrasse 1
Zug
Switzerland

11 December 2008

Henry M. Paulson Jr.
United States of America
Department of the Treasury
1500 Pennsylvania Avenue, NW
Washington, D.C. 20220
USA

Private & Confidential

Dear Hank,

I know I say this every year, but boy, what a year!

Of course there's been a lot to worry about, but let's start by looking back at what you've achieved. Your term as Treasury Secretary has, in my humble opinion, been an absolute triumph. When I quizzed you a few years ago about why you'd accept a lousy $25,000 salary to quit Goldman, no one could have guessed what a lucrative career move you'd made. Shame having to sell $500m of Goldman stock tax free back in 2006, eh? Must have saved you a good $100m in tax and a further $250m by getting out while the going was good. Bingo!

I wish I had had the same foresight with my residual position in Greedspin which has been decimated by wretched short-sellers. That top-notch prime broker John Mack had it right when he fingered those locusts for their "irresponsible behaviour in the market."

And just look at what you've been able to do reshaping the investment banking industry. Okay, it would have been nice to let Morgan Stanley follow Lehman down the plughole, but that would have unmasked the TARP as the Goldman Relief Program and that (probably) wouldn't do. Incidentally, wasn't it a joy to watch those guys at Lehman checking out with nothing but their brown boxes and a bundle of worthless stock certificates?!

But think what it's going to be like in the world of investment banking 2.0. Goldman and Greedspin will have most of the cake to share between them, and I know which way fees are heading. Roping in the old Sage of Omaha confers just the right aura of respectability and allows us to roll out all sorts of "innovative" financial products in the new shadowy banking era. Remember Sandy Weill's rule that in our business, you just need to change the name of the product once a decade!

As for me it's been a bumper year. My decision to up sticks and move to Dubai and set up Sovereign Wealth Advisory Partners couldn't have been better timed. We took a decent share of the fees from the $80bn or so investments made by these chaps in US financials. I don't think I've ever made so much money and the clients lost so much this quickly in my entire career! Of course that brings risk – I was getting nervous up there in the Al Jumoolah Tower, and I kept seeing the same heavies in dark glasses following me up in the express lift. There was also the issue of burnt fingers – given what's happened, these fellows had lost confidence in all things associated with the US of A and had gone all clammy with their money. Things weren't looking too good on the ground either, given the upcoming "built-on-sand" construction bust. So fee prospects in Dubai didn't look too rosy. It was time to move on, which is why I'm now living here in the land of the cuckoo clock. Didn't someone once say, "all successful careers in finance end up in Switzerland?"

It's not just the sovereign wealth folks who are out there looking for me. Those return-chasers who put money into my SuperSize private equity vehicles (RearView VI and VII) complain they got creamed on the 2006 and 2007 deals. But we're still raking in the management fees, and even I felt a bit nervy writing to them about last month's mega-drawdown for the latest round of ByteBack Semiconductor's refinancing. There's a silver lining to this, though. The only place our clients can raise money is in the public equity markets, so as forced sellers they'll push down equity prices just in time for RearView VIII to mop up some tasty deals at the bottom of the market. What a glorious merry-go-round.

The other big group with whom I'm desperately trying to avoid any contact are the investors in the RearView Capital IPO. Okay the share price performance has been in line with that of the Blackstone, KKR and Apollo vehicles, but try telling that to the Chinese Investment Authority. When I said at the time of the IPO that we were entering a golden age for private equity, I should have been more specific. The only thing that had a gilded future was our private equity fees! We are even getting management fees for money we don't manage, for heaven's sake.

As ever at this time of year, my thoughts turn to where we'll find the next great fee generation scam. On the "follow-the-money" principle, which has always worked so well for both of us, the obvious candidate whose pocket is ripe for picking must surely be the dear old Uncle Sam. With the new "save- the-world" regime coming in with mega-bucks spending programs and the Fed printing money like there's no (inflation) tomorrow, this seems like an ideal opportunity for fee generators like us. We just need to get capitalism's invisible hand firmly tucked into the biggest pocket of them all, and we'll do just fine. We've resurrected RearView Infrastructure Partners and are looking to raise money for the Roads-Across-America, Bridges-Everywhere and Broadband-for-Babies programs.

That brings me on to your future. I can't think of anyone with better job prospects than you right now. Not since Bob Rubin moved back to the private side with a sweet deal from Citi (he didn't miss a trick with that non-equity compensation plan), has anyone been in such a strong position. Alongside a highly remunerative role with any one of the major banks, I would very much like you to consider becoming an advisory board member of our RearView Funds, along with a position as trustee of the Stanley and Daphne Churn Foundation. Be assured, the rations are plentiful. Please give this your utmost thought before Daphne and I welcome you and yours here for the ski season in February.

Yours ever, and still dancing!

Stanley H. Churn
Chairman Emeritus
Greedspin Partners, RearView Capital

7.4   FORMER GREEDSPIN BOSS FLEES CHINA
(DECEMBER 2010)

Stanley Churn's private thoughts on the Chinese economy are revealed

(GIR News Flash) Stanley Churn, the controversial former Greedspin banker, has fled China one year after setting up Churn-Woo International, a Hong Kong-based investment bank. The move follows highly embarrassing revelations of Mr. Churn's private scepticism about China's investment prospects in direct contrast to his firm's upbeat public message. Friends say Mr. Churn had talked about "retreating" to Tokyo, where he has recently made a number of large personal investments. His exact whereabouts, however, remain a mystery, and one colleague expressed concern over his safety.

Speculation has mounted in recent weeks about the future of Churn-Woo International after the release of notes of candid conversations between Mr. Churn and the US Ambassador to China via the WikiLeaks website. The comments were recorded by Ronnie Fix, Washington's ambassador to China, who is also a former Greedspin banker and friend of Mr. Churn. Towards the end of a private three-hour lunch at the Grand Hyatt Hotel in Beijing, Mr. Churn described China's economy as "Dubai on speed." He said he wanted to "kill the longs with my shorts," as he expected the Chinese economy to "blow in a matter of time."

"He thinks the authorities can't control inflation and the 'empty' housing market is an Ireland-esque Ponzi scheme," Mr. Fix wrote in his cable to the State Department. At one point, Mr. Churn warned that "an inflation tsunami is about to strike the entire region and the only winner I can see are the desiccated Japanese banks – everyone else will drown." "Investment levels at over 50 per cent of GDP are ludicrous....the Yanks can't stomach more Chinese exports and the flow of slave labour from the paddy fields which has kept the lid on wages is drying up. The only export with growth potential is inflation."

Mr. Churn also bragged that he had excellent access to senior government officials because "we have bribed everyone" and the Beijing officials "are so clueless they have turned to us for advice." At one point, he appeared to joke that his advisory role put him in line for the first Confucius Peace Prize. Later in the same conversation, the billionaire banker said that he expected to make more money from shorting Chinese securities than from any previous investment idea. He described how he was especially keen to short shares on the NASDAQ-style ChiNext board, where there has been flurry of share sales by senior managers of newly public companies as lock-up provisions expire.

The remarks are acutely embarrassing for Mr. Churn, given his comments in recent letters to investors about China's favourable outlook. In one report entitled "No Need to Fear," Mr. Churn wrote that inflation in China was a "temporary issue due to food supply bottlenecks." The housing market was "only a problem in a few cities and the authorities have matters in hand." He described P/E multiples on the ChiNext board of more than 80 times as "cheap at twice the price."

The content of the leaked cables has also raised concern about the role of Greedspin in China. At one stage, Mr. Churn said that he "expected to receive fees from selling the Greedspin off-the-shelf, off-balance sheet accounting packages" to help Chinese banks grow their own shadow banking system.

Since the Wikileaks reports were made public, there has been a spate of arrests of Churn-Woo associates on treason charges. Chinese officials said that Mr. Churn's comments were "unhelpful" and that he "did not understand China." An offer has been made for Mr. Churn to attend the Nobel Laureate Wing of the state-run China Relearning Centre in Beijing.

The Churn-Woo Dragon Growth fund was launched in January 2010 with much fanfare at a gala dinner at the Shanghai Exhibition Centre. Grammy-nominated girl-band à la Mode provided the after-dinner entertainment. Commentators at the time noted the unusually high fee structure of the fund. The fund's launch came after the 80 per cent rise in the Shanghai SE Composite Index in 2009. In 2010, the index has declined by 13 per cent.

A number of economic commentators have publicly raised doubts about China's growth model. Lombard Street Research has pointed to construction data showing starts up 80 per cent in September 2010 versus the previous year in contrast to sales down over the same period. JP Morgan estimates that loan growth is continuing to run at over 30 per cent when RMB 2tn of off-balance sheet debt sold to trust companies is included. HSBC highlights the extreme level of the value of Chinese housing stock relative to GDP in China, comparable to the Japanese and Irish real estate bubbles.

Mr. Churn has never been far from controversy. In 2003, he was sued by a former school friend over allegedly misleading advice during the leveraged buyout of General Chocolate Industries. A warrant for his arrest remains outstanding in Dubai, where he advised a number of sovereign wealth funds on investments in US banks in the early phase of the credit crunch. More recently, he was forced to apologize for comparing increased taxation of wealthy individuals with Hitler's invasion of France.

Mr. Churn was not available for comment. Friends said that his decision to leave China was made at the request of his wife, who intends to remain in Hong Kong.

7.5 OCCUPY BUNDESTAG (DECEMBER 2011)

Returning to Greedspin, our irrepressible banker is full of fee-generating ideas

Mr. Stanley Churn

New Overall Conditions for the Banking Business

Speech to Greedspin Partners Meeting
Cayman Islands, 13 December 2011

It is now seven years since I left Greedspin to pursue a career elsewhere in the financial services industry. I can't tell you how glad I am to be back here in my new role as Special Advisor to the Chairman and CEO, particularly after my recent unhappy experience with Churn-Woo in China. While I have been away, it's no exaggeration to say we've seen the best of times and the worst of times for the investment banking industry. Today the outlook appears bleak not just for Greedspin but for the very future of capitalism. However, if anything on Wall Street is certain – if history has taught us anything – it's that challenges mean new fee opportunities.

First, though, we need to face up to the challenge. Our IB business is under attack as never before. There is class war taxation, vindictive regulation (from Vickers to Volcker), fines for misselling and a dearth of M&A. Politicians in Europe even want to introduce a financial transactions tax. Goldman has just made a quarterly loss (for only the second time since it went public). Jon Corzine is in hot water over his missing client billions. Insider trading slurs have even touched the dear old Sage of Omaha. Worst of all, though, the Teutonic sado-monetarists are gaining the upper hand and threatening to put an end to easy money. I need not remind you that our entire business model is constructed on the foundation of bubble-inducing public policy actions, and we must do all that we can to ensure a return to business as usual. I even heard "Helicopter Ben" Bernanke saying recently that "monetary policy cannot be a panacea." Oh for those halcyon days of Alan "can't spot a bubble 'til it's burst" Greenspan and Gordon Brown's "not just light touch but limited touch" regulation.

To combat the situation, we need to counterattack on a number of fronts.

Sovereign Advisory Group (SAG)
Our European conflict resolution teams need to be more creative in the absence of any additional bail out cash from the Germans. Our US mortgage specialists are currently working on a series of bespoke leverage structures of impressive complexity for the EFSF. In addition, we are developing new linguistic

constructs which everyone can agree on because no one knows what they mean. Whoever came up with "macro-prudential regulation" is a genius. "Economic governance" is almost as good – the Germans thought it was a stick with which to spank those with unsound finances, while the French thought it was about state intervention in industry. There is a lawyer in the US who has done some very interesting work on what are called "incompletely theorized agreements," which sound like just the sort of "more Europe" policy fudge we need.

Since real money will eventually be required, we need to persuade German politicians that the cost of supporting the "sinners" is lower than the cost of dis-integration. We can get our German corporate clients to lobby politicians that a return to the deutschmark equals auf Wiedersehen to exports. I have seen some good work in this regard coming out of Operation Occupy Bundestag team. Austerity impact studies on communities where German politicians own holi-day homes, together with worst case crime projections look promising. Where there is insistence on rule-based fiscal procedures and sanctions, our French-based teams are ahead of the curve on covert opt-out countermeasures.

Our efforts to influence the ECB on "Lederhosen" bonds will be greatly enhanced now that there is a Goldman man at the helm and five of the six executive board members are from countries whose future depends on this solution. Our OTC Off-Balance Sheet Accounting™ packages which served so well in the age of shadow banking can be retooled to keep fiscal deficits off the books. Perhaps we should poach the team from Goldmans, which all those years ago did wonders shrinking the Greek national debt, thereby snatching them a berth in the euro roach motel. With respect to the sinner nations, our GIPSI Privatization teams have a wonderful opportunity (N.B. PIIGS is no longer designated a client-friendly acronym, and compliance is on the look out for any smart-arsed analyst who seeks to evade this injunction).

In the meantime, we must keep our ear to the ground and maintain the traditional timely flow of information around our various departments in order to be positioned ahead of the pack if the euro-area starts to fall apart. We may need to recruit an "expert network" of Rajaratnam-style moles in eurozone central banks. Once our "sleepers" awake, recent investments in nanosecond intranet communications systems should pay off handsomely. If things do fall apart, then let us hope for maximum disorder. Rest assured Greedspin will always end up on the right side of the trade.

Financial Institutions Group (FIG)
Our biggest challenge within FIG is to implement the fee-rich, capital rais-ing agenda and lobby hard against the madness of bank balance sheet (RWA) shrinkage. Our efforts to infiltrate the European Banking Authority (EBA) have clearly had little impact. Where are the Greedspin alumni when we need

them? Incidentally, this year's Chuck Prince Booby Prize in banking must surely go to those chumps. Not only did they run a stress test which gave top marks to Dexia, but they failed to introduce compulsory capital raising on TARP lines when they set a new capital ratio target. If the ensuing "shrivel-like-a-prune" approach to bank balance sheet management persists, then Europe is in for a rough ride. In PR terms, we can emphasize how we are "supporting our banks" as we "become better and more effective corporate citizens."

Infrastructure Finance Group (IFG)
Infrastructure spending has always been of special interest to me. The themes of "investing for our future" and the "growth agenda" have positive PR spill-over effects, while fee generation options are plentiful, and especially so if investments by pension funds in this area become mandatory. Repeated use of terms like "key workers" and "front line services" goes down particularly well with the current bunch of politicos. Accusations of capital misallocation levelled at the Broadband-for-Babies private finance initiative and the subsequent National Audit enquiry should not distract us from the task at hand.

Corporate events team
We need to evolve our post-EU summit party planning strategy in the light of changes in leadership in a number of countries. While recognizing the networking benefits derived from the work of our Corporate Events Team, DSK-style parties fines and Italian bunga bunga evenings are no longer appropriate for the less warm-blooded technocratic leaders now in charge. Frau Merkel wouldn't approve.

PR
I have been particularly impressed with new services on offer from our flacks. As regards our own image perception, the "period of remorse and apology" agenda will continue until further notice, notwithstanding earlier instructions to the contrary. Given the hostile tax, regulatory and political environment, it makes sense to massage down headline profits for the group via investment vehicles with assorted labels including "public," "trust," "key," "infrastructure," "health," and "education," either alone or in random combination.

Finally on a personal note, I would like to respond to the scurrilous accusations made by the Chinese financial regulator concerning the disappearance of Churn-Woo client funds. I can say clearly and categorically that I never gave a written instruction to misuse client funds, and I never intended that anyone authorize the misuse of client funds. I hope I make myself clear.

Wishing you Season's Greetings and a prosperous New Year for us all.

7.6   SEASON'S GREETINGS (DECEMBER 2012)

Stanley Churn, now head of Greedspin, is out of sorts in the era of the "Citizen banker"

From:	"Stanley Churn" [sc@greedspin.net]
Sent:	12 December 2012 11:09 AM CET
To:	Hank Paulson
Subject:	Season's Greetings!
Attachments:	📎 Greedspin Annual Report 2012 DRAFT

Fool Churn, Fool! There was I, thinking a return to Greedspin would replenish the retirement coffers post the China fund fiasco. It was going to be just like the golden age of our youth. Another bad patch, followed by a shakeout of the infirm, and yippee – once more unto the races! Not this time, though. Now the only league tables we head are toxic ones: LIBOR-rigging, money laundering, insurance misselling, "unauthorized" trading losses.... Behaviour which was once just part of the game – if not the game itself – is now viewed with horror by the sanctimonious prigs who regulate us. Yes, the same people who were the cops when the "crimes" were committed! How shocking it must have been to discover LIBOR submissions were phoney as they prepared to nationalize half the sector!

When Ronnie tripped, it fell to me to grasp the reins at Greedspin once again. So, instead of sitting back like you, writing memoirs or watching my people planting vines on the estate, I'm stuck here taking blow after blow. All we can do is grovel, like the Burghers of Calais, before the expense-fiddling politicos and amnesiac regulators. Time-servers! Truly Hank, we are in the hands of fools. These people believe in raising capital and liquidity requirements in a downturn. Worse, they don't appear to want to stop until they have extinguished the very last entrepreneurial spark in the investment banking firmament.

Then there is a whole new ghastly language of Citizenship, sustainability, the community and stakeholders. Why can't they understand? Banking is simple – it's about bonuses and if there's anything left over, shareholders. The rest is frippery.

You know me as well as anyone, Hank. At heart, I'm an optimist. I can steady the great ship of Greedspin. Time will heal, memories will fade. And I'm determined to do whatever it takes to prove these muppets wrong. As I've never been able to resist a good leak, here's my first draft of this year's annual report. It awaits further butchery by compliance ("Track Changes" being the start of it). Who says you can't teach an old dog new tricks!

As aye,
Stanley

Greedspin 2012 Annual Report   DRAFT

Dear Fellow Shareholders,

2012 was not our finest. Mistakes were made which sadly we cannot undo. Difficult challenges lie ahead. As your new captain, I will endeavour to navigate between the Scylla of regulatory and political hostility and the dreadful Charybdis of risk aversion. We must never forget that fortune favours the brave and risk-taking is in our DNA. Though we still have issues to resolve, I believe we can steer our way back toward a sustainable future.

> **Deleted:** golden

To get there, we will employ contrasting tactics. The ship's telegraph is firmly set at "risk-off" in highly-regulated jurisdictions until market conditions change. We will be a utility bank which is passionate about Citizenship. By contrast, the throttle will be at maximum "risk-on" in the emerging markets where traditional Greedspin practices can flourish in a higher growth environment.

> **Deleted:** talks a great deal about

> **Deleted:** less challenging regulatory

Citizen Greedspin

Delivering the Global Citizenship agenda is at the very heart of our mission. It involves philanthropy, customer-consciousness, communication and being green.

Greedspin Giveth is at the centre of our philanthropic efforts alongside the *1,000 Puppies* [CHECK – why isn't it 10,000?] and *10,000 Corner Stores* campaigns. For *Giveth*, compensation below board level has been reduced by $100m to support nominated charities such as Save the Children. *1,000 Puppies* has so far donated 550 pets to children of valued clients and our *10,000 Corner Stores* programme continues to provide small businesses with derivative products which can help them mitigate unimaginable risks at low cost.

> **Deleted:** the Churn Family Foundation

We will continue to sharpen our focus on customers. Customer satisfaction scores illustrate the huge opportunity we have. Senior executives are learning modern presentation skills at our new $10m Ethics Centre. Technology also has a role. New unstructured data software has been introduced to detect inadmissable terms used on all Greedspin IT platforms. References to "muppets", "numbties" and "morons" have no place in our databases and will in future undergo automatic substitution by the term "valued client".

> **Deleted:** how appalling we are

In our external communications, we will no longer refer to "acting in shareholder interests" exclusively without also referring to customers, employees and being a good citizen. All releases will be monitored to ensure that they contain a minimum number of approved words and phrases selected at random from the following list:- "communities", "sustainable", "struggling homeowners", "strengthening the customer experience", "philanthropic works", "supporting small businesses", "partner", "civic engagement", "citizenship" and "stakeholders".

Whilst our commitment to the long-term objective of a sustainable planet remains non-negotiable, the *Green Greedspin* agenda will be moderated sensibly according to local conditions. *Green Greedspin* has achieved notable progress during 2012, driving our legacy and sustainability agenda. Lower levels of IPO activity in our M&A departments in developed markets have resulted in markedly lower emissions of dangerous gases. Aggregate toxicity levels throughout the organisation have declined by 20% since the outbreak of the financial crisis, in line with the overall headcount reduction.

Greedspin 2012 Annual Report   DRAFT

Emerging Markets – Back to Basics

Emerging markets continue to represent our major growth opportunity. Attractive demographics, catch-up growth potential and low levels of consumer debt make these markets exciting. Unlike developed markets, emerging markets have _enormous growth potential_ and we can play an important role in risk intermediation and wealth transfer.

Deleted: yet to mortgage their future

Innovation is vital, no more so than in the emerging markets. In Trade Finance, our new ByPass^{SM} transfer solution represents a paradigm shift. We want to be able to help clients resolve complex cash management issues when doing business in emerging market trade corridors and technology channels. With the new *Getting to Know Our Customers A-to-Z* checklist in place, we will become the "No-Go bank for drug cartels" and truly the "Go-Go bank for stakeholders".

In 2013, we will launch our new emerging market consumer lending platform. Our goal is to make credit decisions in 30 seconds. Applications can be made more easily via our new Tweet&TextLoan^{SM} service which reduces unnecessary paperwork. We will be more imaginative when it comes to collateral. Emerging market customers can already post motorcycles, tractors or trailers as collateral. A pilot scheme is being trialled with a wider range of collateral options, encompassing household pets and other loved ones where appropriate. There are millions entering the consumer class each year and our aim would be to build a business _which will endure for the long-term._

Deleted: quickly and then realise value via a trade-sale or IPO when the time is ripe.

Regulation – Striking a Balance

Our relations with regulators have been _an area of great focus_. We wish to work together to create the right conditions for a thriving, sustainable future. Efforts to improve mutual understanding via _greater co-operation_ are essential. Greedspin alumni employed by regulators and central banks have been a great support to our business historically. In turn, we can provide lucrative career options for _retired_ bureaucrats in our compliance and risk departments.

Deleted: too antagonistic

Deleted: revolving door employment policies

Deleted: tired

Our litigation department has been merged with Public Relations to give a more joined-up defence against incoming fines and claims. Whilst it is still too early to revoke the "period of remorse and apology" agenda, I am looking for our teams to take a much more robust approach in order to preserve diminishing capital. We need to remind regulators that raising capital requirements whilst at the same time imposing large fines will not produce the sustainable banking system we all desire.

Deleted: for our prosperous retirement

Remuneration - Just Rewards

Our employees are our most important asset and their _security_ is of paramount importance. We are investing in a new, state-of-the-art entry card security system at our offices throughout the world. The new system will be integrated with the *Octopus*^{TM} personal productivity database to _improve efficiency._

Deleted: insecurity

Deleted: to enable real time "rank and yank" functionality. When individual performance deteriorates, duffers will in future risk instant fob deactivation

As regards the central issue of boardroom pay, I am looking to recruit to our remuneration committee experienced figures from _people-oriented businesses_ to overhaul senior executive pay.

Deleted: the world of advertising

Greedspin 2012 Annual Report **DRAFT**

Conclusion

I would like to thank our 110,000 [CHECK – is it still that many?] employees. They have continued to work hard [in communities]/[supporting small business]/[on civic engagement]/[helping struggling homeowners]*. Through their [philanthropic works]/[citizenship]*, they have been strengthening the customer experience in order to generate sustainable returns for key stakeholders. It is my greatest honour to be their partner.

> **Deleted:** shareholders

Stanley Churn

Chairman & Chief Executive
*delete as appropriate

7.7 LUNCH WITH THE GIR[2] (DECEMBER 2013)

The Greedspin banker talks about his career, his never-ending bullishness and a bizarre recreational interest

By Lucy Stinger

I arrive early for my lunch with Stanley Churn at l'Hôtel Palais d'Or in the Swiss mountain resort of Gsaam. Former colleagues of the Greedspin Chairman and CEO had warned me of Churn's legendary impatience and his Five Minute Rule for meetings. Any delay beyond this interval can have dire career consequences. He once fired his chief of staff who arrived late for a remuneration meeting after attending his daughter's nativity play.

At the appointed time, the Churn entourage starts to arrive. The vanguard comprises three bodyguards, a PR minder and his personal assistant. Eventually, through the melée, Churn appears dressed incongruously for the Alpine setting in pin-striped suit, Hermès tie and wing-tipped brogues. Surprising small in stature, his most striking physical traits are his ferocious dark eyes and unnaturally white, pointy teeth.

"I so enjoy the GIR," he begins, before adding the standard put-down, "though I hardly have time to read it these days."

I explain the rules of engagement for GIR lunches, including the insistence that the GIR pays the bill. "How interesting," he purrs, "may I choose the food and wine? Fifty per bottle should cover it." I explain I am vegetarian. "I see," he responds after an uncomfortable pause.

Changing the subject, I ask about business. His teeth flash. "Never better!" One year after assuming the role of Chairman of Greedspin Partners,

---

[2] GIR is an acronym for Marathon's *Global Investment Review*.

he is more optimistic than ever about his firm's prospects. Despite $6bn of fines relating to the sale of risky mortgages and numerous ongoing investigations into malpractice, Churn believes there has been a sea change in the investment banking industry.

"We now see the silver lining," he says, describing the aggressive stance taken by bank regulators. "This is actually wonderful for our business. Do you know we have recruited 8,000 staff globally in compliance this year?" Churn points out that new regulation is raising barriers to competition. "I don't think we will be seeing many new entrants into our industry. That means spreads will stay high as no one can come in and bid them down."

Churn understands barriers to entry. His 500-acre estate, perched above a sharp escarpment overlooking the village of Gsaam, is protected by heavily fortified walls. It dates back to a sixteenth-century monastery which was blown up in the 1880s and rebuilt as a Romanesque Revival Palace, complete with turrets, gatehouse and throne hall, by a fabulously wealthy Russian émigré. Today the grounds also provide sanctuary for 100 ostriches, accommodated in their own neo-Palladian villa, built despite local planning objections.

The waiter arrives to take the order. "I'll have the foie gras followed by a square foot of Wiener Schnitzel. Oh and a side order of Ortolan Bunting. For the lady, something green." Without opening the wine list, he orders "the usual," tapping the leather-bound tome softly with his fingertips.

Financial regulation is also a factor in Churn's growth plans. "If you look at the areas of the world where we can grow this business, they are places where regulation is light to non-existent," he says, citing news that Bob Diamond is expanding in Nigeria. "We can take money from over-regulated markets and reinvest with exceptional returns. Ultimately, countries with too much regulation will lose and we will gain."

A single plate of foie gras arrives and Churn devours it in two large mouthfuls.

"Africa has stunning assets and politicians who are eager to finance their infrastructure plans. We can bring in Chinese investors and provide a helping hand in all the pockets of the value chain." Greedspin has recently taken a lead role in the development of Jacob Zuma's country residence. "There are huge spill-overs for us," Churn declares banging the table with the handle of his fork.

Throughout his career, Churn has demonstrated supreme self-confidence despite career-threatening setbacks. The arch-capitalist began his working life as a bond trader at Greedspin in New York in the 1960s. He rose to become one of the firm's most successful M&A advisers during the 1980s and 1990s. His role in the disastrous merger of General Chocolate and

ByteBack in 2000 led to his departure in 2004, following an official investigation into irregular practices. "I have no regrets about that deal. For General Chocolate, it was a case of either eat or be eaten."

The sommelier arrives with the red wine, quickly followed by the main course. Churn impales his meat, cuts it into squares and dispatches it to his molars. His songbird side order – a dish which is now banned in the EU on animal rights grounds – is skewered and consumed, beak-to-tail, in a single mouthful. "Do you know, they drown it alive in Armangac!" he exclaims as he noisily munches through the bones.

Establishing a pattern which was to be repeated, Churn bounced back from the General Chocolate fiasco in a new guise. In 2005, he re-emerged as the Chairman of RearView Capital Partners, the private equity firm, at a time when huge sums were raised and invested at the peak of the credit bubble.

"I have always tried to find the hot areas of the market where I can facilitate the flow of money. In our business, flows mean fees. It's really very simple."

After the private equity market began to cool in 2007, Churn relocated to Dubai, where he formed Sovereign Wealth Advisory Partners. The firm advised on $80bn of investments in troubled US financials in the early stage of the credit crunch, which resulted in catastrophic losses. A warrant for his arrest in Dubai remains outstanding. Whereas others might have retired after such an experience, Churn remained undaunted. "Ultimately we were merely acting as facilitators, not advisers. The portfolio performed in line with our expectations."

With his new young wife, Susie, his Beijing-born former PA, he then moved to China to set up a new investment bank, Churn-Woo International. After a year, he was forced to flee following embarrassing leaks in the media revealed a wide gap between his own sceptical views on the Chinese economy and the firm's marketing literature. The episode caught the eye of Greedspin's then-Chairman, Ronnie Fix, who welcomed him back to his alma mater as special adviser. Redemption was complete when Mr. Fix was forced to resign after the LIBOR-rigging scandal and Churn was appointed Chairman of his old firm.

In the new age of the caring banker, Churn has shown a rare ability to adapt. Shortly after his appointment, he launched the Citizen Greedspin initiative, with a new emphasis on corporate philanthropy. He is especially proud of his 1,000 Puppies campaign, which involved the donation of pets to the needy. A *New York Times* investigation later revealed that the recipients were mostly Greedspin clients. "It is important to show our caring side to clients," he responds unashamedly when I raise the subject. Critics argue Churn was less caring when it came to laying off (or "disestablishing," as Churn puts it) 20,000 Greedspin employees, but he is unrepentant. "No one is too big to fail, particularly the little people."

He remains a perpetual bull of equity markets and is a firm believer in the power of monetary policy. "The Europeans will eventually realize the folly of their ways and copy the Americans, Brits and Japanese. It is the only way out. Asset prices can only go one way. When it ends, we will be on the other side of the trade. This really is the best of times."

Despite all the trappings of a billionaire – the Swiss schloss, house on Nantucket, Belgravia townhouse, $65m Gulfstream jet, stake in a Premier League soccer club, account at the Four Seasons restaurant in New York – Churn is reluctant to discuss his own wealth. He does point out, however, that the $6bn figure quoted in *Forbes* significantly underestimates his net worth. He is even more reticent of his own philanthropic activities, which he describes as a "family matter."

"I enjoy my Picassos," he says with a glint in his eye, "and, unlike some, I have never had to sell to pay the fines."

I ask about his recreational interests and for once he looks uncertain. His eyes scan the room for inspiration, or perhaps help from his PR adviser. His gaze eventually rests on a landscape painting. "I shoot sheep," he declares darkly.

With that he stands up, baring his teeth in a maniacal grin. "I really have taken up far too much of your time." He leaves before the bill arrives. When it comes, like many former clients, I am left grappling with the awful financial consequences of my encounter with the Greedspin banker.

L'Hôtel Palais d'Or

Fortresstrasse 80, Gsaam, Switzerland	CHF
Foie gras	60
Wiener Schnitzel	120
Ortolan Bunting	1,000
Spinach	14
Puligny-Montrachet 1er Cru Les Pucelles 2002	1,200
Château Pétrus, Pomerol, 2000	46,000
Total	48,394

INDEX

AB InBev, 37–8
Acciona, 148–50, 150n2
agency business models, 63, 70
Ahold, management, 76–9
AIG, 54, 103, 104
airline industry, 4, 27, 41, 50, 50–1n17
Amazon.com, 54, 61, 62n7, 92, 95, 160
Analog Devices, 66–8, 68n9, 74
analysts
    advantage of generalist, 19, 77
    captured by management, 77
    information overload, 77–8
    taking inside view, 78
Anglo Irish Bank
    boastfulness, 113
    description of business, 109–10, 118–20
    exposure to rising rates, 119
    insider sales, 111–12, 115, 120
    Marathon meetings with, 109–17
    promotional management, 110
    rapid loan growth, 114
Anheuser–Busch, 37, 102
Apollo, 127, 146
Applegarth, Adam, 139
ArcelorMittal, 146, 157
Ambev, 37, 101
Assa Abloy, 54, 55, 55n2, 64n8, 70, 87
asset growth
    anomaly, 9, 10
    driver of mean reversion, 10
    inversely related to investment returns, 8, 10
    as a new investment factor, 9
asset price bubbles
    bursting bubble indicators, 146–8
    Chinese equities, 167, 181–3
    commodities, 6, 127
    construction bubble, Spain, 148–50
    Federal Reserve, responsible for, 27
    involvement of retail investors, 129, 147
    IPOs as bubble indicator, 128
    leads to greater investment, 10, 19
    private equity bubble, 122–7
    technology bubble, 4, 97
Atlas Copco, 85–6
auto industry, 26, 156, 172

Axelrod, Robert, 25, 27

Baidu, Internet search engine, 69–70
Bank of America, 163, 180
Bank of Ireland, 113, 151–4
banking
    cleansing process, 154–6
    Germany, 135–8
    seven deadly sins, 141–4
banking crisis
    asset-liability mismatches, 141–2
    exposure to asset-backed paper, 135–8
    off-balance sheet activities, 143
    reaching for growth, 142
    short-term funding, 139–40
Banuelos, Enrique, 133, 135, 135n12
base-rate neglect, 12
beer, see brewing industry
Beijing Baofeng Technology, 182, 183n5
Berkshire Hathaway, 58, 103
Bezos, Jeff, 92, 95
Blackstone, 124n8, 127–8, 146, 194
BOSI (Bank of Scotland Ireland), 163
brewing industry, capital cycle of, 37–40
bubble indicators, 146
Buffett, Warren, 19, 52, 54, 76, 81, 82, 103

Capital Account (Marathon), 4, 8
capital allocation, management, 19–20, 46, 56, 76,
    78, 80, 82–4, 99, 126, 167, 174
capital cycle, 1, 4
    analysis
        avoiding investment bankers, 18, Chapter 7
            passim
        focus on supply, not demand, 17
        generalists make better analysts, 19
        importance of capital allocation skills, 19
        industry competitive conditions, 18
        long-term approach, 19
    behavioural finance
        competition neglect, 11
        extrapolation, 13
        inside view, 12–13
        myopia, 15
        overconfidence, 11, 14

capital cycle – *continued*
  favourable conditions
    competitive moats, 60–1
    cooperative behaviour, 26
    cutting capital expenditure, 48
    industry consolidation, 37–9
    pricing discipline, 26
    pricing power, 67, 70–1
    product differentiation, 66–7
  fundamentals of, 17
  industry capital cycles
    airline industry, 50, 50n12
    banking, 107, 151–4, 155, 161
    brewing industry, 37–40
    cod fishing industry, 28–31
    commodity 'supercycle', 6–9, 31–6
    homebuilders, 5–6, 81, 158
    oil industry, 40–3
    semiconductor industry, 65–8
    shipping Industry, 3, 33
    wind turbine industry, 47
  stylized capital cycle, 2–3
  tenets of analysis, 20–1
  unfavourable conditions
    airline industry, 27
    bankruptcy protection, 27
    capital raising and M&A, 35, 42n8
    career risk, 16
    failures of capital cycle approach, 20,
      159–60n5
    impact of low interest rates, 27
    political involvement, 26, 30, 159
    poor supply side, 50
    prisoner's dilemma, 16, 25–7
    skewed incentives, 15
    substitution, 41
    technological change, 30, 41
    value investors ignore, 6
  see also creative destruction
capital expenditure
  capex to depreciation ratio, 43, 47
  capex to sales ratio, 66
  creates value traps, 54
  mining companies, 32, 34–5
  oil companies, 41, 43–5
  pro-cyclicality of capital spending, 50
  strengthening competitive position, 61
career risk, 16
Carlsberg, 37–8, 40n6
Carswell, Simon, 151
CDOs (collateralized debt obligations), 131, 139,
  142
Chaoda, 172, 173n2
Charlemagne Capital, 128, 146
China – Chapter 6 passim

Baidu, 69–70
bubble created by government, 181–3
Chinese banks, 179–81
Chinese IPOs, 169–73, 176–9
commodity supercycle, 6–8
corporate over-investment, 175
demand for commodities, 32–3, 36
earnings manipulation, 168–70
high level of fixed asset investment, 36, 167
poor investment returns, 51, 167–8
state-owned enterprises, 174
China Telecom, 169, 170n1
Cinda Asset Management, prospectus of, 176–9
Citigroup, 54, 127
CLOs (collateralized loan obligations), 131, 165
cobweb effect, 3
cod fishing industry, 28–31
cognitive dissonance, 11, 12, 81
Colgate Palmolive, 56–7, 70
Comba Telecom, 173, l73n2
commodity bubbles, 127
commodity prices, 31–3, 34
commodity supercycle, 6–8
competition neglect, 11–12
corporate culture
  danger of poor culture, 103–4
  as an intangible asset, 104
  link between culture and equity returns, 102
corporate governance, 94, 98, 117, 188
creative destruction
  impeded by monetary policy, 145, 158, 162
  politicians obstruct, 145, 157
  Schumpeter's theory of, 1, 145
Credit Suisse, 35, 45, 46, 48, 92, 161, 169

Danske Bank, 84, 152
Denmark, 5, 74, 83, 85, 87
Deutsche Telekom, 127, 146
Dodd, David, 10
dotcom bust, 5, 6, 19, 52, 61
Drucker, Peter, 89
Drumm, David, 111n1, 113
Dunlap, Al, 97, 104

earnings per share (EPS), 15, 43, 49, 56, 69, 79, 89,
  100, 118–19, 164n8, 187
  Goodhart's Law, 79
  poor management metric, 79, 89
EBITDA (earnings before interest, tax, depreciation and amortization), 36, 39, 123–5, 189
economists, flawed paradigm, 108
EETC (Enhanced Equipment Trust Certificates),
  121
Electrolux, 86
Ellis, Charles, 28

energy companies, capital spending, 43–5
energy markets, oil prices, 40–3
equity investment
  agency models, 58–60
  corporate culture, 102
  dilution from new share issuance, 49
  evidence of speculation, 126–30
  niche businesses, 73–5
  quality companies, 62–4
  US earnings growth lags GDP, 48–9
European banking sector, cleansing process, 154–6
European banks, failure of capital cycle, 155
evolution of cooperation, 25–7
Experian, 64, 65n8

fade rate
  Holt's market-implied fade rate, 45–6
  market misjudges mean reversion, 46
Fama, Eugene, 9
family control
  problems with family control, 93–5
  solution to principal-agent problem, 91
  succession planning, 94
Fannie Mae, 121
Fastenal, 103
FCC (Fomento de Construcciones y Contratas),
  148–9
Ferrovial, 129, 147–50, 151n2
Fiat, 46, 47n11, 81, 98
FitzPatrick, Sean, 108, 110–14, 117, 119–20
Fortescue Metals Group, 7, 8n15
Freddie Mac, 121, 143
French, Ken, 9
Fresenius Medical Care (FMC), 64, 65n8
fund managers, labelling, 53–5

game theory, 16
Gates, Bill, 103
Geberit, 58–60, 60n6, 64n8, 70, 100
German banks, 135–8
  afflicted by moral hazard, 137
  excessive fragmentation, 136
  serial incompetence, 136
global brewing industry, 37–40
global financial crisis, 5, 10, 83–4, 108, 117n3,
  122n4, 141, 145, 149, 167
Goldman Sachs, 81, 122n4, 127, 181
Goodhart's Law, 79
Goodwin, Fred, 83
Graham, Benjamin, 10, 18, 53, 54, 147
Greenberg, Hank, 103
GreenPoint Financial, 121, 122n6
Greenwood, Robin, 12

Handelsbanken, 22, 104, 131, 141–4

Hanson, Samuel, 12
HBOS, 132, 152
hearing aid market, 59–60
Heineken, 37–9
Heskett, James, 102
Hicks Muse, 124
homebuilding industry, capital cycle, 5–6, 81, 158
Hong Kong Stock Exchange, 169, 170, 171, 183
Hornby, Andy, 132, 132n9

ICBC (Industrial and Commercial Bank of
  China), 180
ICG (Irish Continental Group), 153–4
IKB Deutsche Industriebank, 135–8
Ikea, 85, 87
inside view, 12–13
insider ownership, 88–91
interest rates
  creative destruction, 156–8
  ultra-low, 174–7
Internet companies, profitability, 61–2
Intertek, 60, 60n6, 73, 74
investment, China's share of GDP, 175
investment banker – Chapter 7 passim
  capital cycle analysis, 18–19
  skewed incentives, 15
investment industry
  focus on earnings and not cash flow, 72
  focus on operating margins, 61
  poor forecasting ability, 69
  preference for large cap stocks, 53
  preference for simple valuation measures, 69
  short-term horizon, 55–7, 72
  value and growth as false categories, 53–4
IPOs (initial public offerings), 3, 15, 125, 127, 182
  capital cycle, 34–5
  Chinese manipulation of, 22, 168–70
  frenzy, 128
  insurance sector, 172
  private equity, 146
  red flag, 18, 49
  Spanish property, 133
Ireland
  post-crisis investment opportunities, 151–4
  property bubble,109, 117
  see Anglo Irish Bank

JP Morgan, 165

Kahneman, Daniel, 12–13, 81
Kamprad, Ingvar, 87
KKR, 127, 146
Kotter, John, 102
Kroner, Niels, 141
Kurlansky, Mark, 28

Lafarge, 81
Lagarde, Christine, 155
Landesbanken, 135–7, 155
Lapthorne, Andrew, 8
Legrand, 64n8, 70
Lehman Brothers crisis, 7, 22, 80–1, 84, 91, 91n7,
    180, 184
Li, Robin, 73
limits to arbitrage, 16n31, 16–17
Linear Technology, 66–8, 68n9, 74, 77
London Stock Exchange, 7, 60, 128

M&A (mergers and acquisitions) activity
    brewers, 37, 39
    Johann Rupert's view on, 95–9
    mania, 128–9
    metals and mining, 35
    pro-cyclicality, 49, 80–2, 129, 147
management
    Ahold, 76–9
    analysts too close to, 77
    capital allocation, 19–20, 46, 56, 76, 78, 80,
        82–4, 99, 126, 167, 174
    corporate culture, 102–4
    cyclical missteps, 80–2
    escalation of corporate pay, 88
    family control, 91–5
    frugality, 101–3
    importance of capital allocation skills, 76, 82
    incentives, 78–9, 91
    insider sales, 130, 147
    learning from failure, 76–9
    management meetings,99–102, 109
    Nordic management, 85–8
    performance metrics, 79
    principal-agent problem, 88–91
    pro-cyclical buybacks and M&A activity, 49,
        80–2, 129, 147
    qualities of a good corporate manager, 84
    quality of, and stock performance, 85–8
    understanding capital cycle, 82–4
managers, selecting, 19
Marathon
    analysing management incentives, 87, 88–91
    analysing management quality, 84, 95–6, 102–4
    concern over private equity, 123–6
    concern over securitization, 120–2
    generalist vs specialist approach, 19, 78, 79
    holding period, 19, 55–7
    identifying bubbles, 127
    investing in "under-the-radar" companies, 73–5
    investing in family owned businesses, 86, 91–5
    investing in Internet businesses, 60–2, 68–70, 160
    investing in quality companies, 63–4, 70–3
    IPO indicator, 128

lack of exposure to Chinese equities, 171, 173,
        183
    meeting with management, 19, 99–102, 109–17
    perils of investing in low return companies, 47
    private ownership, 16
    purchase candidates, 46
    rejection of "value" and "growth" dichotomy,
        17, 20, 45, 53–5, 69
    rejection of detailed forecasting, 69, 77
    underweight European financials, 138, 154
    unsuccessful investments, 76, 158, 159
    wariness of investment bankers, 18, 101, 184
Marchionne, Sergio, 46, 47n11
Mauboussin, Michael, 12
McAteer, William, 110, 115, 116
mean reversion, 10–11
Merrill Lynch, 34, 143
metals and mining industry, 34–5
Miller, Bill, 54
mining companies
    commodity prices, 31–3
    supercycle, 6–8
    metals and, 34–5
Minsky, Hyman, 26, 119
Molin, Johan, 87
Molson Coors, 37–8
monetary policy
    creates corporate zombies, 156
    encourages search for yield, 163–6
    inflating bubbles, 27
    investor implications, 160–3
Montebourg, Arnaud, 157
Montier, James, 109
Munger, Charles T., 58, 60, 120

Nokia, 51, 83, 85–6
Northern Rock, 138–40

off-balance sheet lending, 137, 143, 196, 198
oil prices, energy markets, 40–3
overconfidence, 11

Partners Group, 128, 146
payroll processing, 71, 74
performance
    earnings per share (EPS), 15, 43, 49, 56, 69, 79,
        89, 100, 118–19, 164n8, 187
    quality of management, 85–8
    total shareholder return (TSR), 89, 90, 91
Persson, Stefan, 87
PICC, 171–2, 173n2
Piëch, Ferdinand, 93
Piketty, Thomas, 163–4, 164n8, 166
politicians, protecting industries, 158–60
Ponzi finance, 108, 111, 114, 119, 143

Porter, Michael, 1
Priceline.com, 61, 62, 62n7, 70, 160
pricing power, 21, 26, 37, 66–7, 70–1, 98, 153
principal-agent problem, 88–91
prisoner's dilemma, 16, 25n1, 25–7, 30, 159
private equity
  firms, 122–6, 130, 142, 205
  potential conflicts of interest, 125–6
  private equity mania, 122–7, 130–2
  use of securitization, 131

quality companies
  portfolios shifting to higher, 63–5
  stock performance, 85–8

Rausing family, 86, 87
recency bias, 13, 72
Reckitt Benckiser, 91, 104
Reed Elsevier, 64, 64n8
rent-seeking, family control, 94–5
Richemont, 95–6, 99n12
Rightmove, 63, 64, 101, 160
Rinehart, Gina, 93
Rollen, Ola, 87
Rowan, John, 112, 113, 115, 117
Royal Bank of Scotland (RBS), 83, 116, 152
Rupert, Johann, 95–9
  on China, 99
  on investment bankers, 98
  on the luxury business, 98
  successful stewardship of Richemont, 96
  views on management, 96–7

Sachsen LB, 135–7
Sampo, 22, 76, 81, 83–4, 87
Scandinavia
  management, 82–8
  superior investment returns, 85
Schumpeter, J.A, creative destruction, 1, 145
securitization, 120–2
  fuels buyout boom, 130–2
  oversupplying firms with cheap capital, 121–2
  snares German banks, 135–8
self-dealing, family control, 94
semiconductor business, escaping capital cycle,
  65–8
skewed incentives, 15

Slim, Carlos, 95, 95n11
Smith, Adam, 91
Soames, Rupert, 47
Sorrell, Sir Martin, 89
Spain
  collapse of property bubble, 148–50
  demographic changes, 133n10
  folly of Spanish construction companies, 149
  loss of competitiveness, 135
  real estate bubble, 132–5
state capitalism, 20, 159, 174
steel industry, European, 157
Stenbeck, Jan, 93
Stora Enso, 55, 55n2
structured investment vehicles (SIVs), 137, 143
style labelling, fund managers, 53–5
succession planning, family control, 94
supercycle, commodity, 6–8, 31–6
supply focus, capital cycle, 17
supply side response, commodity prices, 31–3
Svanberg, Carl Henric, 87
Svenska Handelsbanken, 22, 104, 131, 140–1
Swensen, David, 124

Taleb, Nassim, 68, 68n11
Tetra Pak, 86, 87
"tit for tat" policy, 25–7
total shareholder return (TSR), 89, 90, 91
Tversky, Amos, 13

Unilever, 63, 64n8, 160

value investor, 2, 6, 10, 15, 19, 21, 52, 54, 69
Vestas Wind Systems, 47–8
Volkswagen, 26, 93, 156

Wahlroos, Björn, 21, 76, 83–4, 87
Wal-Mart, 62, 92, 168
Welch, Jack, 100
wind turbine maker, capital cycle, 45–8
Wolters Kluwer, 64, 65n8, 85
WorldCom, 4, 54

Yellen, Janet, 166

ZIRP (zero interest rate policy), 162
zombie capitalism, 22, 145, 156, 162